WHY WORK

MOTIVATING AND LEADING
THE NEW GENERATION

MICHAEL MACCOBY

A Touchstone Book
Published by SIMON & SCHUSTER INC.

NEW YORK   LONDON   TORONTO   SYDNEY   TOKYO

TOUCHSTONE
SIMON & SCHUSTER BUILDING
ROCKEFELLER CENTER
1230 AVENUE OF THE AMERICAS
NEW YORK, NEW YORK 10020

DESIGNED BY IRVING PERKINS ASSOCIATES
MANUFACTURED IN THE UNITED STATES OF AMERICA

10   9   8   7   6   5   4   3   PBK.

LIBRARY OF CONGRESS CATALOGING IN PUBLICATION DATA

MACCOBY, MICHAEL, 1933–

WHY WORK: MOTIVATING AND LEADING THE NEW
GENERATION / MICHAEL MACCOBY.
P.   CM. — (A TOUCHSTONE BOOK)
EARLIER ED. HAS SUBTITLE: LEADING THE NEW
GENERATION.
BIBLIOGRAPHY: P.
INCLUDES INDEX.
1. LEADERSHIP.   2. EMPLOYEE MOTIVATION.
3. ORGANIZATIONAL EFFECTIVENESS.   I. TITLE.
[HD57.7.M33 1989]   88-38003
658.4'092—dc19   CIP

ISBN 0-671-47281-X
     0-671-67560-5 PBK.

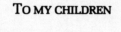

To My Children

CONTENTS

PREFACE   ON METHODOLOGY   9

INTRODUCTION   A THEORY FOR OUR TIME   19

CHAPTER 1   WHAT MOTIVATES?   51

CHAPTER 2   THE INNOVATOR   87

CHAPTER 3   THE EXPERT   117

CHAPTER 4   THE HELPER   133

CHAPTER 5   THE DEFENDER   151

CHAPTER 6   THE SELF-DEVELOPER   167

CHAPTER 7   STRATEGIC INDIVIDUAL DEVELOPMENT   197

CHAPTER 8   LEADERSHIP FOR OUR TIME   213

APPENDICES

A. Follow-up Interview Questionnaire   239

B. A Note on Value Drives   241

C. Statistical Results from the Values at Work
    Questionnaire   245

D. The AT&T Managerial Interview Questionnaire   251

NOTES   255

INDEX   261

ON
METHODOLOGY

I began Why Work to expand my studies of motivation and leadership into the new service workplace, and to test my theory of social character types with larger samples of employees at all levels of industry and government. My earlier books studied managers in high-tech industries, workers and managers in manufacturing and government, and peasant farmers in Mexico.* The approach taken in all of these books is to combine the study of human development with what improves effectiveness at work. I have sought knowledge that can be used to improve work relationships in terms of two different criteria: economic/ technical and social/human. The first has to do with what makes companies competitive so that they can create wealth and provide employment. It has to do with managing resources more productively and satisfying customers and clients. The

---

*See my previous books, Social Character in a Mexican Village, with Erich Fromm (Englewood Cliffs, N.J.: Prentice Hall, 1970); The Gamesman (New York: Simon & Schuster, 1976); and The Leader (New York: Simon & Schuster, 1981).

second has to do with what improves working life: what stimulates the fullest development of human skills and character, and strengthens democratic values in the surrounding society.

There is, of course, a serious question as to the degree to which these two criteria are mutually compatible, or conversely, the degree to which trade-offs must be made between them. The purpose of the projects I have undertaken in the workplace, of which the research for this book is a part, is to further both economic and human goals.

Why Work makes use of three methodologies—surveys, interviews, and participant study. Chapters 2 through 6 are based in large part on a survey on values that motivate people at work. It was given to over three thousand employees from 1981 to 1986 at eight companies and more than ten federal, state, county, and municipal agencies. These samples were not random, but were composed of volunteers who took the survey with the understanding that the group results would be reported back to them. In the companies and three agencies, I discussed the findings in the context of motivation and resistance to organizational change. In the other agencies, either leadership that sponsored the survey changed, or there was insufficient interest and the findings were never reported back.

The questions used in the survey were based on analyzing more than 100 interviews on what satisfies and dissatisfies people at work, how they want to be managed, how they relate to customers, clients, and co-workers, and about their family background and goals at work. These interviews were given by myself (thirty interviews) and the research associates I have trained to study social character, who were members of the Seminar on Social Character of the Project on Technology, Work, and Character. The interviews were given during the period from 1977 to 1982 at AT&T, an insurance company, three federal agencies, and a county health agency. The interviews were analyzed in meetings of the seminar. On the basis of these discussions, I formulated the survey questionnaire which is reproduced in the Introduction (pages 42-43).

The survey questions were presented by the Merit Protection Board of the U.S. Civil Service with seven different samples representing all levels of the federal bureaucracy. After each testing, people who answered the questions discussed their validity—for example, did the choices in fact reflect their values? I fine-tuned the wording until everyone felt comfortable with the questions, before giving the questionnaire to business groups and federal agencies.

The *reliability* of the survey was established by retesting a sample twelve months later, and agreement was found in 62 percent of first choices; in 96 percent of the cases, either the first or second choice remained the same. Reliability was also checked with seven different samples of managers from a single company, and no significant differences were found in response pattern among the samples. (Indeed, as reported in the Introduction, we have found that the pattern of responses is always similar for companies in the same line of business, and that differences can be explained by the values selected for and reinforced by organizations.)

To further test the *validity* of the questionnaire, those interested in a confidential follow-up were invited to write in their names and telephone numbers on a second page, attached to the questionnaire. Fifty-two percent responded. This percentage was higher for managers (66 percent), who want feedback that might improve their effectiveness, and lower for clerical workers (31 percent), who might be either wary that their answers would be traced and used against them, or merely less hopeful that the interview would be useful to them. A sample of 130 from government and business, representing each self-selected value type, was interviewed by my research associates about their family background, attitudes toward work, supervision, service, and self-development. The questions we used for these interviews are reproduced in Appendix A. The Social Character Seminar and I found that in almost all cases, our view of the person from the interview fit his or her view of self in terms of dominant values. Parts of these interviews and others

11

used to explore management style (see below) are quoted verbatim in the chapters in this book on character types, with minor editing to make them grammatical and reduce repetition.

Why Work also makes use of an interview study of managerial style that is reported in Chapter 8. The study began in 1979, when I worked with a group of diplomats at the United States State Department led by Harry G. Barnes, Jr., then director-general of the Foreign Service, to define good leadership for the State Department by studying its existing leaders. Together with the group, I designed a series of interview questions to be used in the study. The questions explored the leaders' strategic goals, their style of communication and decision-making, their motivating values, and their work history. The group then set out to identify good leaders within the Department. First they described personal experiences with good managers. Then they formulated general criteria for good leaders, including skills such as communication, negotiation, waging interbureaucratic power struggles, knowledge of the political and economic subject matter of foreign policy. They also included character traits such as perseverance, a drive to achieve, fair-mindedness, objectivity, a sense of humor (the emotional equivalent of a sense of reality), high tolerance for frustration, optimism, enthusiasm, the willingness to listen to different viewpoints, capacity for growth, and high energy. This list led to nominating fifteen good leaders who were interviewed and compared to a control group of twelve people in similar positions. The research team then analyzed the results and arrived at the conclusion that good leadership depended on values as much as competency, or to put it another way, competency combines skill and values.

During 1983–1985, I used a version of the State Department managerial interview questionnaire in Sweden to interview twenty-eight national leaders, including eight chief executives of large companies, six political leaders, seven heads of national unions, and seven general directors of national government agencies. This was part of a study the Swedish Council on Management and Worklife Issues asked me to help design to determine the kind of leadership Sweden needs for the future. The results of that study have been published in Swedish.*

During 1985–86, Robert H. Gaynor, then vice-president of personnel for AT&T Communications, and I used a customized version of the managerial questionnaire to engage sixty top AT&T executives in three-hour interviews where they explored their approach to management and their own careers. This AT&T questionnaire is reproduced in Appendix D. Gaynor and I also discussed with the executives the relationship of managerial styles and their visions for the company. These discussions led to the development of the concept, presented in this book, of entrepreneurial leadership, as opposed to administrative leadership, as the leadership style needed for our time. Subsequently, I have used a version of the managerial interview as a tool to develop leadership at a large conglomerate and a supermarket chain.

The interview with Russ Nagel of Westinghouse Furniture Systems used in Chapter 2 resulted because he invited me to Grand Rapids to study his innovative leadership.

Altogether, I have interviewed over 70 business executives and 30 government leaders with a version of the managerial questionnaire in Appendix D.

In four of the businesses and three of the government agencies where I have given surveys and interviews, I had been invited as a consultant to help improve management and the quality of working life, and so I was able to carry my research beyond the survey and interview, and place it in the context of attempts to change organizations.

As a consultant to AT&T, I learned about the leadership of Larry Lemasters, described in Chapter 2, and in 1981 Lemasters asked me to help him begin the process of transforming the

---

*The interview with Jan Carlzon of SAS in Chapter 2 was part of that study.

Stock & Bond Division, which eventually became American Transtech.

I categorize consultants into three varieties: off-the-shelf, interactive, and participative. Although at different times consultants can be all three kinds, usually they specialize in one of these approaches. Off-the-shelf consultants have a product or service to sell, such as quality circles, zero-based budgeting, a training package, or a workshop on motivation. Interactive consultants are called in to help solve a problem. Typically, successful interactive consultants work with worried leaders and help them bind their anxiety with new processes and techniques. They study the problem, interview a number of managers, and craft solutions that appeal to the values of managers. (Examples of solutions they employ: reorganization, decentralization, turning cost centers into profit centers, and changing the incentive pay system.) Participative consultants join project teams, bringing not a product but skills and knowledge needed to address the problem. They do not just provide reassuring solutions, but rather join their clients in analysis and problem-solving, adding a missing competency. In the process they teach their skills to people in the organization.

As a participative consultant, I have worked with managers and union leaders, strategizing, designing organization to support strategy, and studying employee values and leadership styles. I have applied the methods of psychoanalysis* and anthropology, exploring the conscious motives and unconscious values which determine approaches to work and social relationships, and attempting to help leaders understand the interrelationship of psychological, social, economic, and technological factors in creating successful organizations.

---

*In my previous books, I have used the Rorschach test to explore cognitive style and unconscious themes. Despite the Rorschach's value, I decided not to use findings from the test in this book because I wanted a methodology that can be understood by readers who do not have the specialized training needed to interpret the Rorschach for themselves.

In 1980, I became the sole joint consultant to the Bell System and the Communications Workers of America in their attempt to improve the quality of working life by giving employees greater freedom and involving them in management decisions. In 1984, I continued as joint consultant to AT&T and CWA to create a competitive entrepreneurial company with work that proved more satisfying and personally developing.

I have found from surveys, interviews, and consulting that work has different meanings for people and that they are most strongly motivated when the demands made on them fit their values. To learn what motivates people at work, I find I must study both the individual and the organization, and especially the role of leadership. Correspondingly, if people are to develop themselves at work and realize their potential for leadership, I believe they must understand themselves and others in relationship to a changing workplace. I have written *Why Work* to contribute to this understanding.

Businesses where employees were studied for this book include AT&T, US West, a large big-eight accounting firm, an innovative insurance company, a TV broadcasting company, a large supermarket chain, the information services division of a large oil company, and a company producing high-tech services. The government agencies include the Internal Revenue Service, the Commerce Department, ACTION (Peace Corps, VISTA, Older Americans Volunteer Programs), the Federal Aviation Administration, NASA, the Departments of State, Agriculture, Justice, and Defense, the Federal Trade Commission, the Library of Congress, a statewide health department, two hospitals, a county health department, a city tax office, a social-work office in California, and a municipal library. Besides these, I surveyed high school teachers and seniors, and drew on interviews conducted by research associates and students of social character with police officers in two metropolitan departments, entrepreneurs in the United States and Sweden, employees of Scandinavian Airlines, and middle managers in Japanese banks and trading companies.

In summary, I have studied people in organizations that have hired me to help them become more effective, and I have administered surveys in those companies and government agencies where I have been invited to speak about the issues described in this book. I have also made use of findings from a number of separate studies that employ social-character theory and methods. While I directed some of them, others were done independently, in which cases I was a consultant to the research. I am grateful to the following research associates, students, and colleagues who have participated in the studies which are the basis for *Why Work*:

Dr. Richard Margolies, a clinical psychologist, has been my principal research associate. He helped me design the survey and interview questions, and he interviewed many government and business employees. He wrote papers on the expert and helper types, and offered useful suggestions about revising drafts of these chapters.

Dr. Cynthia Elliott Margolies, a clinical psychologist and my other research associate, conducted interviews and wrote papers on the self-developer and defender types. She was particularly helpful in the study of the self-developer.

Barbara Lenkerd Cortina, an anthropologist, and Dr. Margaret Molinari, a sociologist, contributed interviews of government employees. Ms. Lenkerd and I jointly authored a report on the ACTION Agency, "Ideals and Interests: Final Report on the Participatory Work Improvement Program at ACTION/Peace Corps, 1977–1980" (Discussion Paper Series, John F. Kennedy School of Government, Harvard University, May 1984), and Dr. Molinari authored a study of government auditors which helped develop understanding of the bureaucratic character, reported in Michael Maccoby *et al.*, "Bringing out the Best: Final Report of the Project to Improve Work and Management in the Department of Commerce, 1977–1979" (Discussion Paper Series, John F. Kennedy School of Government, Harvard University, 1980).

Dr. Mauricio Cortina, a psychiatrist, studied doctors and nurses in a county health center. Dr. Jody Palmour, a philosopher, allowed me to use his excellent interviews with police officers. Dr. Douglass Carmichael has been a valuable participant in the Social Character Seminar.

Using the questionnaire in Appendix A, Marilyn Stahl, Tony Wagner, Scott Camlin, Dr. Veena Kapur, and Ruth Fort contributed employee interviews. John Paul MacDuffie interviewed managers and workers at Westinghouse Furniture System.

Linda Streit and Tony De Nicola provided statistical analysis of some of the survey data. Gay Mount worked with me on the State Department study of leadership. Dr. Douglas Wilson, a clinical psychologist and management consultant, shared his interviews with entrepreneurs in California as did Åke Beckérus and Berit Roos in Sweden.

Jan Erik Rendahl, a psychologist, studied change and social character in the Swedish criminal system. With Dr. Anders Edstrom, an economist, he has also studied social character at Scandinavian Airlines, and I refer to their findings.[1]

In Australia, Trevor Williams applied the social-character questionnaire to managers in Austrialian Telecom. The pattern of responses proved similar to those of U.S. telephone company managers.

Berth Jönsson, Bo Ekman, Russ Ackoff, Lennart Strömberg, and Gunnar Hedlund have contributed to my thinking about holistic business strategy in Chapter 8.

Gene Kofke, Tapas Sen, Bill Ketchum, Ronnie Straw, Jim Irvine, and Maureen Tierney have worked closely with me to develop the quality of working life at AT&T.

Professor Harvey Brooks has contributed to my understanding of technology and work.

Professor David Riesman has been, as always, a supportive critic and has shared his studies of leadership by university and college presidents.

Steve Roday offered a number of useful suggestions. Robert H. Gaynor and Anne Maccoby have been constructive critics of drafts of this book. Alice Mayhew has, as always, made clarifying editorial suggestions.

PREFACE

Not only has Diana Hanson patiently prepared the many drafts of the manuscript, but she has also been a creative researcher and editor.

Sandylee Maccoby has been a helper in the best sense, supportive and challenging.

A THEORY FOR OUR TIME

Although the demands of work and the aspirations of younger workers are changing fast, neither leadership styles nor theories of motivation are keeping pace.

No one doubts that motivation is essential to the success of organizations and people at work. When competent people want to do what is *necessary* to satisfy customers, cut costs, and increase profits, both the organization and the individual win. When I began the research for this book, I believed that by satisfying employees at work, productivity would improve. I no longer believe that is always true. Many managers and workers are not motivated to do what is necessary for companies to succeed. The values and competencies that served them in the past get in the way of adapting to a different economy.

The global market demands that companies produce higher-quality products and services. America needs better, more cost-effective services in health, education, welfare, and law enforcement. To achieve these goals, businesses and bureaucracies must eliminate expensive levels of administration and balance control with self-management. Employees must not only work hard, but care about cutting costs and satisfying customers. New work relations require sharing knowledge and continual learning. As organizations flatten out, there will be less opportunity for promotion. The traditional incentives of hierarchy, money, status, and power will be in short supply.

I found that the values of many young Americans do fit these new demands. They represent a growing generation in the workplace defined not by age but by values that have developed in families where both parents work.

These are men and women whose main goal at work is self-development. From childhood they have sharpened intellectual and interpersonal skills to succeed at work and to get along with people. These self-developers are motivated to solve problems cooperatively with co-workers, customers, and clients. They are ready to learn and succeed in the new workplace, which demands a combination of technical knowlege and teamwork.

But the self-developers are frustrated and turned off by bureaucratic organization and leaders who do not share their values. They resent work that does not allow them to improve their skills and maintain their marketability. They want to be free to respond individually to customers and clients, to be entrepreneurs instead of narrow specialists. They want to be treated as whole persons, not as role performers. Yet they are wary of being swallowed up by work. Motivated to succeed in family life as well as in a career, and to balance work with play, they continually question how much of themselves to invest in the workplace. They want to know why they are working, as opposed to expressing themselves outside of the job.

The title *Why Work* promises answers to questions continually asked by members of the new generation. In this book, I present a theory of motivation to fit the changing economy and the new social character.

THE NEW GAME: TECHNOSERVICE

Global competition, deregulation, and information and telecommunications technology (especially computer networks or telematics) are driving changes in the rules and roles of the game in the most advanced sector of the economy. To compete, managers must change the traditional bureaucratic-industrial hierarchies with their uniform roles and standardized outputs. Managers have to play the new game, which I call *technoservice*, and define as follows:

technoservice n. [fr. *techno*, a combining form from the Greek *techne* meaning *art*, *skill*, *craft*, and the modern *technology*, industrial science or systemic knowledge of the industrial arts, and *service*, fr. OF *servise*, service, fr. L. *servitium* meaning labor for the benefit of another.
    1. The use of systematic knowledge and information-communications technology for the benefit of customers and clients.
    2. The most advanced way of working at the end of the twentieth century, brought about by international competition, and information and communications technology. Technoservice is characterized by customizing products and services for customers and clients both internal and external to the organization. Technoservice organization is characterized by networks and teams; flexible work roles with authority based on competence and knowledge; flat hierarchy, front-line freedom and responsibility to make decisions to satisfy customers and adapt to different conditions; work measurements based on customer satisfaction and profitability; management as strategic planning; and leadership that develops a motivating corporate culture which supports teamwork.
Ant: standardized work, mass production, industrial bureaucracy.

technoservice adj. 1. Of or pertaining to technoservice, as a technoservice organization or technoservice management.
Ant: Bureaucratic-industrial, bureaucratic, regimented.

Both the old and new games coexist in our transitional economy, but the technoservice game is transforming the culture of work. Consider tools, rules, and relationships. The technology of the old industrial-bureaucratic game is electromechanical: people are organized as extensions of machines that produce standardized products, including services and information, with economies of scale. In theory, uniform, fragmented roles are controlled and coordinated by levels of management up to the chief executive, the big brain, who runs the machine. In practice, each individual, worker and manager alike, attempts to maximize autonomy, and successful work relationships depend on negotiations at all levels. Customers of mass-production industry are treated en masse. Needs are stimulated by advertising and standardized products are differentiated by minor variations in product and packaging. Those who want something special, like the luxury car, pay for extra craftwork.

The technology of the technoservice game is electronic and information-intensive: computers, programmed telecommunications networks, computer-aided design, and artificial intelligence. People are organized in teams. Employees must have the authority to make decisions that fit both customer needs and the strategic goals of their own companies. Successful work relationships depend on the ability of different specialists to cooperate in solving problems, and the information and trust created between the center and the front line. Since employees at the front line of technoservice sales and development are sources of market information and intelligence about competitors, strategists at the center must listen to them. There are degrees of technoservice depending on the extent of automation and customization. In simpler forms, front-line employees such as telephone operators or airline clerks use computerized networks to satisfy individual customers. In more advanced forms, salesmen, engineers, accountants, and technicians use computerized systems to serve customers. In the most advanced forms, teams of engineers, programmers, and specialists in organization create value-added networks that automate production and service. Customers might be: a credit card company or a bank needing to make a quick check on a customer's credit; a supermarket where purchases are electronically tabulated and the information sent to a central storehouse where inventory decisions are made by computer; a factory where orders or designs sent over a telephone network are transformed into computer commands to the manufacturing technology; an airline that wants a reservation system that not only produces tickets but also hotel space and special services.

In this form of technoservice, the customer develops and uses the technology together with the producer, who *facilitates* the customer's use of the network by teaching new ways to use the technology. By add-ons and programming, the customer changes or customizes the tool. Given continual changes in technology and organization, relationships between employees, customers, and clients are ongoing. They do not end with the sale. The corporate culture *requires* teamwork since the technology is at once complex and interconnected: what occurs at one point in the network or system affects the whole.

Teamwork includes not only customers, but also synergistic alliances between companies: technology companies allied with specialized marketing companies; large computer and telecommunications companies with small technical consulting and research and development firms. Sometimes, competitors in one arena are customers in another and partners in a third.

TECHNOSERVICE VERSUS SERVICE

There are senses in which all work is a service. In the broadest sense, the machinist serves the factory owners, the bricklayer serves the contractor, just as the salesman serves both customer and company. In another sense, we serve God and humanity through our work. However, these are not the senses in which economists define service work. Service work is a bureaucratic category based on the type of output. Seventy percent of working Americans are now employed in "service," and this percentage is increasing. The Bureau of Labor Statistics does not have a formal definition of the service sector, but it divides employment into two categories: goods-producing and service-producing. The former includes manufacturing, mining and construction. The latter includes transportation, public utilities, government, retail and wholesale, finance, health, insurance, entertainment, real estate, and personal and professional services. *Service* is thus a huge conglomeration of occupations, from the elite: doctors, lawyers, investment bankers, executives, movie stars, diplomats; to the middle level: airplane pilots, accountants, auditors, middle managers, air traffic controllers, teachers; to the service workers at the front line: cabin attendants, librarians, secretaries, insurance salesmen, police, garbage collectors.

Although service workers do not manufacture products or construct buildings, they contribute to both industries as engineers, architects, and designers. However, service work is in fact done in all industries, including those that produce tangible products. The distinction between production and service blurs the critical transition from industrial-bureaucratic to technoservice modes of work within industry as a whole.

Technoservice is not the same as service, in the broad sense, the spiritual sense, or the economic sense. The term is more sociological, describing a mode of working and a business logic that is spreading into the industrial as well as the service sector because of automation and customization.

Many service-sector companies that process standardized "products" at high volumes, such as fast food and insurance claims, are organized as industrial bureaucracies. If they use computers, it is to speed up and monitor routine work, not to give employees tools to provide better service. But these companies are finding that there is no payoff from office automation if the style of work remains unchanged.* Workers become bored

---

*Economists are showing that a major reason for lack of U.S. productivity growth is the inability to realize the potential of office automation. See, for

and make mistakes. Policing is costly. Some successful companies understand this new game (see American Transtech in Chapter 2). In the future, competition will force service-providers to be knowledgeable about their customers, and respond quickly to new market opportunities in order to anticipate and satisfy different customer needs. Since these service outputs depend on circumstances and negotiations, they cannot be completely standardized. The old work organization, with uniform, formatted jobs and levels of bureaucracy to process decisions, is too slow, cumbersome, and deadening to succeed in the technoservice economy.

If employees are to help customers solve problems, their jobs must be designed to allow more freedom. In banks with automated tellers, clerks must make decisions about small loans. In offices where professionals do some of their own word processing, secretaries must contribute as administrative and research assistants. Some companies that gain enormous profits through mass production of standardized products have learned that their marketing, engineering, and legal services must be organized in the new way.

Correspondingly, competition and automation force manufacturing into the technoservice game. Industrial companies that sell expensive customized products to demanding business customers have to orient themselves to marketing and service, building relationships with dealers and customers (as in the case of Westinghouse Furniture Systems, described in Chapter 2).

Global competition and technology transform the production process itself. Because competition requires they be produced at lower cost, AT&T has transferred the assembly of telephones and small PBXs to low-wage countries like Singapore. Four types of products remain at AT&T plants in the United States: innovations, customized products, automated processes, and

---

example, Martin Neil Baily, "What Has Happened to Productivity Growth?" *Science*, vol. 234, October 1986, pp. 443–450.

microelectric chips produced in "clean rooms" where technicians and engineers cooperate to monitor a delicate computer-aided process.

Automation in plants wipes out the bureaucratic-industrial rules of job design. When repetitive, individualized jobs are automated, the ones that remain require people who understand the process, and can anticipate or respond quickly if something goes wrong. They must take responsibility for the whole product, not just a specialized part, and work cooperatively to ensure quality and avoid breakdowns. To do this profitably requires work relationships different from those that function for mass production. This requires more education for workers, who no longer just follow rules but diagnose systems. It narrows the gap between management and nonmanagement. When managements fail to understand this, stressed employees feel overwhelmed and underprepared, and automated factories continually break down.*

The most advanced mode of production in a society inevitably influences the national culture, affecting beliefs, relationships, education, language, art, movies, and TV programs. Just as the industrial mode made hierarchical bureaucracy and specialization seem "right" for schools, government, and the orga-

---

*Larry Hirschorn, in *Beyond Mechanization* (Cambridge, Mass.: The MIT Press, 1984), makes the argument that automation transforms production work to service, and he shows that most companies have difficulty changing the bureaucratic organization.

In his study of why computerized, flexible manufacturing systems (FMS) are less successfully implemented in the U.S. compared to Japan, Ramchandras Jaikumar places the blame on the bureaucratic-industrial organization and the fact that American management fails to "treat manufacturing as a service." To exploit the new technology, not only must workers be more competent and responsible, but management must use the system to customize its offerings to particular customers. "Postindustrial Manufacturing," *Harvard Business Review*, November–December 1986, pp. 69–76.

See also Richard Walton, et al., *Human Resource Practices for Implementing Advanced Manufacturing Technology*, Manufacturing Studies Board, 1986. Available from National Academy Press, 2101 Constitution Avenue, Washington, D.C. 20418

nization of knowledge in universities, now technoservice makes people think in terms of competitive teamwork, customer satisfaction, continual learning, and innovation. People, especially those with money to spend, expect customized treatment, and the market becomes more demanding. Professionals like doctors, lawyers, and architects are pressured to change. Future computer programming advances will accelerate the trend to technoservice in professions as well as industry.

As computers take over routine professional diagnosis and problem-solving, human productivity depends increasingly on the added value of understanding and helpfulness.[1] People prefer useful, impersonal robots and computers to unhelpful, impersonal experts.

In the industrial bureaucracy, productivity results from simplifying jobs, automating, and cutting labor costs. In technoservice, productivity gains are more complex. They result from more efficient use of materials, less waste, and higher-quality work. This requires better organization, communication, and cooperation.

Beyond this, productivity results from *productive relationships* with customers. System designers are successful when they understand the needs of users who want data services or automated systems for different purposes, such as inventory control, traffic flow, insurance claims, and banking transactions. Individual service providers have always found this to be true. Doctors cure patients who cooperate in terms of diet and exercise. Teachers succeed when they can stimulate students to put in more effort. Lawyers solve problems, win cases, with clients who understand the issues and provide useful information.* To

---

*For a good discussion of productivity in service, see Thomas M. Stanback, Jr., Peter J. Bearse, Theirry J. Novelle, and Robert A. Karasek, in *Service: The New Economy* (Totowa, N.J.: Allenheld, Osmun and Co., 1983). They write, "If the borrower keeps accurate and complete records, the bank is likely to be able to extend loans quickly on more favorable terms, at less cost and risk to itself. Similarly, a better informed and more cooperative client is likely to get better legal service and at a lower cost" (p. 4).

27

be sure, lawyers still measure productivity by billable hours, and doctors by income per hour, but this is because they have not yet felt the discomfort of competition.

Client and patients increasingly complain of professionals who are unresponsive. A recent Harris poll indicates that 39 percent of Americans say they stopped going to a particular doctor, or changed doctors, because they were dissatisfied. Their most important reasons were that "the doctor didn't spend enough time with me," "didn't have a friendly personality," or "didn't answer questions honestly or completely"— signs of poor relationships.[2] Scandinavian Airlines became profitable because it followed a strategy of serving business customers (see Chapter 2), while People Express began to slide in large part because it sacrificed service to maintain low-cost travel. A market saturated with the values of technoservice will force managers and professionals to redefine productivity and question their own values. The new market will demand workers, managers, and professionals who are highly motivated not only to produce quality goods and services but to create productive relationships.

OUTMODED THEORIES OF MOTIVATION

The major theories of motivation at work still taught at business schools and in managerial courses are *partial man* theories. They are designed by academics for experts in bureaucracies. Like functional departments in an intellectual bureaucracy, these theories focus on one motivating value at the expense of the whole person. The academic theories see man as *economic man*, *sociological man*, *political man*, and *psychological man*. They are partial theories about partial man who is motivated by money, power, status, or a hierarchy of needs. Each of these theories is partially true; none is fully true. They are designed for partial people in narrow, routinized jobs at the bottom, and specialized functions at higher levels.

These theories do not explain how to motivate people to become more involved in the management of the business and to work interdependently. They do not explain differences in values that determine the quality and intensity of motivation for technoservice.

At the top of organizations today, managers are attracted to *economic man* theories of motivation because money is what they themselves control best. Top managers would like to believe they can design a system in which each employee, by working to maximize individual gain, makes the whole company prosper. It is an idea that brings to mind the image of a well-made watch. Yet the theory of economic man does not even explain top management motivation.

Because they are motivated to maximize the bottom line, it appears that chief executives in most American companies are pure economic men. This is misleading. Although they want to make as much as they can, top managers are not motivated to be more effective by the promise of more money. The executive making $250,000 does not work harder to make $500,000 or $5,000,000. The bottom line has meanings for chief executives other than money. Like most of us, their sense of self-worth depends in large measure on the esteem of people they consider their peers. Chief executives spend much of their time with other CEOs, bankers, and financial analysts who judge them on their quarterly statements. Doing poorly is humiliating. Doing well gives them a glow of success.

The theory of economic man has lasted because it engages so many drives and has some meaning for everyone. It has been the most reliable theory of motivation for the industrial age.* The meaning of money may be different according to our values, but everyone wants it. Money provides a sense of security. It is

---

*See, for example, the labor economists Sar A. Levitan and Clifford M. Johnson, *Second Thoughts on Work* (Kalamazoo, Mich.: W. E. Upjohn Institute for Employment Research, 1982). They write: "In wealthy industralized nations, the concern for relative income gains is a far more powerful source of work motivation than any basic survival needs" (p. 28).

proof of mastery and the means for pleasure. Money means freedom from indignity. With enough of it, one can tell any boss to go to hell. Freedom-loving Americans dream of making enough money to be financially independent, and the entrepreneurial spirit remains strong. Some of the most courageous businessmen are willing to carry a huge load of debt and risk their own money in hopes of a big payoff. Some of the most gifted of the new generation march into business school with the dream of making a quick killing as investment bankers or traders in securities and commodities.

But within technoservice organizations, everyone cannot become financially independent, and money alone will not motivate the good relationships required for effectiveness.

Sociological man is the structural complement to economic man. This theory maintains that people are motivated by their organizational role and their desire for status gained as they advance up the hierarchy. This was the approach to motivation of Frederick Winslow Taylor and his followers, who designed industrial bureaucracies at the turn of the century according to principles of "scientific management."

The theory worked well enough as long as American corporations controlled their markets and profited from grinding out standardized products. It fit the values of immigrant workers and snobbish experts educated to measure success in terms of promotion. But today the status hierarchy dampens productive motivation of people at lower levels with high school or college degrees. Furthermore, managers at higher levels come to believe their position proves they know more, and they are unable to make use of the knowledge of others.

The theory of *political man* holds that people act to increase their power and influence. Its roots lie in Machiavelli's *Realpolitik*. The Prince is motivated to gain power. Marxist theories of political man also say that managers design work to maintain control over the workers, and claim that workers would be more motivated if they gained control of the means of production and the fruits of their labors.

But a sense of ownership does not necessarily motivate employees, especially in large companies. Despite Marx's theory, many Yugoslavian workers who "own" their companies and elect the managing director feel alienated and turned off by boring work. Despite ownership, they have little or no say about how work will be done. Nor do most workers understand why management makes decisions that change technology and jobs. Workers who owned the Vermont Asbestos Company sold their shares to make a profit. They saw no compelling advantage to ownership.[3] To feel whole at work, people must have a meaningful say over conditions that affect them. Ownership is not necessarily the key. Workers can gain the right to have a say in a constitutional system, through contract, or by agreement. Whether or not they own the company, to participate meaningfully they must be educated about the business.

The experience of work in industrial bureaucracies has caused a sense of powerlessness and provoked employees to protect themselves by using power against power, either collectively in unions, or individually by rising up the hierarchy to gain a strategic role. The theory of political man then describes a defense mechanism against exploitation and manipulation.*

Psychological man is the twentieth-century theory that motivation is caused by needs. It appears to integrate the other theories, but it does so within the old bureaucratic-industrial context and ends up as another partial-man theory.

Abraham Maslow's psychological man is by far the most popular and influential theory of motivation taught to managers. Maslow describes a hierarchy of needs and presents a typology.[4] He calls the lowest-level needs physiological: feeding, drinking, sex. These are needs for relief of tension, pain, and discomfort.

---

*See Michel Crozier, *The Bureaucratic Phenomenon* (Chicago: University of Chicago Press, 1964), for a description of the bureaucrat as a political man. See also Melvin L. Kohn and Carmi Schooler, *Work and Personality: An Inquiry into the Impact of Social Stratification* (Norwood, N.J.: Ablex Publishing Corporation, 1983). They show that the bureaucrat's ideal is a job with authority and autonomy.

Next come what he calls the safety needs (security, dependency, protection, etc.), which are felt once the physiological needs are gratified. These are the needs of economic man. If both the physiological and safety needs are satisfied, Maslow then postulates that the next level of needs for love and affection will emerge. Once these are satisfied, a person will experience needs for status, achievement, and autonomy, the sociological and political needs, and finally self-actualization, the need to express one's creative potentials. All managers from big business and government learn this theory, either in business school or in advanced executive seminars, and the hierarchy-of-needs chart can be found in offices around the globe.

According to Maslow, people are motivated by money, status, and power only at lower levels. But through success, partial man can become whole and transcend the bureaucratic condition. This theory is used by both conservative and liberal managers. Conservative managers cite Maslow's hierarchy of needs to justify and rationalize their reluctance to change organization. They argue that workers are still at lower levels and do not want more demanding and responsible roles. In reply, liberal managers contend that with affluence, the needs of workers have moved up the hierarchy, and unless organizations provide more opportunity for self-actualization, these people will not be motivated.

Maslow's theory appears to integrate all the others and satisfy everyone. What is wrong with it?

Two things. First, it does not fit the facts.

Second, while it works well enough for the industrial bureaucracies, it seriously misleads technoservice management.

Starting with the first objection, the evidence does not support the concept of a need hierarchy. Superficially, the concept appears to make sense, but the theory ignores all the cultural and psychoanalytic evidence of the role of values, of human character. Human development is not a result of climbing the corporate ladder, or vice versa. What we choose to do depends more on our ethics than on satisfying needs. No evidence shows that satisfaction of lower needs triggers higher needs, or that these needs can indeed ever be satisfied. One thinks of hungry artists or generous villagers who transcend lower needs without satisfying them. One never satisfies needs for safety, food, or love, once and for all. We may learn better ways to satisfy these needs, we may raise the aesthetic quality of these needs, but they never disappear. Nor can we ever achieve all our potentials. How we develop depends on opportunity, discipline, and commitment.

Once character is formed, satisfaction of needs does not necessarily change the motivation to work. And when it does, the result may be negative rather than positive. Empire builders are never satiated. Conquests whet their appetite for more. Narcissists of any type can never receive enough acclaim. Nor do people become more productive if they are given what they have not earned. This I observed when an idealistic innovator, a believer in Maslow, gave half his multimillion-dollar company to the workers. He expected that the sense of security would move them to higher levels of self-actualization. In fact, as owners, they complained about too much work and criticized the innovator for not giving them more money and time off. Filling "needs" increased dependency and did not stimulate greater responsibility or creativity.

Maslow's partial person is contradicted not only by everyday experience, but also by neurophysiology and cognitive psychology, which show that humans from birth strive to organize experience, infuse it with meaning, and master the environment. Our very perception of the world requires from infancy that we actively organize ambiguous stimuli. Human development results from opportunity combined with discipline, knowledge, and practice. In fact, we often grow by frustrating, not satisfying, our needs. Needs have been made to sound biological, genetically determined, even though we continually manufacture new ones. Instead of automatically serving all our needs, we would be wiser to analyze each of them in terms of whether or not they do contribute to self-development.

For the second objection, the theory misleads. If technoservice managers embrace Maslow's theories, they will be misled into believing that what worked for the industrial bureaucracies will fit their new game. It does not fit. For instance, in the industrial bureaucracy, one can treat the lower-level workers as economic man, motivated by security needs. If this treatment does not guarantee good workmanship, it does at least gain compliance and high output. Middle managers need their self-esteem bolstered; they can be controlled with the symbols of success and the chance to exercise power. The financially independent at the top are so driven to succeed that they need no further incentives; they are fully capable of negotiating their own rewards to satisfy themselves. Although this does not fit every case, it has been good enough to keep the industrial bureaucracy running, especially in Maslow's time, when American business dominated world markets and could pass the cost of inefficiencies on to customers.

Like Maslow, Tom Peters and R. H. Waterman, the authors of the bestseller *In Search of Excellence*,[5] talk of middle managers as motivated by status and self-esteem. But they go further and emphasize that all of us need meaning in our lives and will sacrifice a great deal to institutions that provide it for us. The "excellent companies" embody strong values emphasizing excellence, winning, and the respect for individual dignity. The employee either accepts these values or gets out.

Most of these successful companies reflect the value of strong owner-entrepreneurs. The organization is held together when the employees identify with the culture-shaping paternal leader. However, the new generation of self-developers will be motivated not by praise from fathers but by opportunities for self-expression and career development, combined with a fair share of profits.

I believe that Peters and Waterman do in fact describe the spirit of successful American companies as studied by them in the late 1970s. But some of these companies have not done well in the 1980s and the others will continue to be successful only if their culture matures beyond the paternalistic model.

Technoservice not only requires higher levels of motivation, but it also asks people to work cooperatively, share information, solve problems, and care about customers, fellow employees, and the success of the business, even if that means sacrificing short-term personal gain. Motivation for technoservice requires attention to psychological concepts totally lacking in partial-man theory; trust, caring, meaning, self-knowledge, dignity.

MOTIVATION FOR TECHNOSERVICE: SOCIAL CHARACTER TYPES AT WORK

To discover what motivates people at work, one must focus on the values that drive behavior and determine why and how we work. In this study I have used the theory and methods of social character research, as I did in my previous books,* to describe those values. Through family, school, and workplace, a culture molds human drives—that is, dynamic behavior patterns—into values that are adaptive to work and social relations. The values shared by a group are the "social character" of that group.

In my books *The Gamesman* and *The Leader*, I studied managers in business and government. For this study, I used the managerial character types described in those books as conceptual tools, expanding and modifying them where they did not fit, to develop a typology for managers and employees at all levels of business and government. The social character types described in Why Work integrate the high-tech managerial types with values of people at all levels of business and government,

---

*Social Character in a Mexican Village, with Erich Fromm (Englewood Cliffs, N.J.: Prentice-Hall, 1970); The Gamesman (New York: Simon and Schuster, 1976); The Leader (New York: Simon and Schuster, 1981). The theory of social character was developed by the psychoanalyst Erich Fromm (1900–1980).

from executives and professionals to the front line of operators, agents, and clerks.

Social character research is a systematic method of differentiating people in terms of value differences that cut across demographic categories. These differences determine motivation and style of leadership. However, if these differences are not named, they will not be noticed and taken seriously in the design of organizations and the education of leadership.

Since each human being is unique, categorizing people into types can be limiting. Yet we cannot avoid it. We think about and describe people in terms of age, sex, intelligence, race, religion, and national origin, even as we recognize that no one can be fully understood by these stereotypes. But these categories only marginally explain motivation (e.g., working mothers want day-care facilities; younger workers want higher wages instead of pension benefits).

Many managers use their own categories to explain motivation, such as, "She's a real marketeer; she loves to put on shows," or, "He's an engineering type; he has to measure everything." The most effective managers continually modify their categories according to experience.* The purpose of my social character types is to refine these categories, sensitize perception, enrich experience, and deepen understanding of people at work.

A typology is a conceptual tool. It should not be used to pigeonhole or caricature people, but to understand better what is meaningful and satisfying to them. Social character types are "ideal" types, exaggerations based on dominant values. They are like photographs that show one figure in high focus while the rest of the picture is blurred. Unlike other typologies based on needs or temperament style (such as Carl Jung's introvert-extrovert dichotomy), social character describes shared values

---

*Donald A. Schön shows how professionals use and modify practical theories to solve problems in *The Reflective Practitioner: How Professionals Think in Action* (New York: Basic Books, 1983).

and how they are formed. The theory helps us to understand ourselves within a particular culture. It shows us how different patterns of upbringing cause variations in the dominant values that motivate us at work. Although most people are a mixture of types, the *Gamesman* research team of psychologists and psychiatrists agreed that in over 80 percent of the cases they studied, including practically all of the most successful managers, one of the four types predominated. The other 20 percent fell into many small mixed types, and for the purpose of generalizing, we left them to one side.

In *The Gamesman*, I described managerial social character based on 250 interviews with managers in ten successful high-tech companies at the cutting edge of change in the early 1970s. (Four of the companies—Hewlett-Packard, International Business Machines, Schlumberger, and Texas Instruments—were also included as exemplary models in *In Search of Excellence*.) These managers participated in the study and helped shape the conclusions because they were interested in better understanding themselves, what made them effective at work, and how their work shaped their values. After analyzing their responses, I distinguished four variations on corporate social character. I called these types *craftsman, jungle fighter, company man,* and *gamesman,* terms the high-tech managers were able to use meaningfully to describe differences in motivation among themselves.

Craftsmen value making, building, designing high-quality products and systems. They tend to be responsible, self-contained, prudently conservative, and paternalistic. Craftsmen fit easily into a system of masters and apprentices. As leaders, they tend towards perfectionism. They seek one best way to do things, and find it difficult to delegate.

Jungle fighters live in a psychological world where they see everyone as either predator or prey. The worst fit that television stereotype of the American businessman, J. R. Ewing of *Dallas*. At their best, like the lion, they defend their workplace families. Some of the builders of American industry were jungle fighters, and today there are still lion-like entrepreneurs such as Ross Perot of Electronic Data Systems in Dallas, who risked his life to protect his employees imprisoned in Iran.[6] Protectors at the top can create freedom for front-line employees, but jungle fighters at middle levels resist sharing power and block the open exchange of information necessary to effective technoservice.

Company men value harmony, cooperation, and identification with the organization. They are other-directed careerists who climb the corporate ladder by making themselves useful to bosses. They flourished in the age of rapid growth of fat American corporations. Their drive for consensus can smooth over conflict and drag the organization toward mediocrity. As corporations struggle to become lean and competitive, the negative side of the company is fueled by fear of the future.

Gamesmen see a developing project, human relations, and their own careers in terms of options and possibilities, as if they were a game. Their characters are collections of near-paradoxes understood in terms of adaptation to the needs of the business. They are detached and playful, but compulsively driven to succeed; team players, but would-be superstars; team leaders, but often rebels against bureaucratic hierarchy; tough and dominating, but fair and unprejudiced.

Each of these types has both positive and negative potentials. The positive side is more productive and flexible, the negative side is more defensive and rigid. Formative experiences and current opportunities determine which side will be expressed. When there is a good fit between the requirements of work and values, people become more successful, respond to opportunity, and gain the incentive for more positive development. When conditions no longer allow a type to adapt, negative traits become stronger. People feel frustrated, unappreciated, resentful, and defensive. Consider, for example, the hard-working, self-reliant farmers who, no longer able to prosper, become increasingly isolated, angry, and paranoid about the politicians and bankers whom they blame for their disaster.

In my subsequent book, *The Leader*, I predicted the emergence of a new social character type for whom the dominant meaning of work would be self-development. Since writing that book, my associates and I have interviewed many self-developers at work, and through surveys I have charted the growth in their numbers.

THE NEW TYPES

In the process of interviewing employees at all levels of business and government for this book, I found that the high-tech managerial types of *The Gamesmen* described above did not quite fit. Like the craftsmen, many accountants, doctors, executives, salesmen, and clerks valued mastery and excellence, but not necessarily designing and building products and systems. The values of government lawyers and whistle-blowers are in some ways similar to those of corporate jungle fighters. Both feel they must fight to defend their dignity, vanquish people who might harm them, and protect those who are loyal to them. But in contrast to the jungle fighter's striving to be the head monkey, the most positive values of the defender transcend the jungle and promote the public good. So I developed a new social character typology in which my original types become subtypes.

I decided to make the gamesman a subtype of a new type I called the innovator, because the term *gamesman* for many people suggests only the compulsive drive to win and willingness to gamble, in contrast to the positive values of playful creation and daring strategy to develop markets and organizations embodied in the term *innovator*. Furthermore, I wanted a gender-neutral name that comfortably fit women as well as men.

I named the new types according to positive values that motivate them at work and determine their leadership style. These types—*expert, helper, defender, innovator,* and *self-developer*—are broader than those of *The Gamesman*, and one can see more easily the possibility of a combination of types. Experts include craftsmen; a subgroup of helpers with defender values are institutional helpers or company men; lion-like jungle fighters are a type of defender; innovators are creative gamesmen.

The following chart shows the relationship between the social character types of *The Gamesman* and the broader types of this book.

SOCIAL CHARACTER TYPES

Type	Dominant Values
EXPERT	Mastery, control, automony
Craftsman	Excellence in making
HELPER	Relatedness, caring for people
Company man, institutional helper	Survival, sociability
DEFENDER	Protection, dignity
Jungle fighter	Power, self-esteem
INNOVATOR	Creating, experimenting
Gamesman	Glory, competition
SELF-DEVELOPER	Balancing mastery and play, knowledge and fun

Most people balance more than one of these value types, and the best employees are a mixture of all of them. Usually, however, one type describes the dominant meaning of work for people. In subsequent chapters, the strengths and weaknesses of each type, their character development, and how each views service, work relationships, and management are described.

For *experts*, service means providing technical excellence and professional knowledge. Their highest values relate to mastery and achievement. Their search for autonomy in an organization pushes them up the hierarchy through functional specialization and toward professionalism. Typical experts are surgeons, foreign service officers, auditors, air traffic controllers. But would-be experts are found among salespeople, computer operators, and policemen.

For *helpers*, service means helping people, responding to their needs. They value relationships above all and seek to make the workplace a family. They represent a secondary American value, oriented to caring rather than to individualistic achievement or self-development. Typical helpers are teachers and nurses, but they can be found in most fields.*

For *defenders*, service means policing and protection. They are most concerned with values of survival and are also strong in the defense of human dignity. They include both the corporate empire-builders and their critics like Ralph Nader and government whistle-blowers.

For *innovators*, service means creating and implementing competitive strategy. They value the game for its own sake and the glory of winning. They are naturally enterprising, like Steven Jobs, the cofounder of Apple Computer, and Lee Iacocca of Chrysler.

For the new generation, the *self-developers*, service means facilitating a problem-solving process with customers and clients. It is also an opportunity to learn, grow, and gain a sense of competency and independence. Self-developers value an egalitarian workplace where authority belongs to the one who is in the best position to know.

---

*A subgroup of helpers, *institutional helpers*, combines the values of helpers and defenders. For them, service means helping leaders. Although they are not a distinct character type, I included them as a separate category in the survey questionnaire on values at work I developed for this study (see pages 42-43) because they seemed sufficiently different from the helper. However, people who find meaning in helping the leader *do not* necessarily care about people. The most productive institutional helpers care about defending the organization and its values. The less productive merely want to share the leader's strength; their desire to help is the company man's need to identify with the powerful organization. I have not written a separate chapter on the institutional helper. Since most are mixtures of either helpers or defenders, I include positive examples of institutional helpers in Chapters 4 and 5.

THE QUESTIONNAIRE: VALUES AT WORK

To test the conclusions drawn from the interviews and from observations and to study the distribution of the new character types, a short questionnaire was constructed based on brief descriptions of each type. The questionnaire asks employees how and if they identify with the values motivating each type, and whether or not they are able to express these values in their own jobs.

The first part of the questionnaire is reproduced below. Fill it out so that you can compare yourself to the people described in the next chapters.

How Well Does Each Statement Describe Your Approach to Work?

	Very well	Some-what	A little	Not at all
A. You approach your work as an expert. Whatever your job, you want to provide high-quality work and to exercise your skill and competence.	1	2	3	4
B. You approach your work as a helper. You want to help people.	1	2	3	4
C. You approach your work as a defender. You want to defend against those who do not respect the law, who do harm, or who undermine the values essential to a good organization.	1	2	3	4
D. You approach your work as a helper to those in positions of leadership. You want to strengthen your organization by serving well those who have the authority to make decisions.	1	2	3	4
E. You approach your work as an innovator who knows how to play the bureaucratic game. You want to win by making the organization more successful.	1	2	3	4
F. You approach your work as the means to a self-fulfilling life. You want your work to further your own development	1	2	3	4

Which of the above approaches to work are most important to you? Please write the letters of those choices.

	1st choice	2nd choice	

	Very much	Some- what	A little	Not at all
To what extent does your current job permit you to take this positive approach?				
First choice	1	2	3	4
Second choice	1	2	3	4
To what extent does the following statement apply to you? You came to your job with a positive approach but have found that the system and its leaders keep you from working in this way.	1	2	3	4

The questionnaire has been administered to over 3,000 people. The results from seven interesting samples are given in Appendix C. The first combines 650 employees from ten different service sector businesses and government agencies (*Service Sector* sample). The second describes about 300 middle and upper managers from a telecommunications and information service company (*Telecommunications* sample). The third includes 180 middle and upper managers in a high-tech service company which designs information systems (*High-Tech* sample). The fourth is a sample of 135 agents and managers of the Internal Revenue Service (*Government* sample), the fifth includes about 700 managers from the National Aeronautics and Space Administration (*NASA*). The sixth presents 46 leaders (80 percent under age forty) brought together for a seminar by a major foundation (*Young Leaders*), and the seventh consists of 106 college students who were summer interns at a major technology company (*College Interns*). Besides these, the survey has been given to other groups from business, government agencies, and schools.

The distribution of character types varies among samples. This happens because organizations can be considered as *psychostructures*. That is to say, types are selected and select themselves to fit the styles required by a role that serves a particular organization's goals. For example, a higher percentage of teachers (75 percent) than Internal Revenue Agents (51 percent) say that the phrase "I want to help people" describes them very well. On the other hand, a much higher percentage of the IRS (44 percent) than teachers (8 percent) check "defender" as describing them very well. The percentage of innovators is higher in business than in government. Indeed, most of the innovators I have met in government eventually left for business.

Different types approach the same job differently. Defender-revenue agents or government auditors are more aggressive in attacking suspected criminals than are the experts. Helper-teachers show more interest in slow students than do experts, who respond most to achievers like themselves.

Almost everyone surveyed identified to some degree with each of these values, but the *most important* to most people in both business and government are, first, those of the expert (about 50 percent), and then the self-developer (20 percent).* These express the individualistic values of traditional and new-generation Americans. Helping (15 percent) or helping leaders (7 percent), innovating (8 percent), and defending organizations (1 percent) are less frequently chosen as most important. The Service Sector and High-Tech samples are even more expert-oriented, with 92 percent of the NASA managers indicating that this description fits them very well, and 72 percent listing it as most important. The Young Leaders and College Interns identify most with the self-developers. (Over 90 percent of the Young Leaders and 93 percent of the Interns say this describes them very well.)

Most employees of all types, especially those at higher levels,

---

*Checking an approach as "most important" is considered to indicate the primary way people see themselves.

feel they can express their preferred orientation at work. Three-fourths of all the samples believe their job allows them to take their favored approach very much or somewhat. What dissatisfied about 60 percent (very much or somewhat) is leadership, lack of communication with and too little participation in management.

This means that although most American employees feel they can be experts or self-developers at work, the majority also believe that the system and its leaders keep them from working as productively as they can. This seeming contradiction can be explained. Most Americans have a basically positive attitude toward work. In companies and government bureaucracies, there is room for expertise and self-development. But people feel that red tape and overcontrolling management limit them. They are dissatisfied with organization and authority, although the meaning of this dissatisfaction is different for the different types.

Although there are few entrepreneurial innovators in either business or government, a larger percentage at higher levels consider this approach as most important to them than do people at lower levels. Ten percent of the top managers see themselves as innovators, versus 6 percent of middle managers, 2 percent of skilled workers, and 0 percent of clerical workers. In the Telecommunications sample, 17 percent of upper management see themselves as innovators, versus 6 percent of lower management.

For the most part the types are distributed fairly evenly among the age groups—with two noticeable exceptions. There are fewer female helpers among the younger generation than the old. That is to be expected now that women are gaining options beyond the traditional helping roles.*

---

*However, in the IRS sample, more women (17%) than men (4%) see themselves as primarily helpers, and this difference is reinforced by second choices (women, 40%; men, 22%). The difference is explained by the fact that women have traditionally been selected for helping roles in the IRS, such as service specialists who give information to taxpayers. More of the men were in roles like revenue agents and criminal investigators that called for defenders.

The major age difference is seen in the self-developers. They are a higher percentage of the under-forty employees (25 percent) than of the over forty (14 percent). At age thirty, it is 30 percent. This difference between younger and older employees holds for all samples, and among the young leaders, there is an overwhelming emphasis on self-development. We also found an even higher percentage of self-developers among the sample of College Interns (40 percent) and High School Seniors (35 percent).

This age pattern fits my thesis in *The Leader* (1981) that values among new-generation careerists have become more oriented to self-development than to merely moving up the hierarchy. Of course, it might indicate that older people have become less interested in self-development, but the first explanation is supported by Daniel Yankelovich's surveys over the past fifteen years, which show these values have been spreading.[7] It is even more convincingly shown by the correlation of self-developer with the two-wage-earner family and by the interview findings reported in the following chapters, which demonstrate how these values were formed in childhood as people adapted to different family constellations and social mores.

OUR TIME

In the 1960s, social character began to change. Why did values change? Why does the change continue?

First, general prosperity in the sixties undermined the frugal, self-sacrificing, and dutiful values of the social character formed in the first half of the century. The majority of the country became a consumer-oriented society, experimenting continually with new forms of pleasure. Television flooded minds with images, ambitions, and wants. Affluent parents accepted and paid for their children's new needs for clothes, travel, and education. Employees with more years of schooling expected to continue their learning at work.

Second, political movements of both New Right and New Left attacked bureaucracy as dehumanizing and set the stage for organizational change. Writing for the Left in 1962, Tom Hayden called for a new community, acceptance of one whole man by another whole man, not those forms of partial contact fostered by bureaucratic life. On the Right, Michael Bernstein's 1961 "Goldwater Manifesto" spoke for the "total man" against the crippled liberal bureaucrat dependent on institutions and unable to stand up for liberty.[8] Both models of freedom aroused the national psyche. The movements of the 1960s began on the University of California, Berkeley campus with a demand for free speech and an attack on dehumanization, starting with the IBM registration cards which were fed into computers. (Students were incited to "fold, spindle, and mutilate" their cards.)

The ambition to be more of a whole person at work was fed by TV shows, like those in which Mary Tyler Moore and Bob Newhart brought viewers into their service-oriented workplaces, a TV station and a group therapy session.

Third, the sixties brought a new sense of individual rights and criticism of authority. Welfare policies and workplace protections lessened fear of speaking out. The civil rights and antiwar movements reinforced the challenge to traditional authority. Activists identified authority with old men who hoarded power, sent the young men to war, and lied to the public about Watergate. Haunted by the threat of nuclear war and made indignant by reports of ecological damage, young people questioned the authority of science and technology that threatened the planet.

Fourth, electronic technology, much of it developed in the space program, created new opportunities for entrepreneurs. Young engineers and scientists outstripped their elders and became impatient with outmoded ideas. These irreverent innovators modeled a new style of participative management in high-tech companies.

Fifth, and perhaps most important, the mass entry of women into the workplace signaled the end of the family with a sole

47

male wage earner, and with it the traditional sex roles and the paternal model of managerial authority.

The dramatic rebellions of the sixties are over, but despite some backlash, trends begun then have continued. Although America is pulling back from sexual excess and self-indulgence, and rediscovering the need for discipline and good leadership, the forces changing values at work have not receded.

The percentage of dual-career families and those with a sole female working have been steadily increasing. The percentage of households with a sole male breadwinner has decreased from 69 percent in 1954 to 33 percent in 1984, while that of families in which both husband and wife work has jumped from 28 percent to 50 percent and those with a single female wage earner have increased from 4 percent to 15 percent.

The self-developers tend to come from families where both parents worked. At an early age, they have had to adapt to strangers and develop interpersonal skills. Increasingly, American children are being raised to become self-developers by parents who are away at work much of the day. In the last ten years alone, the percentage of working mothers with children under one year of age jumped from 30 percent to nearly 50 percent.

The new social character no longer models itself on the paternal image at work, or on the maternal image at home. The two-wage-earner family requires shared authority and trade-offs between work and family. Self-development means that both men and women must create their own models of maturity. It means a different motivation at work.

We are in a period of value transformations, pushed along by changes in work and family structure. Traditional and new value orientations exist side by side in organizations. Self-developers tend to be younger, but it is important to emphasize that a significant percentage of the young still identify with the traditional generation. There is a communication gap between value types, even within the same age group. The traditional experts and helpers see the self-developers as egotistical and superficial, and do not recognize their greater flexibility and co-operative potential. To motivate the new generation, we need new organizations and leadership. To work more effectively, we need to understand ourselves and each other.

CHAPTER 1

WHAT MOTIVATES?

Why do we work?

Work ties us to a real world that tells us whether or not our ideas and visions make sense; it demands that we discipline our talents and master our impulses. To realize our potentialities, we must focus them in a way that relates us to the human community. We need to feel needed. And to feel needed, we must be evaluated by others in whatever coinage, tangible or not, culture employs. Our sense of dignity and self-worth depends on being recognized by others through our work. Without work, we deteriorate. We need to work.

Through work we express ourselves and practice commitment. When activity that springs from a spirit of play, like music or painting or sports, moves to the category of work, this implies a seriousness of purpose beyond pleasure in activity for its own sake. However, we differentiate work that expresses a vocation, work we love to do, from work we agree to do as a means of gaining a livelihood, having status as employed, or paying our dues so that we can do "our own work."

Hope also drives us to work. We expect rewards according to our values. We hope our work will bring us money, pleasure, appreciation, fame, power, knowledge, independence, a better world, and possibly the satisfaction of creative fulfillment. The underside of hope is fear of not reaching our goals or measuring up to expectations. The urge to work is an emotional necessity directed by our values and opportunities.

Thus, the strongest universal motivators to work are self-expression, hope, and fear. Neurobiological research illustrates how necessary hope is to the survival drive. David Ingvar's research with Position Emission Tomography (PET Scan) shows computer-generated pictures of the neocortex during different states of mind. Ingvar finds that the brain turns off when people cannot anticipate a positive future.[1] We cannot solve problems without hope. People who face a dead end need to spark a facsimile of hope. Some retreat from life and seek hope where they can, in compulsive gambling or in a lottery ticket. Hope can come from denying unpleasant reality and escaping to a wishful future. But even optimism that is irrational becomes habit-forming, because it allows people to function. It motivates them to act, if not to work.

Of course, hopefulness depends not only on seeing opportunity, but also on a feeling of optimism. We all know people with sunny, optimistic dispositions, and we like to be around them. This emotional attitude of hope seems to be a natural quality or an inborn gift in some people. The attitude of hope attracts us to possibilities for growth, opportunities for productive relationships. For most of us, a hopeful attitude was nurtured by loving parents who satisfied our infant needs and promised us a bright future if we worked for it. Hope is bolstered by disciplined learning and achievement that make us feel we can take advantage of opportunities. It is strengthened when as adults we take responsibility for creating a better future in every way we can. For those people whose hope wavers, and that is true some of the time for most of us, leadership can rekindle hope, at least for a while. Despite his fuzzy visions, Ronald Reagan's optimism encouraged many Americans who wanted to believe him. Thus, the perennial appeal of motivational speakers preaching, "We can do it." But positive thinking can also become a narcotic, blurring unpleasant realities that require painful decisions and action.

Good leaders cannot create motivation in others, but they can direct and amplify it. Optimistic and supportive leaders bring out a positive attitude in those they lead; but worried, pessimistic leaders make everyone feel worse.* A skillful coach can pump up a team's intensity and drive to win. But the leadership that helps motivate best depends primarily on understanding the values of those led.

To understand what motivates ourselves and others, we must identify our dynamic values. Such an understanding leads the way to both organizational productivity and development of our individual potential at work.

Values are slippery concepts. They can be defined narrowly as "a principal, standard, or quality considered worthwhile or desirable."[2] We also think of human values in a broader sense as energized patterns of perceiving, thinking, wanting, and acting shared by members of a society. I call these patterns *value drives*.

All of us are born with dynamic tendencies, drives that direct our actions. For example, we respond to pain with flight or fight; we are driven to repeat pleasures, master the environment, communicate and so on.** While all human beings share these dynamic tendencies, they are expressed and directed by different values according to the culture, acting through family, school, and workplace.

---

*Goran Ekvall and Jouko Arvonen, in "Leadership Styles and Organizational Climate for Creativity" (Stockholm: The Swedish Council for Management and Worklife Issues, working paper, 1984), show that 75 percent of the workplace climate, defined as feelings of optimism, openness to and support of subordinates' ideas, etc., is determined by leadership style.

**Some psychologists and ethologists object to the use of the term *drives* as unobservable and prefer using *behaviors* or *behavior patterns*. In Appendix B, I explain why I use *value drives*.

The creation of value drives is a biologically necessary function of culture. Human decision-making is less genetically programmed than that of other creatures. Shared value drives (social character) allow us to act instinctively, as it were, in ways which are common to members of a culture and facilitate effective social relations. Otherwise, we would be overwhelmed with conflicting impulses and paralyzed by the constant demand to evaluate and decide what to do and how to interpret the behavior of others. Enough must be programmed into us to participate in the culture. But we also need flexibility to adapt to change. In our education, we human beings need a balance between structure and freedom.

As we grow up, we can develop value drives by defining ourselves, deciding what we should do or not do in different situations, and disciplining ourselves with good habits so that we can achieve desirable goals. However, few people make the effort to define and shape their values (see Chapter 7). Most people do not question the values taught them: they accept the rules of family, school, and workplace. Only when these rules conflict or don't work will most people start thinking about changing their values. Now is such a time for many people.

VALUE DRIVES

Psychologists and psychoanalysts study motivation through experiments and clinical observation. I have tried to integrate their findings in the light of my own experience with the emotionally disturbed in the consulting room and ordinary people at work.

Most psychoanalytic views of motivation are limited by the sample of humanity upon which they are based—the emotionally disturbed, mostly from a common culture and social class, i.e., the white, urban upper-middle class, studied in an artificial setting such as the hospital or the psychoanalyst's office. The psychoanalyst is not likely to study value drives as they operate in healthy, productive people, but as they are expressed in perverted form, by patients with unconscious conflicts and addictive, irrational needs.

Thus, psychoanalytic theories apply the psychology of illness to healthy situations. These theories assume that attitudes expressed by mature people at work are all formed in early childhood. In contrast, in the tradition of Erich Fromm, David Riesman, and Erik Erikson, I expand psychoanalytic theory to nonpatients and, as an anthropologist, observe the workplace in different countries and social classes. Social character is a theory for understanding both health and sickness.

My observation and study of children and adults, the emotionally disturbed and the healthy, peasant farmers and high-tech managers, have challenged me to make sense of similarities and differences in human motivation that are not explained by the existing theories of motivation. I have formulated a theory to fit the scientific evidence and my own experience. I see its purpose as an intellectual tool for others to develop or refine their own working theories of motivation. The search for goals and behaviors common to all cultures leads me to group value drives into eight categories: *survival, relatedness, pleasure, information, mastery, play, dignity,* and *meaning.* (See Appendix B for a note on how I arrived at these categories.) This is not a hierarchy; everyone expresses each drive in some form. Furthermore, value drives may be in conflict. At certain times, one drive will dominate. The value of survival usually takes precedence over the others, but not always. For example, a person may risk death to preserve dignity or freedom, or to protect others, or death may be accepted because it has religious meaning. Some people risk their lives for the pleasure in mastering mountains or winning car races. The value drives underlie achievement and illness. Paranoics sacrifice relationships in their drive for elusive total security; their investment in defense leaves little energy for health, education, and welfare.

Because all eight value drives are what make us human, we

cannot rank any of them as necessarily higher versus lower. But each drive can be expressed in a style that is either lower—primitive and childlike—or higher—mature and developed. Higher values expand consciousness and inner freedom, increase hope and creative power. Work is a means for developing our value drives and becoming more integrated and purposeful.

NEEDS AND DRIVES

In common language, we speak of needs, not value drives. How many times a day do we use the phrase, "I need"? We say, "I need to work," or "I need to eat," not "I am driven to work." But the term *need* refers to both a force we feel and to a value; I use the term *value drive* to emphasize this and stimulate readers to evaluate their needs. Human needs are never purely physiological; we always express a value when we speak of a need. A need statement can always be transformed into a value statement. If I say, "I need something," ask me what will happen if I don't get it. The answer, "I'll be lonely, less capable, humiliated," describes a value—relatedness, mastery, dignity. Even necessity ("I need it to survive") expresses a universal value of life. We can correlate some common needs with their common values.

Need	Value
Eating, drinking, sex	Survival, pleasure
Dependency, protection, love	Relatedness
Achievement, glory, fame	Mastery, dignity

To evaluate needs, we can distinguish three types: developmental, maintenance, and addictive. These can either strengthen or weaken us, depending on the values they express. *Developmental needs* activate us and increase energy; they include the need to know, to achieve, and to create through art and science. *Maintenance needs* keep us going and maintain a sense of dignity through good habits. They include eating (in moderation) and sleeping, exercising mind and body, and practicing good manners. Both developmental and maintenance needs require discipline, and both strengthen us. *Addictive needs* weaken us; they are needs for drugs and also the perverse needs for sadistic power, effortless luxury, narcissistic adulation, and false hopes. When our drives are directed by productive values, we make decisions and practice habits that serve our best interests; we create developmental needs. When we are driven unconsciously by irrational values, we have addictive needs. Even needs that are developmental at one stage of life, like dependence on a good teacher, can later become addictive bonds that sap our initiative and self-confidence.

FEELING MOTIVATED

Normally, we are not particularly conscious of being motivated to work. But when faced with a problem to solve, or an opportunity to exploit, we are suddenly aware of being motivated. Pressure makes us aware of our values. Frustration brings out our drives. We are stymied by a problem and feel a need to solve it. We are threatened and feel a drive to prevail. We are insulted and feel a need for self-assertion and dignity. But drives can also be repressed and unconscious. Today, many people repress the fury generated by attacks on their self-esteem. This repression is caused by a conflict of values; for example, wanting to keep your job clashing with a wish to punch the boss in the nose, an impulse which goes underground. It does not disappear, but festers into some form of bad-humored resentment. Workaholics are driven by irrational drives such as the need to gain a parent's approval. Those of us less irrationally motivated express the work ethic in the need to achieve and create.

We are most motivated when work satisfies our developmental needs. We feel the most productive energy when there is an opportunity to satisfy these needs through a balance of work and play. Our energy either is strengthened and focused by these activities, or it is dissipated through addictive needs and frozen by repression.

THE EIGHT VALUE DRIVES IN THE WORKPLACE

Different situations at work stimulate different drives. Furthermore, different character types are motivated by patterns of value drives which, as we shall see, have been reinforced by different types of family subcultures. For example, the dominant drive for the expert is mastery, for the helper it is relatedness.

VALUE DRIVES

Survival
  Sustenance
  Nutrition
  Livable environment
  Healthy rhythms of sleep and
    wakefulness
  Relief of stress and maintenance of
    health
  Avoidance of danger
  Self-defense
  Defense of one's group

Relatedness
  Attachment
  Care
  Protection
  Recognition
  Communication
  Sociability
  Community

Pleasure
  Comfort
  Sex
  Tasty food and drink
  Exercise and rest
  Novelty

Fun
Beauty

Information
Sensory stimulation
Directions, cues, signals, signs,
   feedback
Knowledge
Understanding

Mastery
Competence
Control
Ownership
Autonomy
Achievement
Power

Play
Exploration
Fantasy
Adventure
Competition
Experimentation
Creativity
Innovation

Dignity
Respect
Self-esteem
Glory
Integrity

Meaning
Universal
Cultural
Individual

Survival: the drive toward sustenance, nutrition, a livable environment (temperature, air), healthy rhythms of sleep and wakefulness, relief from life-threatening stress, avoidance of danger, and self-defense or the defense of group by flight or fight. In a rich society like the United States, worries about survival focus for many not on getting enough to eat, but on maintaining health through diet, exercise, and relief of stress. Indeed, with affluence, survival becomes a less dominant concern.

However, the human organism is quickly mobilized by real and imaginary threats to survival. Indeed, a problem for the organizational careerist is that threats to employment security or even promotion are reacted to with the same rush of endocrine that neolithic men and women felt in the face of attack by wild animals. When our survival drive is triggered, emotions of flight or fight and catastrophic images dominate thought and behavior. The possibility of layoffs and unemployment, even uncertainty during reorganizations, alert the survival drive. Crisis produces adrenaline, which first activates but eventually paralyzes the body. Good leadership can bind survival anxieties by presenting a hopeful vision and directing people to act. The job of the leader throughout history has been to direct survival drives to common goals, to express and defend a vision that infuses followers with hope.

But sometimes it is essential for leaders to break through defenses and mobilize anxiety to save an organization: people must be told that unless they cut costs, produce more, improve quality, the business will go under. This kind of situation is always risky. While survival fear focuses energy, it narrows interest to looking out for number one. For many employees, especially in large organizations, personal security becomes the overwhelming need. Insecurity drives them to unproductive politics, protecting themselves at the expense of the organization.

Like the other seven drives, survival can dominate personality. When this occurs, a person is forever oriented to defense. The jungle fighter is the survival-obsessed character who sees the world in terms of threats to survival and organizes other value drives—relatedness, mastery, meaning—around this orientation. Such people need power over others to quiet their fear. The most positive version of the type is the protector, who expands the drive to survive to include others.

Each character type emphasizes its own style of maintaining a sense of employment security. Traditional craftsmen believe they will maintain security by self-reliance, by controlling nature and the world around them. Modern bureaucratic experts expect to find security in both specialization and seniority. Helpers trust in family-type groups where people stick together. Self-developers, brought up in relative affluence, are least worried about employment security, but they are concerned with maintaining and developing their marketable skills. The fear for them, as for the gamesman, is not survival, but being a loser in the career game. Gamesmen are unique in that danger triggers their productive motivation. The challenge turns them on.

Relatedness: the drive toward attachment, care, protection, recognition, communication, community. Relatedness is essential to sanity. Different modes of relatedness separate illness from health. A neurotic is someone who lives with fantasies more than with people; the totally unrelated individual is psychotic. Psychoanalysis has charted the development of the drive for relatedness. Originally, Freud focused on the individualistic sexual drive, but in his later years, he took more account of the infant's pre-Oedipal drive for relatedness. Since Freud, other psychologists—for example, Rene Spitz, Margaret Mahler, John Bowlby, and Mary Ainsworth—have studied infants and young children, showing how relatedness develops and describing negative results when the drive is frustrated.[3] William James had earlier observed infantile instincts of imitation, sympathetic response, smiling, and attachment, all beginnings of the drive toward relatedness.[4]

From early childhood, we have all sought to be understood and to be connected with other human beings. The drives for care, protection, and recognition inevitably clash with other more individualistic drives for autonomy, mastery, play, dignity. The resolution of these conflicts depends not only on individual character, but also on the culture and its support for diverse, individual expression. When George Foster and I studied Mexican villagers, we found one of the most original potters in the village suffered crippling anxiety because he was too original and feared being ostracized by the other villagers.[5] In contrast, our society supports the process of individuation, breaking away from constraining relationships to express the self. At an early age, we already react to "excessive" care as constraining. Paradoxically, we want to be free, but not lonely, so we seek playmates, work partners, or the camaraderie of a team. As we become more individuated, to avoid isolation we must seek others who share our values and support our aims.

The chance to enjoy sociability at work is a significant motivation for many people. It must be considered in the design of a motivating workplace and the selection of people for jobs. In *The Leader*, I reported that many assembly-line workers in the Harman auto parts factory in Bolivar, Tennessee, said that socializing was the most important aspect of their work, and they rejected more challenging jobs that would have isolated them from conversation. When I repeated this to a group of General Mills managers and workers, I was told a story about two women who spent fifteen years dropping coupons into cereal boxes coming off the line at a factory. When they were told by a manager that the job was to be automated and that they would be relieved of the monotony, they were disappointed. The manager asked if they liked the job. They told him the job had long ago become automatic, but they had spent the work hours talking to each other about their outside lives. Each knew the other's family intimately. What they would miss were the daily conversations. In Cambridge, Massachusetts, mothers working on computer terminals at home preferred bringing their children to a child-care center at a common workplace where they could talk to each other. The vision of futurist Alvin Toffler of the electronic cottage industry may appeal to expert programmers and workers, but the loneliness of the word processor turns off many in the new generation. If given a choice between working at the office or at home by telecommuting, only 7 percent of employees would choose to stay at home.[6]

The satisfaction of work relations is not limited to lower-levels of organizations. People underestimate the glue of fellowship in organizations, especially at the top. In Los Angeles, marketing managers of a large technology company became independently rich buying and selling real estate. Yet they did not leave the company. The reason: they enjoyed being part of a team. In traditional companies, the father-son mentoring relationships provided deep satisfaction. Among competitive peers, those who have overcome obstacles together feel bonds of affection that facilitate teamwork. Top managers in large corporations have told me that being part of a supportive team and sharing values is one of the most satisfying aspects of their work, but they seldom generalize this experience to the design of lower-level work.

Relatedness for helpers includes contact not only with co-workers, but also with customers and clients. When the Communications Workers of America (CWA) organized social workers in New Jersey, Morton Bahr, the union president, noted that a new type of resolution was introduced at meetings. In contrast to expert-type workers in the union who demanded better pay and improved working conditions for themselves, the social workers demanded more help for their clients. Responsive caring and coaching are forms of behavior that express mature relatedness.

The development of the drive for relatedness requires the ability to question authority and break the chains of dependency. Many who work in organizations, especially the experts and the helpers, fail to achieve a sense of independence. They experience the organization as a protective family, and their drives for security and relatedness merge into powerful transferential feelings toward the leader, inappropriately seen as a parent, feared and loved as though one were still a child. The strong transference motivates one to please the parent. This is why the entrepreneurial leaders cited by Peters and Waterman could motivate subordinates so effectively by expressions of approval. The new character, the self-developer, is more critical of parents and authority, more intent on gaining independence, and therefore less moved by transferential drives. Self-developers are less likely to seek mentors, but also less likely to be mentors.

Pleasure: the drive toward comfort (avoiding discomfort and pain), sexual satisfaction, tasty food and drink, stimulation, novelty, fun, beauty. Physiologically, there are three types of pleasure: appetite, as in sweet taste or sexual arousal; tension reduction, as in orgasm; and activity pleasure, as in the harmonious exercise of mind and body. Pleasure and pain are the infant's first way of learning and they forever influence all value drives. For the adolescent, sexuality is of course most demanding, experienced in continual frustration and frequent fantasy. Pleasure is developed aesthetically as good taste, a love of beauty, and a sense of harmony. It is developed ethically as the pleasure in staying within the rules. It is developed creatively as the pleasure in learning, innovating, designing, building, crafting, and helping things grow. However, the drive for pleasure is easily transformed into addictive needs that undermine productive values.

Historically, economic conditions have placed limits on the expression of the pleasure drive. In an era of scarcity, the Puritan Ethic demanded self-restraint, ascetic control, and mastery of the pleasure drive. Of course, today, in an era of relative abundance, such prohibitions are no longer considered necessary by most people.

By lifting the limitations placed on private and public pleasure, we fertilize the economy of a society, allowing an infinite number of needs to flower. But we also increase the possibility that addiction to pleasure might undermine drives for mastery and self-control.

What implications does the strengthening of the pleasure values have for the workplace? The liberation of the pleasure drive means that people want and expect work to be more fun. If the workplace fails to fulfill needs for pleasure, workers seek pleasure in ways that divert them from work. Correspondingly, where work is more fun and, as we shall see, playful, people invest more of themselves at work.

Information: the drive toward sensory stimulation, messages (direction, cues, signals, signs), feedback, knowledge, understanding. From early infancy, we seek information in the form of sights and sounds that exercise our faculties, and messages that reassure us. As we grow older, we need information to orient ourselves to the world we live in and avoid danger, find pleasurable experiences, and master skills. Also, the brain transforms information into memory and uses it to project visions of a desirable future, the hope essential to motivation. This ability to gather information from our environment is necessary to feeling human. Psychologists have found that putting a person into a dark, soundproof room disintegrates the individual's sense of self.

Culture and language shape the drive for information. In different cultures, people attend to and name the world according to their needs and traditions. Peasants notice and react to small differences in crops and animals, information that would not register in the urban mind. In peasant villages, information about neighbors, gossip, is highly valued as a form of social control. In modern organizations, gossip becomes the main source of information when people lose trust in the messages coming down from the top.

Managements often puzzle over how difficult it is to communicate information to the troops. Yet, when the message is trusted or appreciated, there is no communication problem. In a company building with 3,000 employees, the executive in charge worried about improving communication. But he noticed that one winter day when an announcement was made at 2 P.M. that because of blizzard warnings, employees could leave early, the building cleared out within ten minutes.

We are most motivated to acquire information that satisfies our values. Experts scan for information in their area of expertise that maintains their sense of mastery, and they filter out what they consider irrelevant information, such as human problems. In contrast, helpers like information about people. The ears of defenders perk up when there is information about threats, plots, dangers to their sense of security. Innovators seek information to design new approaches, and self-developers have from childhood sought new experiences and information that expand their horizons, scanning for trends so that they can prepare for an ever-changing future.

All of us seek useful feedback, information that tells us how we are doing, how we are evaluated. People are motivated by the opportunity to get results. They enjoy seeing the score and the chance to improve it. They want to know plans so they can adapt. Lack of information is troubling. Yet some managers tend to hoard information and remain stingy with positive feedback.

As we grow, we acquire, store, and transform information more effectively to adapt to our environment and realize our aspirations. As we learn to identify and solve problems and test hypotheses, we transform information into meaningful knowledge.

There is the reverse side of the need to know: the addiction to information as predigested experience, a cognitive fast food. This is a danger for the new generation, raised on instant knowledge from television and the computer. Members of the new generation need discipline to filter and edit useful information, and beyond this, to develop deeper interest in and understanding of the world and themselves.

Mastery: the drive toward competence, control, ownership, autonomy, achievement, power. Mastery is directed not simply toward the external world, but also toward the self. Survival and hope of success demand competence; moderation and discipline of drives require self-mastery. If we are to adapt to the world, maintain dignity, and enjoy life, our drives must be tamed or managed. Children struggle to walk, talk, and manipulate their environment. Watch the frustration of infants when they cannot move around or make themselves understood. Mastery of language skills allows us to participate in a human group. Expertise and craftsmanship are mature expressions of mastery.

The need for achievement strengthens and develops the mastery drive. People are motivated by challenges that stretch but do not exceed their skills. David McClelland's research shows that people with a strong need for achievement continually push themselves to master new tasks and develop competence.[7]

But mastery requires some control over the job. Where the drive for mastery is frustrated at work, it is either expressed elsewhere or perverted. In 1971, an auto worker with a strong pride in his skill told me that the fast-moving assembly line blocked any attempt to care about craftsmanship. He and others expressed their sense of mastery in a perverted way by trying to stop the line or sometimes by putting a coke bottle into a gas tank. But when work engages the drive for mastery, company and worker benefit. Today in Fremont, California, at the Nummi plant (New United Motor Manufacturing Inc., General Motors in partnership with Toyota) assembly workers can stop the line at any time if they spot poor workmanship. Managers report that the gain in quality and motivation is much greater than the loss in downtime on the line.

Control and power are a form of mastery. The corollary of Lord Acton's dictum that "power tends to corrupt and absolute power corrupts absolutely" is the equally certain law that powerlessness perverts. This concept will be developed further in Chapter 7, Strategic Self-Development. The meanings of power differ for different types. Defenders seek power as an addictive need to dominate or, more positively, to protect themselves and subordinates. Experts want power as authority to do the job in their own way. Innovators want power to organize new approaches to serve customers better, and to improve the quality of life at work. In the technoservice economy, innovators know that to gain real power, they must create it for others. Unless their subordinates have power to satisfy customers and innovate, their own power will be constrained.

Play: the drive toward exploration, fantasy, adventure, competition, experimentation, creativity, innovation. This drive might be grouped with mastery, since play can contribute to mastery by serving as a means of trying out new skills and strategies.[8] But a distinction would be lost. While mastery is necessary to cope with the world and accommodate to authority, pure play belongs to the realm of freedom. Play implies self-expression through exploration, experimentation, and invention. In its most developed forms, play merges with mastery to become creative work: the innovation that depends on disciplined technique necessary to express artistic, scientific, and economic intuitions with beauty and elegance.

In our society, parents and teachers sometimes make children sacrifice play to mastery. Accommodation and conformity dampen the spirit of play. When the drive for play is repressed, it does not disappear, but may emerge as mischief. Or it goes underground as fantasy, excape to the canned creations of the media or to an inner, isolated world, and the personality becomes impoverished. My first experience as a psychotherapist was with children who could not learn, and I found that they had also lost the capacity to play. They feared both the external world of parents and teachers who judged their work, and the internal one of their own angry fantasies.[9] Play which might express these impulses they felt was dangerous. Treatment for these children included playing the roles of feared authorities in such a way that the child could laugh, gain control over impulses, and realize that learning and performance were not matters of life and death. Then they could tolerate fantasies of terror, anger and revenge. Through play, the children gained a sense of freedom and a sense of humor that rekindled their self-esteem and hope and allowed them to put energy into mastering schoolwork.

Since free play is so individualistic, its development requires teaching that respects the unique individual or a temperament stubborn enough to resist regimentation.

In America, the idea of making work into play has long been the ideal of entrepreneurs. The play spirit is a unique strength in this country. It sparks a spirit of exploration, competition, innovation, and adventure. It provides a sense of fun and meaning to businessmen who enjoy making deals, marketers who play with product concepts, and researchers who test out hunches.

In the regimented workplace, people joke and play jokes as a form of rebellion. If this drive is engaged at work, and if there is a sense of game spirit, people easily become motivated.

The new generation wants more play at work, or work as play, and management that can provide it, at least some of the time, is rewarded with more motivated employees. People who are most effective with computers have played with them; they feel at ease with the machine as their tool, not their master. Employee Involvement (EI) and Quality of Worklife (QWL) programs succeed because people enjoy the opportunity to solve problems and experiment. Their training includes liberating the mind to find new ways to solve puzzles. The pleasure is in play as well as mastery. Notably, workers in QWL teams have refused monetary rewards for ideas. They wanted the normal work to include problem-solving and incremental innovation.

However, the drive to play must be managed. Unbridled play becomes unproductive: the gambling gamesman playing with other peoples' lives, the expert's infatuation with high tech as an expensive toy instead of a useful tool. Love of play can cause instability and waste.

The spirit of play is best engaged at work by the chance to experiment and innovate, to question organizational forms and practices and try out new ones. It is the spirit that founded and built America, a society constructed on the impulse to experiment with new models. It can be harnessed at all levels of organizations.

Dignity: the drive toward gaining respect, self-esteem, glory, integrity. We must value ourselves to survive; our sense of dignity, self-esteem, and integrity is essential to productive motivation. Notice the response of shame, pain, and anger when a young child is ridiculed. The drive for dignity appears fragile, easily crushed, but this perception is misleading. As adults, the pressures to survive or accommodate to a job may cause us to swallow humiliation. But while the drive for dignity may be frustrated, it is not extinguished, and takes another form. It is often perverted into fantasy, revenge, and hatred. This frozen rage of people at work can explode into destructive violence.

Dignity needs more explanation than the other value drives because it is ignored by many psychologists, or described only in its narcissistic perversions. Some psychoanalysts confuse dignity with narcissism, which is the drive to love thwarted and turned back on the self. Heinz Kohut, a psychoanalytic theorist of the self, portrays narcissism as a normal drive, when in fact the patients he describes express narcissistic behavior as a reaction to dignity wounded in early childhood.[10] The drive for dignity is a normal one, common to all societies. It unfolds naturally if a child is lovingly valued. Neglected, unloved children can suffer deep wounds to their dignity. Feeling worthless, they compensate with grandiose fantasies of becoming loved by everyone. Oppressed children identify with their oppressors and internalize their guilt, turning their anger against themselves. Overly admired and indulged children have an inflated sense of self-importance, and an exaggerated sense of dignity.

In healthy children, the demand for fairness and justice comes to express the drive for dignity. At about three to six, children recognize that others share the same feelings. The family and culture facilitate this emotion through teaching and games. Children learn to curb their egocentric drives and to respect the dignity of others. It is the role of the parent and teachers to shame disrespectful children, not enough to humiliate them, but enough to ensure they learn good manners. Shamed in early childhood by a caring elder, children avoid being shunned later by a community that harshly punishes disrespect for others and the law. Plato and Aristotle argued that the capacity to feel shame made ethical development possible, since shameless people are beyond the reach of the moral community.[11]

Older children may damage their sense of dignity by playing the fool, letting themselves be pushed around, or betraying themselves to avoid a fight or to gain an advantage. These developments affect adult behavior in organizations. As I reported in *The Gamesman*, climbers within bureaucracies reveal a sense of self-disgust because they give in too easily to the boss. This loss of integrity is disheartening and dampens motivation at work. Another person can wound my dignity, but the only way I can repair it is by acting with courage and self-respect.

Much human destructiveness results from frustrating the drive for dignity. Gandhi pointed out that people without dignity could not practice his nonviolent *satyagraha* (truth force).[12] We must express our rage and either avenge humiliation or activate a sense of humility through prayer. Gandhi, like Jesus, became a model for maintaining dignity despite poverty, both in teaching and in the practice of a simple, healthy, self-sufficient way of life.

Of course, the drive for dignity can dominate the personality. False pride, touchiness, confusion of dignity with special privilege, the compulsive drive for approval, all these strivings for a sense of dignity undermine relationships and destroy teamwork. In contrast, the positive qualities of the playful gamesmen include the ability to lose without losing face, and to detach themselves from the game while enjoying the play, strategy, and tactics. To gamesmen, joking put-downs and locker-room banter serve as homeopathic doses of humiliation that inoculate against serious loss of self-esteem.

In some people, the drive for dignity is so easily bruised that they compensate by overdefending it. Swedes suppress their spirit of play at work for fear of losing dignity. For the Japanese, dignity is "face" and losing it can make life worthless. Machismo is an unending struggle to maintain an exaggerated sense of dignity. This is highly valued in Latin and Islamic cultures, whose men express what seems like a caricature of touchy dignity compared to the English-speaking cultures, whose playful and self-critical humor lightens up organizational life. If we can maintain a sense of integrity, then ability to laugh at our exaggerated need for dignity is a sign of emotional maturity. There is a universal appeal to this shared humor in Charlie Chaplin's silent ballets, which deflate the pompous and create sympathy for the tramp's struggle to maintain dignity at the bottom of the social pyramid.

In the United States our self-esteem depends all too much on repeated success. To Americans of all social and economic groups, the promise of winning is highly motivating. We admire the competitors in business, the arts, entertainment, science, government, and sports who gain the glory of the winner's circle. As a culture, we have a strong need to win and an overdose of optimism. Since we expect to win, to be branded a loser by others or oneself is especially humiliating. In the workplace, good management not only respects employees, but also gives them opportunities to win by setting goals they can reach. The effective manager not only rewards success, but also presents the employee to his peers as a winner. However, the success must be real to be motivating, and the award meaningful to others who recognize and certify one's achievement. Otherwise, awards can backfire.

A manager of telephone operators, a paternalistic expert, described to me his practice of recognizing the operator of the month, which he believed was motivating. I asked the young woman, the current recipient, her feelings; was she motivated by the award? "I'm embarrassed," she said. "All the girls think I'm sleeping with him." In contrast, because of Quality of Work Life programs in suburban Chicago and Salt Lake City, AT&T operators pin on the bulletin boards photos of fellow workers who are helpful to customers and colleagues, with the result of boosting self-esteem, increasing solidarity, and raising productivity.

Competition is, of course, extremely motivating. It stimulates the spirit of play, forces disciplined mastery, holds out the hope of winning, and threatens us with the fear of losing. Today there is enough real competition in the global market to motivate anyone. Forced competition between employees can cause emotional burn-out, and undermine the cooperation essential to everyone's success.

For the independent entrepreneur, winning is determined not by a boss but by the market. New-generation employees are attracted to the entrepreneurial role in part because they prefer the rewards be based on a bottom line they can control, rather than on someone's subjective evaluation of them.

Respect for another's sense of dignity is essential to the trust needed for success in the technoservice economy. There are degrees of trust, from willingness to explore mutual interests and agreement, to joint activities, to teamwork, to friendships that make people vulnerable to each other. The beginning of any productive relationship requires trust that the other person will not take advantage of our goodwill. There must be a sense of mutual respect. If people do not feel respected, they will not even begin to develop relationships which can lead to mutual benefits.

If American managers want workers to take responsibility, they can never discount dignity. Managers must rebuild employees' self-esteem and confidence; they must repair the damage done by autocratic classrooms where working-class children were made to feel stupid, and by jobs where they were told not to think.

Bureaucratic factories and offices have further bruised the dignity of workers by emphasizing hierarchical differences, including special privileges for managers. These privileges are now disappearing in places where the goal is to increase productive motivation. At Ford and GM factories, the reserved space for management cars has been replaced by first-come, first-served parking. Everyone eats in the same cafeteria. A greater sense of equality strengthens and helps to create teamwork. By attacking status, these companies also deflate an exaggerated sense of managerial dignity that blocks managers' learning from subordinates and customers.

At the height of the bureaucratic-industrial era, during the first part of the twentieth century, organization man gained dignity by being the *paterfamilias*, the breadwinner and boss at home. Today, a renewed spirit of individual rights and dual-wage-earner families affirms dignity in relationships of greater equality between men and women. For some people, being a part of a powerful organization, even in a minor role, provides a sense of dignity, but I find increasingly that employees, from the front line to the executive suite, resent submitting to a boss. In recent years, many entrepreneurs in search of dignity as well as fortune have left management positions in large companies.

All those I have interviewed want respect and esteem from others, but each type protects dignity in a characteristic manner. Experts find dignity in autonomy and professional certification that insulate them from bureaucratic indignities. Helpers find dignity in being needed and part of a protective family. Defenders gain a sense of dignity through power, and the willingness and ability to fight those who threaten it. The innovator's sense of dignity comes from a freedom to experiment and create, achievement that promises fame and glory. And self-developers consider dignity their right. They expect to be treated with dignity, and if not, are prepared to leave the situation, be it job or marriage or business interaction.

Success in the technoservice economy requires careful attention to the dignity of both employees and customers. The American spirit of freedom makes service seem like servility. There is a notable lack of the service spirit in bureaucracies, and the helpers in service jobs feel like second-class citizens. Customers feel lucky to get help. Only if they can play the service role with dignity can we expect service employees to respect the dignity of customers.

Meaning: the drive to integrate the other drives and make sense of each situation by infusing value, seeking reasons, finding hope in religious transcendence. All other needs are eventually shaped by the drive for meaning. It is the strategic drive. Although we may not be conscious of it, we give meaning to all our experiences and impulses. Even when we sleep, the drive toward meaning continues in our dreams. The healthy person finds shared meanings that contributes to growth. The neurotic clings to childish, irrational meanings covered by self-deceiving rationalizations. Without meaning that gives hope, there is no motivation. Emile Durkheim observed that extreme economic fluctations that either wipe out small businessmen and make their struggles and hopes meaningless, or create equally meaningless windfalls, cause depression and suicide.[13]

Harry Stack Sullivan differentiated three kinds of human meanings: universal, culturally given, and private.[14] Universal meanings are based on shared human experiences such as the sun as a source of light and life. Culturally given meanings are embedded in language and folklore, and learned by all members of a particular culture; thus, in tropical countries, the sun is also a destroyer, but not in Scandinavia. And finally there are private meanings: individual experiences determine whether dogs will be thought of as dangerous or as warm and loyal companions.

All three types of meaning are formed in childhood, but with development, meanings change. Piaget showed that children at age three give meaning to events according to principles of egocentrism. For example, if they disobey parents and then step on a rotten board that breaks, they think this is punishment for misbehavior. Prescientific man imputed meaning in terms of spirits and gods. The growth of our knowledge determines the meanings we give to events, but the meaning we give to our own self integrates cultural messages and experience and forms our sense of identity.

In wartime, work has the meaning of defending the nation: the same boring work that turns off a worker in ordinary times becomes essential. In the monopolistic Bell System, the meaning of work for managers was expressed in the spirit of service, of providing all America with the best telephone service in the world. In the competitive marketplace, gamesmen at AT&T and the Bell Operating Companies are motivated by the chance to innovate and be winners, but this does not inspire some employees, who feel they have lost the sense of service. Because of different meanings, one worker may be motivated by the same work that turns off another, as in the story of two medieval stonemasons. One was bent over, drained after a day of work, while the other sang to himself. Asked what they had been doing, the first said, "I have been lifting heavy stones all day." The second said, "I have been building a cathedral."

Today, there are still bricklayers and stonemasons motivated by working on buildings that serve meaningful functions, and who speak of their pride in buildings that require quality craftsmanship, and of being turned off when working on poorly designed buildings or those where the desire for profit results in the use of inferior materials.

Meaning has become a problem in our society because of the weakening of traditional religion, family ties, and patriotism. There is confusion about the meaning of work, especially for self-developers. Most Americans no longer consider work as a means of survival or as the dutiful support of a family. Business leaders explain their own work by such socially meaningful terms as creating wealth for owners and employment for workers, providing the public with needed products and services, and supporting innovation. But they try to motivate workers by telling them they must work hard to beat the competition and help keep their jobs. This is not enough.

When everyone shares a positive meaning at work, the workplace becomes more attractive and motivation is strengthened. But character types are differentiated by the meaning each gives to work: expertise, helping, defending values, innovating, self-enhancement.

HOW TO MOTIVATE

Value drives explain both our enthusiasm for and our resistance to change, our willingness or reluctance to commit ourselves to a project, to push ourselves to perform, to learn new competencies.

Managers can be measured by how effectively they harness value drives. Indeed, the term *manager* comes from the Italian *maneggiare* (from Latin *manus*, hand), to handle, to wield, to touch, to manage, to deal with, to break in horses, to handle horses—to train and direct animal force. For human beings, these forces combine mind with body, head with heart. Directing human motivation requires understanding value drives and creating opportunities to engage and develop them. This is as true for managing ourselves as it is for leading others.

Companies hire people who have shown that they are motivated to work hard and well. The task of management is to understand this motivation, develop rather than frustrate it, and direct it properly. Although radical individualists may consider this to be manipulation, most employees welcome leadership that provides them the opportunity to express themselves, develop their competencies so that they can get better jobs, and play on a winning team.

People at work want bosses to use power, but they want it used productively, to create power for them also. Leaders who claim they have no power or do not want it are not seen as becomingly modest; they are considered weak bureaucrats who should be replaced by someone who does have power. People at work eventually resent a leader who manipulates, motivating by seduction, false promises, misleading use of the transferential relationship, and unreal visions of opportunity.

Productive motivation results when we *want* to do what is *needed by the organization*. To motivate people for technoservice, one must provide opportunities for them to express and develop their value drives, recognizing differences in social character. Half the technoservice workforce are still experts who are motivated to work autonomously and control others. Leaders must help them develop an expanded sense of expertise, so they will learn from others and share what they know. On the other hand, to motivate helpers, opportunities for meaningful relationships are more important than promotions. But helpers must learn to think about cost-effectiveness and profitability; they are motivated to learn new skills if convinced this will make them more helpful. To motivate the new generation, managers must provide opportunity to develop marketable skills in a climate of mutual respect and reciprocity. Beyond this, self-developers are motivated by the chance to expand their knowledge, improve their well-being, have fun at work, and live a more satisfying life outside. All types must be motivated to work interdependently.

To strengthen and direct motivation for technoservice, managers can make use of four conceptual tools: *responsibilities*, *rewards*, *reasons*, and *relationships*.

MOTIVATION TOOLS IN MANAGEMENT

Responsibilities
Neither beyond nor beneath competence
Risk-taking, experimentation
Development

Rewards
Meaningful
Equitable
Reinforcing productive behavior

Reasons
Competitive strategy
Business results
Corporate values
Social significance
Individual feedback

Relationships
Bosses
Co-workers

Subordinates
Customers
Suppliers

RESPONSIBILITIES

Responsibilities is the ambiguous term that describes both tasks and challenges on the one hand, and authority or turf on the other.

Managers sometimes define responsibility in terms of control: "I am responsible for this organization" means, "I am in charge here." "This is your responsibility" means, "These are your tasks," and sometimes, "This is your turf." But responsibility has another implication, the ability to respond. In this sense, we speak of responsibility to meet a challenge, solve a problem, or serve a customer.

People are motivated by opportunities to express themselves meaningfully through work. This implies that responsibilities should engage value drives of mastery, information, play, dignity, and meaning. They should be neither beyond competence nor beneath it. Without competence, people are unable to respond adequately, and responsibility becomes a burden, not a motivator. Without competence, people do not willingly accept accountability for their performance. A beginning medical student does not want responsibility for a surgical operation. Conversely, despite all the ideology about everyone sharing work roles, the highly qualified pilots at People Express did not want the responsibilities of baggage handling. To motivate productively, a manager must match person with job, facilitate learning, and define the rules of the game to encourage the kind of risk-taking necessary to satisfy customers, avoid costly accidents, or experiment with new procedures. If small errors are punished, people will avoid responsibility; if errors are not understood, people will not learn. This match is more likely to occur if people participate in designing their jobs and choosing their own styles of implementing policy.

Most people are motivated by opportunities to develop their competencies through experience and education. To continue motivating a person whose competence has increased, and who is better able to respond, tasks must be expanded. In the bureaucratic-industrial world, this is done by promotion to a higher level with "responsibility" for and authority over more people. In the traditional workplace, experts carry out this responsibility by narrowing the responsibilities of those beneath them, frustrating subordinates. The paradox of industrial bureaucracies is that to motivate the careerist through promotion, subordinates must become demotivated through loss of responsibility.

In the technoservice world, motivation does not require promotion up the hierarchy. Responsibilities can be expanded, for example, to deal with more customers, make loans, cut deals, teach other employees, and solve problems that bureaucracies usually hand to experts. There is less need for management, since individuals and teams learn to manage themselves and share management functions. This may be frustrating for the expert, who measures success by promotion and status, but not necessarily for the new generation, more interested in the challenge of a bigger job and learning from new experiences, with the possibility of future ventures in other companies.

REWARDS

The promise of rewards motivates by sparking hope. Rewards are also a validation of individual worth. They satisfy needs for dignity and meaning. They reinforce relationships. Poorly administered, they can demotivate. Consciously, experts want rewards to represent the fair market value of their performance and prove their achievement. Unconsciously, they experience rewards as parental approval and a bonus cements transferential loyalty to the boss. However, if an expert considers that a "sibling's" higher reward is unfair, the result can be disgruntlement. For this reason, some companies, like IBM, keep salaries and bonuses secret and forbid employees to compare them. Helpers feel that material rewards contaminate good relationships and should be the same for all, or based on seniority. Helper-teachers resent merit pay schemes: no administrator can measure the value of help, and they believe that differential pay undermines solidarity. Defenders consider rewards in terms of justice: not getting their fair share is a blow to dignity. And the innovator-gamesmen treat their rewards as the score, and money as a liquid resource to be used, like any other resource, to create wealth and independence. Self-developers see money as part of the total reward package they would like to negotiate. Money is weighed against other rewards: opportunity to develop skills, time off, health care, child care, exercise facilities, and a friendly atmosphere.

The new generation wants clear commitments from management, contracts for responsibilities and rewards. This contract makes explicit performance and profitability goals, and how they will be rewarded. It provides for both individual and team awards. It also describes what subordinates expect from each other, not only in terms of performance, but also in terms of values and attitudes. For the new generation, this must include sharing information, participating in decisions that affect one's job, and work that maintains one's marketability.

Money is not the only, or necessarily the most effective, reward. (The State Department finds that the Germans they hire at the U.S. Embassy in Bonn sometimes prefer a higher-sounding title to a job with more money.) Experts yearn for high-sounding awards, plaques, professional validation to frame and put on their walls. Helpers will work long hours, weekends, and holidays for signs of love and appreciation. Once self-developers earn what they consider essential, they may be motivated by more free time.

A factory manager in Southern California asked apathetic young workers what it would take to make them really productive. These workers felt they had interesting craft jobs and a fairly good relationship with each other and with management, but they were not motivated to make more money. One of them said, "If you are serious, what I want is a chance to enjoy life more, with more time off." The others agreed. "We have seen our fathers old and tired at fifty because they worked too hard. Don't expect us to wear ourselves out. If you want us to really work, give us at least three months a year unpaid leave, so we can live another life in the woods or on the beach. Just guarantee our jobs will be available when we return." I sat in on the meeting of company management when this idea was proposed and rejected for the reason that "it would be treating workers like school kids getting a three-month vacation and it would undermine discipline."

In the bureaucratic-industrial organization, rewards set according to measured individual performance cause employees to maximize their gain even at the expense of organizational effectiveness and profitability. In the Bell System, for example, an engineer would be rewarded for not spending over budget, even if such spending would have increased profitability. It was like a reward system for a football quarterback in terms of first downs rather than touchdowns—there is time for one more play, the team is behind four points, and it is third and one to go for a first down on the ten-yard line. He can run for a high-percentage first down or try to pass for a game-winning touchdown and risk losing the first down and his reward.

In the technoservice company, rewards should promote winning by increasing involvement in the business and reinforcing teamwork, as well as individual performance. This calls for rewards based on profitability, but for these to be credible, employees must understand the business and the direct relationship between their work and profitability. A team bonus reinforces cooperation. In contrast, if, for example, a salesman receives his commission even though the customer is unlikely to pay or if he promises service someone else must deliver, there is no incentive for teamwork and those who follow in the salesman's wake feel mistreated and unmotivated.

Does punishment or the fear of punishment motivate? The

answer depends on both the degree of punishment and the type of person. It is well known that if punishments for failure are too severe, people will play it safe. But even less severe punishment may backfire. Experimental psychologist Harry Harlow demonstrated that when a monkey has learned to solve a problem out of a natural curiosity, both rewards for success and punishment for failure disrupt performance.* The monkey is thinking about the banana, not the problem. Some people, particularly experts who are motivated by rewards, are disturbed by punishments. Others, particularly gamesmen, are motivated by risks and perform better if failure means punishment. The adrenaline seems to energize them. Given the difference in meanings to different types, the principles for determining rewards and punishments are:

1. They should be meaningful. People should feel they have been compensated, recognized, and appreciated for a real contribution. Rewards should be designed according to differences in values.

2. They should be considered fair by everyone in the organization. This means that differences in pay should be considered equitable. As leadership asks for more commitment, employees will become more sensitive to salary differentials. In American companies, CEOs make 40 or 50 times as much as a skilled employee, compared with a ratio of 5:1 or 7:1 in Japan or Sweden. That huge difference undermines the motivation of employees who are asked to perform as though they own the company.

---

*H. F. Harlow, "Mice, Monkeys, Men, and Motives," *Psychological Review* 60 (1953), pp. 23–32. In an experiment on using information to solve problems, I found that anxious people did better when rewarded for success but not punished for failure. However, less anxious people (like gamesmen) did better when the stakes were higher—when they were punished for failure and rewarded for success. M. Maccoby, "The Pay-Off Matrix in Concept Attainment" (unpublished honors thesis, Harvard University, 1954).

3. They should reinforce productive behavior: exceptional effort, teamwork, innovation, service to customers, developing skills, and long-term profitability. If managers want to reward individual achievement, they must describe the criteria so that the whole team understands what behavior is expected. It might be a combination of improving profitability, helping others, and innovating. Both rewards and punishments should reinforce a sense of accountability, but people should not be punished for failing when they take the kind of risk that is necessary for success.

REASONS

Reasons stimulate drives, especially the drives of survival, information, dignity, and meaning. Many people at work do not know about competitive realities; if they know their jobs are at stake, that company survival depends on sales, quality production, or lower cost, they are driven either to save the company or find a better job. If they believe that a project can gain them fame and glory, they are driven to succeed. If they believe that failure will cause ridicule, they require no further motivation than to avoid humiliation. Information about competitors can stimulate the drive to play as well as to survive. People like to know how they are doing against the competition. If the game is meaningful, they are motivated to improve their score.

By explaining reasons for decisions and actions, leaders manage meaning, and one task of managers is to provide reasons that are meaningful to each value orientation. To be credible, these reasons must describe real practice. Experts find meaning in the search for excellence; they are motivated by management which supports this goal. For helpers, it is the chance to make a real difference in the lives of those they serve. For innovators, it is adventure, challenge, and the chance for glory. Self-developers, more than the other types, are motivated by feeling included in the whole process, knowing the reasons why things are done and thereby seeing possibilities for entrepreneurial ideas and personal growth. These are the kinds of reasons presented at American Transtech (see Chapter 2). There, at frequent team meetings, everyone has the chance to reflect not only on the reasons for doing things, but also on the reasons for success or failure. Each quarter, the CEO meets all 2,000 employees and reviews the finances. In contrast, some of the best young computer programmers left a major company because they were not told the reason for their work, how it fit into the business. They found their work meaningless.

Thinking is never solely in the present time. What is meaningful in the present is related to the past and anticipates the future. A manager makes work more meaningful and motivating not only by providing information about the business and feedback on performance, but also by explaining reasons for current policy in relation to future goals and organizational values. These values should describe the product or service (e.g., quality, safety, helpfulness) and the process of work (e.g., craftsmanship, cooperation, innovation, individual development).

RELATIONSHIPS

People are motivated by relationships with bosses, peers, subordinates, customers, and suppliers. The trust essential to effective technoservice depends on a sense of security and respect for individual dignity. Of course, employment security builds trust, but where market conditions make this impossible, there must be guarantees that people will not lose employment because of their productive ideas, that people who work themselves out of a job will always be given another. Respect for individual dignity does not just mean avoiding insults, overcontrol, and distrustful treatment. It also translates into clearing away nonfunctional status differences and symbols of authority. Relationships motivate by creating a sense of support and influencing behavior. Innovators build teams at every level.

Different types vary in terms of the relationship that motivates most intensely. Experts develop transferential attachments to father-figure bosses whom they try desperately to please. Brief expressions of approval and disapproval have a powerful motivating impact on experts because the father figure's judgment is so important to them.

Bonuses based on performance evaluation inevitably cause feelings of resentment, so much so that one wonders why they are so widely used. The answer, I believe, is that they give managers a feeling of control over subordinates: if I can decide whether or not to give you a bonus, then you will want to please me. Such motivation makes the subordinate a child, and intensifies the father-figure transference to authority; it reinforces insecurity and servility, not productive performance.

But paternal approval is not a satisfying relationship for self-developers, who are motivated by encounters with customers where they have a chance to learn, and by egalitarian teamwork. In fact, all types are motivated by relationships marked by respect for individual dignity, recognition of good work, and opportunities to learn and participate. In Sweden, where government benefits assure workers they will not lose money by being absent from work, the corporate doctors find that when they feel needed and their views are solicited, workers come to the factory or office even with mild symptoms of illness. Workers who lack this kind of relationship stay at home with mild symptoms.

In the chapters that follow, we examine each of the social character types in detail: the meaning they give to their work; their relations with co-workers, managers and subordinates; their strengths and weaknesses; and how their values were formed. We start with the innovators because they have designed the new models of technoservice organization.

CHAPTER 2

THE
INNOVATOR

Innovators and self-developers are creating the new workplace. The best models of technoservice organization, like AT&T's American Transtech, Westinghouse Furniture Systems, and Scandinavian Airlines (SAS), have been led by innovators who have reorganized their bureaucracies so that employees on the front line are empowered to solve problems for customers. By making supervisors and middle managers facilitators and resources rather than bosses, and encouraging innovation at all levels, these innovator-entrepreneurs have changed the game and motivated the new generation.

Each type examined in this book can be an entrepreneur, an enterpriser. Each type has innovative potential. The expert-entrepreneur takes risks to discover new uses for methods, products, and services. The helper-entrepreneur finds new ways to help people. The protector-entrepreneur builds a team of loyal followers and leads them into new territory. Entrepreneurial self-developers spin off new ventures. But only the true innovator redesigns the organization, inventing new rules, roles, and relationships.

The thirty innovators of the 330 people we interviewed share behavior patterns. They are organizers, instigators, and strategists. Their vision involves motivating people—not necessarily developing them, but bringing them to life. In the process, they create power for themselves and others.

Only 5 percent of the Service Sector sample checked the innovator as their most important approach to work. The percentage is higher among the High-Tech managers (12 percent) and Young Leaders (17 percent). Among the IRS sample, the percentage is zero.

In this chapter, I present three chief executive innovators. Unlike the individuals described in the following chapters on other character types, these innovators and their companies are identified so that the reader can gain a better understanding of the technoservice organization and how it is designed. However, the values of these leaders, their approach to service, management, and work relationships, is similar to that of innovators at all levels of employment. While innovators at lower levels may become boxed in, this usually is only temporary. They refuse to act like bureaucrats. They either find projects where they can be entrepreneurial, or they leave the organization that does not allow them to innovate.

LARRY LEMASTERS OF AMERICAN TRANSTECH

In 1979, American Transtech (now a fully independent AT&T subsidiary with 2,000 employees) was a bureaucratic backwater, the stock and bond transfer division of the Bell System.* This division of some 600 white-collar employees handled 3.2

---

*Before the breakup of the Bell System, AT&T included about one million employees in its twenty-two operating companies (e.g., New York Bell, Pacific Bell, Ohio Bell, Illinois Bell); the long-distance company, Long Lines; the million AT&T accounts, issuing stock certificates, transferring them, sending dividend checks, and answering inquiries from stockholders. Many expert managers had passed through the division and built a layered bureaucracy.

The new boss, Larry Lemasters, in his early forties, was an innovator who had shaken up management at Ohio Bell by creating a spirit of teamwork among installers and maintenance workers. When I first met him at Ohio Bell in the late 1970s, Lemasters was disgruntled by the listless, unmotivated workers he observed. He believed the problem was bureaucracy: managers followed regulations and did not like to listen to workers. There was too much monitoring and not enough roadblock-removing. He had recently participated in producing a film called *The Death of the Bell System*, a movie with professional actors who played turned-off workers. (Example: "Why should I tell them anything? They don't listen anyway.") Then Lemasters brought groups of workers, managers, and union leaders together to watch the film and to respond.

The Death of the Bell System evoked new ideas from the groups and Lemasters encouraged them in experimentation, less monitoring, and more self-management. As a result, in Lancaster, Columbus, and Cleveland they accomplished faster turnaround times, made fewer errors, lost less equipment, and had a higher output in fewer hours, and Ohio Bell saved money. One year in Cleveland alone, Lemasters saved 6 million dollars.

Then he arrived at AT&T Stock and Bond to face another cynical, turned-off staff. He was convinced that "people could work more efficiently, if only given an opportunity to utilize their pent-up potential." He recruited internal and external consultants and asked them to consider every possibility for improv-

manufacturing company, Western Electric; the research and development organization, Bell Labs; and the central AT&T headquarters staff, of which Stock & Bond was a part. In 1982, AT&T and the Justice Department settled an antitrust suit by agreeing to separate AT&T, together with Western Electric and the Bell Labs, from seven independent companies formed from the original operating companies (e.g., Nynex, Ameritech, Bell South).

ing productivity and morale, including socio-technical analysis of the computerized system. Lemasters's motivation included personal ambition, boredom with bureaucracy, dislike of inefficiency, and enjoyment of the drama: the game of change, the exercise of power.

He began by raising consciousness of dissatisfaction. Employees distrusted management. They complained of secrecy, disrespect for the lower levels: typical complaints in large bureaucracies. Before Lemasters arrived, these complaints had been shared privately. Now they became public and legitimate. Lemasters was creating the desire for change and giving it meaning in terms of dignity and mastery. He formed diagonal-slice project teams, which included each organizational level but were chosen so that no one was a supervisor or subordinate of a team member. One team interviewed employees about their feelings regarding work and supervision and videotaped some of the responses, which were then viewed by the entire organization. Lemasters led the meetings. Mutual evaluation sessions revealed feelings of employees that there was too much control, not enough freedom, and too little training.

After eight months, the thirty top managers met at a hotel, watched the videotape of employees criticizing them, and explored their goals and values. They found that by making values into bipolar dimensions, they could measure value gaps. For example, the group felt, "There is too much rivalry and not enough teamwork." So teamwork was identified as a value; its opposite was maximizing self-interest. Authority based on knowledge was identified as a value, as opposed to authority based on hierarchical position. Innovation was made a value, as opposed to conservatism.

These values were written on a blackboard as a scale:

1 2 3 4 5 6 7 8 9 10

self-interest	teamwork
authority based	authority based
on hierarchy	on knowledge
conservatism	innovation

The group voted on where they would rank the organization on each scale. In each case, the mean vote was about 4. They then defined the task of management as closing the gaps between the values of their present conservative hierarchical bureaucracy and those of the new innovative team. This included the successful introduction of a redesigned computerized data system to give employees the information and freedom to serve customers and solve problems without having to ask for approval. It included training for managers to become teachers and facilitators rather than monitors and policemen.

After the meeting, task forces were chosen from volunteers. One group visited and reported on innovative participative factories at Hewlett-Packard, Cummins Engine, GM, and the Dana Corporation. Another group designed a survey of ten questions called the Barometer for periodic measurement of morale and management effectiveness.

HERE IS THE BAROMETER QUESTIONNAIRE:

1. In my dealings with people at other levels, I am treated courteously.

[ ] [ ] 1 2	[ ] [ ] 3 4	[ ] [ ] 5 6	[ ] [ ] 7 8	[ ] [ ] 9 10
Strongly disagree	**Disagree**	**Neither agree nor disagree**	**Agree**	**Strongly agree**

2. I am informed about changes that will affect my job.

[ ] [ ] 1 2	[ ] [ ] 3 4	[ ] [ ] 5 6	[ ] [ ] 7 8	[ ] [ ] 9 10
Strongly disagree	**Disagree**	**Neither agree nor disagree**	**Agree**	**Strongly agree**

3. I am involved in decisions that affect my job.

[ ] [ ] 1 2	[ ] [ ] 3 4	[ ] [ ] 5 6	[ ] [ ] 7 8	[ ] [ ] 9 10
Strongly disagree	**Disagree**	**Neither agree nor disagree**	**Agree**	**Strongly agree**

4. I get training when I need it.

[ ] [ ] 1 2	[ ] [ ] 3 4	[ ] [ ] 5 6	[ ] [ ] 7 8	[ ] [ ] 9 10
Strongly disagree	**Disagree**	**Neither agree nor disagree**	**Agree**	**Strongly agree**

5. Overall, how would you rate the morale in your unit?

[ ] [ ]	[ ] [ ]	[ ] [ ]	[ ] [ ]	[ ] [ ]
1 2	3 4	5 6	7 8	9 10
Poor	**Fair**	**Average**	**Good**	**Excellent**

6. Over the last six months, how would you rate the honesty of communication between you and your supervisor?

[ ] [ ]	[ ] [ ]	[ ] [ ]	[ ] [ ]	[ ] [ ]
1 2	3 4	5 6	7 8	9 10
The worst	**Getting worse**	**About the same**	**Getting better**	**The best**

7. Over the last six months, how would you rate the recognition people get for a job well done?

[ ] [ ]	[ ] [ ]	[ ] [ ]	[ ] [ ]	[ ] [ ]
1 2	3 4	5 6	7 8	9 10
The worst	**Getting worse**	**About the same**	**Getting better**	**The best**

8. How would you rate the fairness of the appraisal process?

[ ] [ ]	[ ] [ ]	[ ] [ ]	[ ] [ ]	[ ] [ ]
1 2	3 4	5 6	7 8	9 10
Poor	**Fair**	**Average**	**Good**	**Excellent**

9. Changes in policies and procedures are well thought out before they are made.

[ ] [ ]	[ ] [ ]	[ ] [ ]	[ ] [ ]	[ ] [ ]
1 2	3 4	5 6	7 8	9 10
Strongly disagree	**Disagree**	**Neither agree nor disagree**	**Agree**	**Strongly agree**

10. I feel I have a good sense of what is going on at Stock & Bond.

[ ] [ ]	[ ] [ ]	[ ] [ ]	[ ] [ ]	[ ] [ ]
1 2	3 4	5 6	7 8	9 10
Strongly disagree	**Disagree**	**Neither agree nor disagree**	**Agree**	**Strongly agree**

11. How would you rate your confidence in Stock & Bond's top management?

[ ] [ ]	[ ] [ ]	[ ] [ ]	[ ] [ ]	[ ] [ ]
1 2	3 4	5 6	7 8	9 10
Poor	**Fair**	**Average**	**Good**	**Excellent**

The younger self-developers took the lead. They eagerly volunteered for those project teams, testing their skepticism about Lemasters. They spoke out in taped interviews and published the highly critical results of the Barometer.

Lemasters pushed the process tirelessly, talking with managers for hours, challenging their expert attitudes, encouraging them to engage their subordinates in the change process, overcoming their disbelief and complacency. After a year and a half, operating costs had been cut by 30 percent. Lemasters eliminated a layer of management and found jobs for the unneeded. People at all levels of Stock & Bond began to come alive.

All this was accomplished in the monopoly world. With AT&T's divestiture, Lemasters saw an opportunity to innovate in a growing market, to enter the stock and bond business, serving not only AT&T but also the seven regional Bell companies: Nynex, Bell Atlantic, Bell South, Ameritech, Southwestern Bell, U.S. West, and Pacific Telesis. The objective was to also gain other corporations as customers. He found himself in a very competitive market. With his managerial team, including new entrepreneurial recruits and consultants, he sized up the competition and designed an organization that could do the job at lower cost. In 1983, American Transtech became a fully separate subsidiary owned by AT&T.

Cutting costs, including levels of management, was not enough to ensure profitability. The management group met and decided they could not remain in business unless they cut wage rates. By moving to Jacksonville, Florida, in 1983 they situated themselves in an area with lower wage rates and rental costs. Although they knew some people would not move, the group decided that the choice was to move and accept a salary cut, with the promise of profit-sharing, or stay and risk losing the business and employment for many of them. Everyone was invited to move and 40 percent accepted.

The average age of American Transtech employees is thirty-four. They are organized into four levels, starting at the first level with the front-line workers. These people are divided into participative teams of twenty to forty people. Most of the teams use computerized systems to interact directly with customers, set their own schedules, including vacation, and measure themselves weekly in terms of their profitability. They know the costs and charges for each type of transaction billed to the customer companies. Transactions range from giving information (How many shares do I have? Was my dividend check sent? Can I reinvest my dividend automatically?), to stock transfers, to drafting letters explaining company policy to be signed and sent by corporate officers. Other first-level teams deal with telemarketing, financial recordkeeping, data security, printing, and mailing. Front-line workers are trained to rotate to different teams, to learn the whole business and avoid forming exclusive groups. Their salaries are based, not on grade, but on skill ("pay for knowledge").

At the next level are facilitators, on call to provide training in technical and group problem-solving skills, trained to counsel workers and be supportive ("catch people doing things right"), and also to sniff out problems before they cause trouble. This appeals to the new-generation employees, who want responsibility for the whole job and unobtrusive management available to them if needed. Meetings are called by managers or team members when there is a need to resolve operations problems or communicate new policy. Team members are encouraged to innovate, even to try out new services.

The third-level managers run the lines of service and staff departments (public relations, advertising, organizational development and training, strategic planning) and have the entrepreneurial role of finding new customers, companies looking for high-quality, low-cost information services and direct mailing.

The fourth level is the chief executive, leader of the strategy team. The whole company of 2,000 employees (1,000 full-time and 1,000 part-time) meets quarterly and receives the financial reports, customer evaluations, Barometer results, reports on the state of the business. Yearly bonuses are given, based on profitability and customer satisfaction.

Lemasters started the process of innovation believing, based on experience, that the people doing the work could help design a more effective way, and in the process, become more enthusiastic, more involved. He used everyone who could help him. As he moved along, his vision become more systemic, including competitive service and supportive organizational roles, measurements and rewards.

Unlike an expert, his vision was not of becoming the big brain that knows and controls the pyramid from the top, but of using the skill and knowledge of all the brains to build a business, of developing each individual's potential. In this sense, he combined the entrepreneurial approach of the helper-developer with that of the innovator. The pure helper would build teams, but not think of redesigning the organization. Employees have responded to Lemasters by accepting a sense of ownership, by feeling that they represent the company to customers. They consider themselves business people, not bureaucrats. This is the kind of motivation that provides a competitive advantage for the technoservice organization.

Innovators see the existing organizational form not as a given, but as part of the technology, a tool to be designed and redesigned to optimize motivation and cost-effective service. Lemasters recognized that the enterprise needed spirit, and he saw his main task as creating a culture in which everyone feels involved, where everyone understands that they make a difference. New teams are now designing approaches to better understand and service large customers. They believe that future profitability depends on creating relationships with clients who trust them to understand their special needs.

JAN CARLZON OF SCANDINAVIAN AIRLINES

Jan Carlzon is chief executive of Scandinavian Airlines (SAS), a consortium formed in 1946 by three joint ventures between government and private companies in Denmark, Norway, and Sweden to take care of their intercontinental air traffic. The mission was extended in 1950 to include both European and domestic business. SAS also runs hotels, catering services, restaurants, tour agencies, and other entrepreneurial service companies.

Carlzon became chief executive of SAS in 1981, at age forty. The group, with 28,000 employees, had been losing money due to a stagnant market, rising oil prices, deregulation, and increased competition in the airline industry. Carlzon was brought in because he had been a successful CEO at Linjeflyg, a domestic Swedish airline, where he used innovative pricing to make a losing company profitable. He started his career as a tour guide while studying at the Stockholm School of Economics, Sweden's business school. In 1969, he went to work as production manager at Vingressor/Club 33, Sweden's largest tour agency. In 1971, when Vingressor became a wholly owned subsidiary of SAS, he was appointed director of marketing, and in 1974 became managing director, at age thirty-three. In his first year as head of Vingressor, he turned a $1.9 million loss into a $3.8 million profit.

Up until 1978, the company was managed by engineers, experts who took the market for granted and concentrated on safety, technical excellence, and cost-cutting, what Jan Carlzon calls the cheese-slicer approach to acceptable profit. But international competition as well as costs were eroding profits. In 1978, a new CEO was hired who believed that profitability and motivation could be increased by decentralization. He set up project teams, but little happened. His approach was too piecemeal and experimental. Uncertainty provoked resistance from those threatened by change. In 1980, for the first time, SAS reported a loss.

Then came Carlzon; he analyzed the business problem and proposed a systemic solution, using consultants to examine what other airlines were doing and to survey customers. He changed the question from how to cut costs to "What generates revenue?" His short answer: "Satisfied customers." The place to begin was to understand what the customers wanted and then determine how to transform that need into a profitable business. From market studies, Carlzon found the strategic segment to be the business traveler. If SAS could attract more businessmen traveling to and from Scandinavia and paying full coach fare, the tourists and first-class passengers would be gravy, and the company would become profitable. Surveys and interviews showed that businessmen wanted reliability, punctuality, and comfort. They resented standing in long check-in lines with tours and families with crying babies, all on supersavers, while they paid full price.

This understanding was the basis for innovation. Carlzon designed an organizational strategy to gain the businessman customer. It included investment in the hub airport of Kastrup in Copenhagen to improve punctuality. A new business class was devised, with more comfortable seats on the plane, free lounges, and special check-in counters. But Carlzon believed that for this strategy to work, everyone had to share a radically different vision of the business. Everyone must understand the first principle of the new game: the assets are satisfied customers, not technology. With these assets, it is easy to get technology; without them, technology is worthless.

Like Lemasters, Carlzon saw potential power in what he called "the front line," where cabin attendants and ticket takers met the customer in the "moment of truth," the some 50 million encounters each year (10 million passengers with an average of five interactions each) that determined satisfaction or dissatisfaction.

Carlzon's vision demanded that all employees understand the

business and recognize that they are needed to make it work. It meant freeing the front line from bureaucratic controls and policing supervision, and developing new training that made room for initiative and response to customer needs. He invited his managers to propose change within the framework of his vision, to change systems so they measured profitability and customer satisfaction, rather than internalized budgetary accounting. Wherever possible, cost centers were made into profit centers. Maintenance was told to sell its services to operations, and urged to find new customers from other airlines. Administrators were encouraged to be entrepreneurs.

Carlzon sold this vision as a whole, first to the board, then to the unions, then to countless groups within the company where he preached the new SAS philosophy:

1. The most important thing for a person to know is that he or she is needed.

2. Satisfied customers and employees are more valuable than billions of dollars worth of aircraft.

3. Everyone—customers and employees alike—wants and deserves to be treated as an individual. That is what good service means: living up to customer and employee needs and expectations at every contact.

4. To free someone from rigorous control by instructions, policies, and orders, to give that person freedom to take responsibility for his own ideas, decisions, and actions, is to release hidden resources which would otherwise remain inaccessible to both the individual and the company.

5. An individual cannot take responsibility without information. An individual who has information cannot avoid taking responsibility.

In the summer of 1984, Carlzon described his job to me in terms of two phases: innovation and execution. In the first stage he defines the problem, strategizes, and offers a systemic solution. In the second, he picks executives, educates, monitors, and develops the corporate culture. This means delegating responsibility to interpret the grand strategy, while he takes the role of preacher spreading the gospel within and outside the company.

Carlzon has vigorously defended his views against criticism from all sides: expert-engineers claim his marketing emphasis undervalues safety; expert—cabin attendants fear that by satisfying the customer they will lose autonomy and integrity. (One cabin attendant complained in a newspaper that the new course was sexually suggestive because it taught cabin attendants how to gently control amorous drunks. Carlzon defended the course and asked why she had not voiced her criticism directly to management.)

Carlzon wants believers. He demands participation. Before he announced his vision publicly, he wanted his managers to criticize it. He said: "If you are responsible for the company, you get a little scared. Even if you know you are right, you want to check up. By listening to people, getting their confirmation, you are on the right track. Actually, in a positive way, you hook people. It is impossible for them to say later, 'I think you made the wrong analysis.'"

Carlzon contrasts participation with democracy. On the one hand, he sees democracy as an arena for a clash of interests. On the other hand, a company is owned by stockholders who invest wealth to create wealth. The chief executive is delegated by the board of directors to run the company for this purpose. Those who join the enterprise, and none is forced to join, must accept this goal and follow the rules. Participation and delegation are management tools.

Carlzon says: "Many people make the mistake of thinking that this kind of distributed responsibility is some kind of undefined democracy. It is not. I think that getting the right people and giving them total freedom is the incentive to get many, many more things to happen within the company than if you try to steer it from a central point."

As do most innovators, Carlzon has an intuitive sense of timing, about when to risk decisions. Carlzon: "A wrong decision can always be corrected. Lost time you can never get back. If you enter an organization like I have done, the crisis is your resource, you have to use it. It is better to do ten things and two are wrong, than to do one thing which you are absolutely sure is the right thing to do."

He wants his managers to be daring. Carlzon: "Many times people say, 'I want to go through this wall,' and they start walking towards the wall and they are two meters away when they tell themselves that it will not work. The authorities will not let us, or the management will not let us. I tell them that the civil aviation board has 6,000 employees, and they get their salaries to tell us where the wall is. You should not take their work upon your shoulders. If you come to the wall, two times out of ten it gives way, and you get through. Then you have the middle managers, and that is a more complicated and interesting situation. When you move into a decentralized situation, a lot of people have to become strategists and preachers. They get insecure because they are not used to it. We are talking about that in our education of 2,500 middle managers, we are teaching them the new management philosophy."

What motivates Carlzon, like Lemasters, is not only the business game, but pleasure in seeing people respond and grow. He says: "There is no doubt that I like this role very much, coming into the organization, trying to grasp the situation, making the overall decisions, and having it achieved through education, information and the new organization. I like to feel people respond to responsibility, how people come to life or grow in this process. My personal reward is to see people get enthusiastic and act on their own and reach goals."

He likens the workplace to a circus, where the brave and competent have a chance to perform on the high wire, risk themselves for glory. In his circus, ideally, everyone should have a moment under the spotlight, and there should be a safety net for those who fall.

Carlzon maintains he does not care about personal power, but this is a matter of definition. *Power* has become a dirty word in the twentieth century, something for dictators. CEOs invariably disclaim interest in power, but contradict this once they describe what they really want. Asked: "Don't you want the power to change things?" he responds: "I think I am honest to myself if I say that I am very results-oriented. I don't get any reward from power as such. I think I can prove that. I very seldom act as having power. I don't think power comes from position. I think that power comes from the results you achieve." It is a different kind of power he wants from that of the CEO who gives orders to people and expects them to jump. In the technoservice world, such power is limited. You cannot order people to be true believers or make good decisions. Carlzon wants not formal but real power, the kind of power essential for winning the game of technoservice.

To gain this kind of power, Carlzon must be able to give up formal power, let go of the controls. He cannot be an expert in everything. His example of a bad decision was when he personally gave orders to improve the freight business and so set the company back a year. Carlzon's favorite book is Erich Fromm's *To Have Or to Be*,[1] which contrasts power *over* and power *to*, having formal power or being a leader who is respected, trusted, and followed.

Carlzon's vision and personality have had an impact beyond SAS, on the whole of Swedish society. His concept of organization and style of management have challenged the traditional Swedish industrial bureaucracies and has become a model for innovators in business and government.

RUSSELL NAGEL OF WESTINGHOUSE FURNITURE SYSTEMS

Under Russell A. Nagel, Westinghouse Furniture Systems was transformed from a failing industrial bureaucracy to a model of technoservice that integrates office and factory to meet the needs of demanding customers. Before Nagel's direction, first as operations manager, then as general manager, the factory in Grand Rapids, Michigan, lost money cranking out office equipment with the goal of quantity rather than quality. Now it is a profitable and exciting "living laboratory" for 700 people, and the fourth-largest company for a growing international market of customers who want to replace the bullpen-type office of rows of desks with more private office modules. Westinghouse office employees play a continual role in designing new products and collaborating with customers and every major producer of electronic and computerized office equipment. Factory workers in the Quality of Worklife program participate in designing production methods, while marketeers try out glitzy multimedia approaches on the whole staff. Nagel has somehow put together two disparate cultures, the marketing world of hype, games, and fun and the production world of craft, care, and quality.

Nagel's team proudly states: "We don't think of the Westinghouse workplace as 'the office of the future.' That is an engineering vision where people are replaced by computers. This is a continually evolving workplace where people continually find better ways of using new technology to satisfy customers. More accurately, it represents a living, working example of the future of the office." "Our business is service" is Nagel's philosophy. "Our product is not an end in itself but a means to help businesses operate more productively." And he tries to involve everyone in thinking about what increases office productivity. He believes the key to success is "total quality," not just in the product, but in every function: relations among people, processes, product design, and sales calls.

Westinghouse Furniture Systems makes 15,000 different products: tables, desks, chairs, office modules equipped for lighting and electronic equipment. At the high-tech office in Grand Rapids, employees work with customers to try out products with computer-aided design (CAD) systems. As one of them says, "It is like putting together the largest Lego set in the world."

Nagel, in his late forties, is an innovator and developer, a teacher and helper with strong values of dignity and productivity. Before joining Westinghouse, he taught math, architectural drawing, and industrial arts at Bedford (Ohio) High School. Starting in 1961 as a junior industrial engineer, he moved up the Westinghouse corporate ladder, holding twenty-five different positions in manufacturing, including general plant manager, before he arrived at the office furniture factory in 1981. After leaving a plant where union and management fights had sparked violence, he took over another factory with poor labor relations, and engaged the union (the United Steelworkers) in a successful Quality of Worklife program. Nagel sees this as his years of experience in the trenches.

He was sent to Grand Rapids to evaluate the factory's potential. Relations with the carpenters' union were faltering, productivity was low, but Nagel liked the people. He felt they had a strong work ethic, but needed leadership. Indeed, nearby competitors Steelcase and Herman Miller are both extremely well-run companies.

Nagel believes that productivity depends on self-esteem, that people feel motivated by pride of identification with a winner. In fact, he creates that kind of motivation and much more. His winning workplace supports mastery and play, quality production and innovation. He has hired bright young people and enjoyed competing with them for new ideas. In the "future of the office" are traditional and new-generation types, men and women, black and white, but these differences do not impede an easy relationship between factory, sales, and executive offices, and workers have in fact been promoted into the office.

Like Lemasters, Nagel started the change process by getting people involved, inviting them not just to solve problems but to understand the causes. He says, "If we can understand a problem, we can solve it." Sixty percent of employees are involved in problem-solving teams.

He supports the team atmosphere with parties and picnics. There is also a wellness program, which has reduced health costs through nonsmoking training, aerobics, and weight control. Factory employees meet monthly to hear reports on results of productivity, new orders, shipping objectives, absenteeism, financial results, quality results, and goals. Questions are encouraged and answered. Every month, Nagel also hosts a union-management roundtable to discuss strategy and listen to union concerns.

The progress has justified investment by Westinghouse in new products and technology. After three years, the new technoservice concept jelled and became an organizing principle for new products, processes, systems. Factory productivity rose 50 percent, resulting partly from quality improvements and automated processes. White-collar productivity improved one-third. Nagel believes that 40 percent of these gains was motivation. "People began to believe we were a high-quality provider and acted that way."

Everyone is invited to improve quality and service, and productivity has continued to grow. Methods experts have interviewed customers and redesigned order forms so they are easier to use and allow the office to keep track of orders better. On-time deliveries have jumped from 65 to 95 percent. Westinghouse experts have trained major dealers to install the furniture systems. Once installers are certified, Westinghouse takes responsibility for their work. Field representatives have video cameras to record the products as soon as they are installed, and send the information to Grand Rapids for review.

Not everyone is fully satisfied. On the one hand, the process has stimulated many employees to want more participation, more opportunity to improve methods. On the other hand, some middle managers are uneasy about the challenge to their authority. Union leaders tolerate the process. After all, their members want it. But they fear an erosion of union power and remain vigilant to make sure people are treated fairly.

Nagel is not surprised that change causes conflict. He feels that change requires debate, that innovation flows from dissatisfaction. He seems pleased by the whole process and his role of innovator-coach motivating a winning team into world markets. He looks for the best resources he can find, for quality is the key to success. He has contracted with German ergonomics experts to make his furniture comfortable and, he believes, more productive for the customer. He scans the world for designers to create stylish fabrics, colors, and configurations. He has hired young managers, including a Rhodes Scholar and an Olympic athlete. Nagel says, "I love to be around young people. They keep you young. They have energy. They keep me on my toes." He laughs. "But they won't get ahead of me. I play the game."

Nagel seems a contradiction of styles: down-to-earth and in the stars; competitive yet comfortable and supportive; humorously self-effacing, yet grand; gamesman and helper. When the newly renovated plant was inaugurated, Nagel invited President Ronald Reagan, who brought Gerald Ford, formerly a congressman from Grand Rapids before he became Vice-President and President. Reagan not only gave a speech but handed out awards to workers.

In the plant, one rides around on a futuristic Customer Transportation Vehicle and watches a swinging film on the future of the office. A conference room has a device which keys in managers' salaries and calculates the climbing cost of meetings. But the technology does not overpower the people. Westinghouse does not try to automate everything. People still make furniture. The ideal is not an automated plant cared for by experts, but an organization of people using the best tools to satisfy customers and also having a good time doing it. Nagel has created a technoservice model for making an aging industry competitive.

GOVERNMENT INNOVATORS

There are few innovators in the government, and these few are frequently frustrated. There is little opportunity to transform the industrial-type bureaucracy of expert specialization, rigid hierarchy, and turfism into a technoservice team organization.

Without a market mechanism, there is no compelling reason to do so.* Without understanding and support from political leadership, innovation is a risk with little chance of reward. Federal innovators sometimes achieve remarkable results in reorganizing a particular function, such as auditing, or office, such as the Passport Office at the State Department, but all too often they give up and move to private industry.

We found innovators in the Departments of State and Commerce, the Federal Aviation Administration, the Veterans' Administration, ACTION, and the National Parks Service. These women and men are results-oriented and dislike bureaucratic routine. They view problems from a systemic point of view, emphasizing how their work fits into the big picture. They are attached to data networking and telecommunications technology. Even if they don't understand it technically, they are quick to grasp how it can be used to improve productivity and make work more exciting by decentralizing information and decision-making.

Our study within the government includes Paul Pepper (a pseudonym), age forty-eight, an innovator, a manager of auditors, who defined his role as making government work better:

"While the function of auditing is to save the government money, I really view my function as seeing that systems work better. This would result in not wasting money. We have all sorts of ways to come up with dollar savings. Cutting waste is one. But improving something is a cost-avoidance type thing where you would have had to spend more money if it hadn't been improved on.

"To me, you look at it like a house with cracks in the wall.

---

*A notable exception in Sweden is the transformation of the Labor Market Board under the leadership of Allan Larsson. This ministry is like a national employment agency which matches job seekers and employers. It has the resources to loan money to businesses to create employment in areas where many people are out of work. Its counselors help people determine where their skills will be best employed, and provide training. Larsson has decentralized the agency into over 200 cities, emphasized a service orientation, and replaced bureaucratic measurements with those reflecting customer satisfaction.

Most managers want to know if there is a crack and if I get time, I'll fix it up. But I'm not going to let the cracks worry me if the termites are eating away at the foundation. I'm more interested in the structural weakness. If there are too many cracks, you will develop a structural weakness. A lot of auditors don't think in those terms. That's the problem. They've got to think systems or they are out there talking about peanuts when we ought to be up here talking about watermelons."

An expert would view the audit as a review by the rules. He would assess whether there has been compliance with appropriate regulations. An expert in Pepper's organization said: "An audit is simply a review to see that what management has stated is correct as can be told by various tests performed. An audit to me is just a probe—to find something adverse, but there are possibilities of finding something good, too. You use whatever authority you have—regulations, handbooks, laws—to represent what is good and bad."

In contrast, a helper in Pepper's group described auditing as: "Dealing with people, sometimes you get satisfaction that you are helping. For auditors, it is hard to get that because most people see you coming and it looks like it is a downer to most folks. The way I do it is that I approach the person and we talk about any problems they have and I let them know that I am here just to do the audit and not to criticize on a personal basis. I want to go by the guide and the restrictions of the contract that they signed so they can improve their organization, and to make sure that they are doing the right things so that they can prosper and get the contract renewed."

The helper-auditor continued: "I don't want to be a policeman. If I wanted to be a policeman, I would be one. I want the auditees to feel the way I would want to feel, so they can treat me accordingly. I like to get a good working relationship because you can't work with people when they are tense and are not sure what you are doing. So I try to explain it fully so that they can be confident that I am there to help and not to hinder what they have done."

107

A defender in Pepper's organization also used the policeman analogy, but he liked the idea of defending honest people from "thieves." "I think that the reason for some of the rules and regulations was this moral ethic that we have. And I think it was to keep people from going astray. As a result, I feel it's important that people follow the regulations. I believe some of the regulations have just been overdone. I'd rather not see them. But I do believe that there should be a policeman around to make sure that people do the right thing. If there weren't, there would just be a world full of thieves who do all the things they are not supposed to do, and laugh at everybody else."

In a previous government job, Pepper developed an early-warning financial-analysis system for a whole industry. He collected information from all over the country, put it into a computer, analyzed it, and fed back the indicators. He discovered indicators that give early warnings of financial disaster for companies that are important for national security.

Like other innovators, Pepper was not satisfied just by having a position of authority. He wanted real power to improve things, as he said, "to make good things happen." Early on, he left one government job because he had a weak boss:

"I felt he had no clout. First of all, he was frightened. I also perceived him as having very little clout with the assistant secretary. And if he had no clout, I had no clout. And if I had no clout, there was only so much I could do. And there were a lot of things I wanted to get done. I had strategies to get them done. But if he understood them, he didn't have the guts or the determination to try to make them happen. I just don't think he really understood what I was trying to tell him. Consequently, he was afraid to do anything, because he wasn't sure if it was right or wrong."

When he became manager of auditors, with the support of a stronger assistant secretary, he saw his task as improving the effectiveness of both internal and external audits (of government contracts and grants). He said of his goal: "Can we make it work more effectively, efficiently, enjoy it more, deliver the system better?"

To improve effectiveness, he realized he needed to educate the experts to expand their view of the mission and their role. He recognized the resistance of experts who want unambiguous rules.

"I'd like to be able to communicate a management philosophy on what is out there and how all these things kind of fit together and how they really don't. You have to learn to live with ambiguity. Most people don't want to do that. Ambiguity runs people down and they dissipate their energies instead of learning how to live with it. I think that's because they have no conceptual image of how things fit into the whole. I think if they could just begin to recognize that, then I think they could begin to deal with it."

With the help of a consultant, he organized team meetings where experts, helpers, and defenders discussed their preferred approaches and agreed to allocate audits according to their respective interests and strengths. Defenders took the suspicious-looking cases. Helpers were assigned audits of internal department operations and minority-owned businesses which needed help in setting up financial systems. In group meetings, auditors learned from each other. Pepper kept pushing the experts to take on different types of audits, to risk making mistakes and learning from them.

"You've got to instill a different kind of philosophy, a different kind of feel, a different kind of perception of the world. Just because you are an auditor, that doesn't make you God Almighty. Just because you are an auditor, that doesn't mean that you are 100 percent right. Just because you're an auditor doesn't mean that you can't be flexible. Because you're an auditor doesn't mean that you're the only one with the solution.

"You must deal with the fact that there are no magic answers. You know, you deal with each situation within certain parameters, and you make a decision, and some you make right and some you make wrong, and if you make it wrong there's no sense crying about it, because that's not going to make it right. There are some things that you just have to learn to live with, and if you blow one, you blow it and move on. I think auditors generally want to be so right, and if they're ever wrong, it's just like their whole world falls in on them."

The audit group became more effective and more lively. Pepper encouraged challenge and debate rare in bureaucracy. He was promoted and moved to another agency, where he continued his innovative leadership another four years before leaving the federal government. Pepper said he was tired of fighting the bureaucracy, where the experts drag you down. What kind of management did he most appreciate during his government career? Pepper enjoyed innovators like himself, but he also appreciated the political civil service and political leaders he considered smart and secure enough to let him innovate. He said:

"I don't like dumb bosses, because I think dumb bosses get frightened. I like a bright boss. I like them to be straightforward. Not mealy-mouthed. If they're bright, they're straightforward. They give you room, and they're willing to talk about challenges. That's what matters. The four or five bright ones I've met in my total career have been those kinds of people. They're generally dynamic themselves. They want to get something done.

"I had a boss—I was hired to replace him. They said he was going out in four or five years. I wanted to learn as much as I could, and he was bright. Now, he wasn't going to do anything, but I could learn one helluva lot from him. He was a very bright guy. And you should see him work with the industry. He knew how to handle people. He knew how to keep himself out of problems and he knew how to keep the agency out of problems. I learned an awful lot from him. He wasn't going to initiate new things. He let me. He didn't stand in my way. Like when I'd say, 'Hey, you know, I've got this idea, what do you think of this?' he'd say, 'Go ahead, try it.' So even though he wasn't dynamic in that respect, he wasn't going to stand in my way. When he thought you were wrong he said you were wrong. And I could live with that kind of guy. The kind of guy that I can't live with is the kind of guy who really doesn't want to make anything happen and won't let you make anything happen."

CHARACTER FORMATION: INNOVATORS AS GAMESMEN

Let's step back and consider the character of the innovator and how it develops.

In *The Gamesman* and *The Leader*, I described organizational innovators as gamesmen, driven by a spirit of play, motivated to be winners. The term *gamesman* causes an emotional reaction, partly because it is not clearly understood. There is no precise translation in most languages. Words like *gambler* (Swedish, *spelaren*) or *player* (French, *le joueur*) were used to translate the title *The Gamesman*. Some people confuse the gamesman with Stephen Potter's manipulative character, who is expert in the art of winning without actually cheating.[2] When I have asked groups of high-tech managers whether they consider it positive or negative to be a gamesman, the response is usually fifty-fifty. The bureaucratic experts are generally most negative, focusing on the manipulative, superficial, egocentric, and threatening aspects of the gamesman, while entrepreneurs and self-developers tend to identify with his daring spirit.

Gamesmen do enjoy risk-taking, but the best are innovators. Like Lemasters, Carlzon, and Nagel, and P. G. Gyllenhammar of Volvo, Thomas Watson, Jr. of IBM, and David Packard of Hewlett-Packard, they create power not only for themselves but for a whole organization. Less attractive are the paper entrepreneurs, the speculators, gamblers whose goal is limited to personal gain and glory, without regard for other people.

Although these two types, innovater and gambler, share the game language and a certain antibureaucratic informal style, there are significant differences. Both express the play spirit at work, but the innovator's approach is more developed. It is more in the tradition of Johann Huizinga's *Homo Ludens*, who creates new forms of organization out of a spirit of play.[3]

The great Swiss psychologist Jean Piaget traced the development of the play drive by observing children's games.[4] My doctoral research built on his discoveries to show the relationship between the development of play and learning.[5] The infant first plays with his body, then plays repetitively with objects, rolling a ball, pushing an object on a string: play for mastery over body and external objects. Freud describes how very young children play peek-a-boo with parents as a way of mastering the trauma of their sudden disappearances, turning powerlessness into a game.[6] At the age of four or five, children begin to play seriously with each other, but there is little cooperation. Each tries to impose his will on the other. Gradually, through experience of conflict and education in games, children develop a cooperative play relationship. But to do so, they must free themselves from their awe of and unquestioning belief in the authority of grownups. They must develop a critical attitude so that they can think for themselves and accept or reject ideas on their merits. This is something innovators achieve more than experts and helpers. For the expert to become more of a gamesman, he must free himself from internalized authority.

In the United States, the United Kingdom, Australia, Sweden and other Western industrial democracies, this development is fostered in games like hide-and-seek, ringalevio, or Red Rover, played between the ages of six and eight. These games encourage cooperation, banding together against the central person, the symbolic authority, to home-free all one's fellows. In the traditional, conformist Mexican village, this type of game is not played. There, central-person games teach the message that the individual cannot escape punishing authority.[7] In the game *cuero quemado* (burnt leather), the "it" wields a leather belt and can strike anyone he catches. In a version of hide-and-seek, the "it" is the deviant who tries to escape while everyone searches for him. These games are mostly played by boys. The village girls' central-person games have descended from medieval Spanish roundelays, where a circle is formed around a virgin, and the symbolic male predator, the wolf, tries to break through and rob her.

By the age of ten or eleven, in the United States as in Piaget's Switzerland, the more independent children develop a spirit of reciprocity. Neither adult pronouncements nor the rules of the game are blindly accepted as God-given truths. Children evaluate rules in terms of making the game fair and fun. They are able to put themselves in another person's place. While the younger egocentric children must win or feel humiliated, reciprocal gamesmen enjoy the contest for its own sake: the interaction, strategy and tactics, the exercise of skill, and the sense of freedom. Innovative gamesmen conceive of the whole game as a system which can be better organized with improved roles, rules, and technology. This is why innovative gamesmen are more likely than other types to strategize systemically. They have learned not only to play the game, but to make better games.

The innovators we interviewed came from families where they felt valued, supported, and encouraged to explore their own paths. As children, they combined a sense of freedom with discipline and love of challenge. They were involved in entrepreneurial activities in school, developing their skills and gaining financial independence from parents. Lemasters, Nagel, and Carlzon were entrepreneurs and leaders in college. Most have far surpassed their fathers in terms of career. Carlzon's father was a chauffeur for a government official, Lemasters's and Nagel's were supervisors in service companies, Pepper's was a merchant seaman.

The innovators share with the new-generation self-developers independence, enjoyment of teamwork, flexibility, enthusiasm, the drive to make work more fun. The differences are that innovators have made the organization of people to create wealth into an art form, a life project. Members of the new generation seek a more balanced life. Their goal is a sense of measured happiness rather than the exhilaration of playing in the big leagues and the drive for glory.

Innovators will motivate the self-developers as long as they recognize the difference between the latters' values and their own. However, if innovators expect commitment like theirs, they will be disappointed. Self-developers may enjoy the game and share the innovators' results-orientation. But for them, it is not all of life, and they want to leave the game at the office. They prefer to invest energy in relationships, avocations, and entrepreneurial activities that give them a sense of independence from organizations. They want to be involved in an interesting project, but not necessarily committed to the organization. As one self-developer put it, "The hen is involved in your breakfast of eggs and bacon, the pig is committed."

WEAKNESSES OF INNOVATORS

Donald Burr, founder of People Express, is a notable innovator. In four years he built a one-billion-dollar airline on a vision of low-cost air travel produced by a highly motivated team. At People Express, before it was bought by Continental Airlines, everyone except contracted-out baggage handlers and plane reservation clerks (non-People people) was a manager, and each person, even the pilots, who were called "flight managers," did a regularly scheduled turn at everyone else's work. Everyone owned stock.

Burr's vision did not inspire some of the pilots, such as the experts, who felt they had paid their dues in Vietnam and deserved the special status and salary pilots have at TWA, American, and United. The pilots pointed out that while they could do the other managers' work, the others could not do theirs. Some pilots at People Express tried to organize a union. Burr saw them as the bad guys, destroying the vision.[8]

114

Some innovators have no patience with people who refuse to accept a vision they believe both is economically positive and expresses higher values of cooperation, individual development, and public service. They become too attached to the games they have designed. They fall in love with their creations. They risk seeing people as chess pieces, not human beings.

Innovators miss the differences in goal and meaning for different types. Speaking of Pepper, an expert-auditor said: "I think out of the directors we've had in this office, I think he's the best by far. But technically, he's probably near the bottom in knowing the office. He doesn't really project to me that he knows the people in the office. You know he has something in mind and this is his goal, and he's going to have everybody work for it rather than finding out what he's got to work with and then finding ways to go."

Experts, helpers, defenders, and self-developers may love the innovator's enthusiasm, and be captivated by the vision, but they resent the hype, the manipulation. Innovators do admit that when they get going, they "run over people," "lose their tolerance."

Other types also bridle at the innovator's drive for glory, what they feel as egomania, hogging center stage. A Swedish manager, an expert, says: "Jan Carlzon acts like he did it himself. He is always taking the credit. He did a good job, but I get tired of seeing him." A Swedish small businesswoman, also an expert, says: "I am rather fed up with Jan Carlzon. He has overacted, as I see it, but I am sure he is a very good leader because he gets people to work. I see him as a very good motivator."

An Ohio Bell expert manager: "Larry Lemasters achieved results, but a lot of people distrust his motives. He always seems to be at the center of everything." (In 1987, Lemasters left AT&T, where his innovative pushing was not universally appreciated.)

Finally, there is the question of whether the innovator's motivations can be maintained without his or her optimistic, enthusiastic leadership. Once the innovator leaves, will the game settle into a bureaucratic ritual? Can the innovator create a self-perpetuating culture? These are challenges for even the most creative innovators. No organization or culture lasts forever. All vital organizations must be continually renewed. There is no leadership that does away with the need for leadership and no organization that can adapt to change by staying the same. The challenge for innovators today is to organize the experts, helpers, defenders, and self-developers into productive techno-service teams. That requires the kind of organizational vision developed by Lemasters, Carlzon, and Nagel. It requires a systematic development of services, people, and organization through participation. To be successful in the long run requires some tolerance and understanding of what motivates other types on the front line and in middle management.

CHAPTER 3

THE EXPERT

The expert's dominant value is mastery, including achievement, hard work, and a sense of self-esteem through recognized success. At their best, experts stand for diligent work and quality of service. At their worst, experts are prototypically inflexible, rules-driven bureaucrats. But even at best, the expert character can be a roadblock to creating effective technoservice. Experts want control over their function, and they resist the delegation, flexibility, and relationships essential to technoservice. To them, the innovator's vision feels like anarchy, and the new generation's drive for independence seems arrogant.

APPROACH TO SERVICE

The experts we interviewed are driven to *perform*. They find satisfaction in mastering a challenge. For them, service is performance, achievement, meeting a standard of excellence rather than helping people. They are less concerned about the customer than about measuring up to standards.

A thirty-five-year-old expert accountant at a big-eight firm bridles at the very idea that it is her job to help customers. She says, "*Helping* is a bad, crummy word. 'Help me' is like saying you can't do it yourself. You're not free. Advice is not helping. You don't go to a doctor to help you. You go to have him cure you. You help an old lady across the street, that's help. But helping isn't tax advice you pay thousands of dollars for." Yet, at the top of the same company, managers tell me that the accountants who do more than give advice, who get involved to help customers solve their problems and implement business strategy, get the business. So it goes for banks, telecommunications, and information services.

The dreams of experts are often about solving problems and taking tests. Lawyer-experts work through cases in their dreams. "I had a nightmare," said a research director. "I was trying to get a key program through and I could not convince management." An air traffic controller has nightmares of being unable to "get the words out to warn the pilots, and they hit." He says, "Every time there is a bad situation, I can count on dreaming about it. Sometimes I drink a lot that night to knock myself out."

The experts of the Bell System interpreted service as providing everyone in the country with telephones and a dial tone. At Bell Laboratories, this also meant inventing new technology that would improve communication. At the operating level, it meant the willingness to maintain that service when it was disrupted by floods, fires, and storms. Yet, even as top executives, experts still measure themselves in terms of profits, stock prices, and return on equity.

The ideal job for an expert allows the exercise of independent judgment and personal control. But it is difficult for a group of individualistic experts to work interdependently. Experts want control.

A woman psychiatrist in a mental health center at a county health department says: "As I see it, they hire you for your expertise. They are very interested in your qualifications. They really want to be sure what you are talking about, and then they spend all their time arranging not to listen." She maintains control where she can: "I medicate patients sent by the nonmedical psychotherapists. But never do I medicate anybody where the psychotherapy is done badly. If you want me on your case, you'll do it the way I think is good."

As defined by *Webster's New International Dictionary,* an expert is "an experienced person...one who has a special skill or knowledge in a particular subject, as a science or art...." *Expert* comes from the Latin *expertus,* meaning tried, experienced. Over 75 percent of the employees surveyed identify with this aspiration as describing them very well. This makes sense. Expert knowledge is essential for good service. For about half those surveyed, becoming an expert is the most important meaning of work. These are the people who have dominated American organizations. They represent a social character adapted to the industrial bureaucracies.

CHARACTER FORMATION

The expert orientation develops in the traditional father-dominated family and is reinforced in school and bureaucracy. A child, boy or girl, seeks to be like and gain the approval of an expert-oriented father who becomes the model for a productive relationship outside the family. The family is a support system for the father. His work determines where the family will live and its standard of living. Father interprets the world of work and the values essential to success and esteem. Over and over again, in many ways, he says, "You must work hard for success. No one can do it for you. You and you alone must take the tests. Those who succeed are the ones who accept responsibility." The child's dominant drive becomes mastery of self and schoolwork, successful performance which is rewarded by paternal approval. The school programs meritocratic hierarchy into the tender young psyche. Grades are the measure of achievement. People are classified as As, Bs, Cs, Ds, and Fs.

Consciously, experts value autonomy, freedom to do things their way, with the integrity to demand excellence. Unconsciously, this striving for autonomy conflicts with the wish for approval from paternal figures. The result is ambivalence to authority. On the one hand, experts resent oppressive control, which limits freedom. On the other, they yearn for the caring father, who provides support and recognizes a job well done.

Most experts say they most admire their fathers or father figures who are models of fairness and hard work. A corporate executive sums it up. "I admired my father, who taught me to be myself and do a good job. I admire my boss. He is thoughtful and supportive, and leaves me alone. He gives me autonomy." What about your mother? "He was strong. She was beautiful. She treated all the children alike. My dad represented the outside world. She lived for the family."

Experts do not want to be controlled, but neither do they want to be so independent that they leave the system of measurable achievement, comfortable rewards, and expressions of approval. The most mature experts grow into the good-father role and take responsibility for subordinates. Of course, this has been easier for men experts than for women experts. The less mature of both sexes remain overly impressed by and dependent on authorities, and correspondingly, they remain stuck in an egocentric view of the world. Oppressed by autocratic fathers, these people seek security and a sense of dignity in controlling their space and maximizing power. Although they want autonomy for themselves, they believe their freedom and effectiveness depend on controlling subordinates. They define responsibility as authority, rather than ability and commitment to respond. The only important relation for them is with authority. It is difficult for them to work interdependently with peers, who are competitors, or customers, who are seen neither as bosses to be obeyed nor subordinates to be directed.

The genius of Franz Kafka was to describe the ambivalent strivings of expert bureaucrats, one moment servile, the next stubborn and proud. The bank clerk of *The Trial* and the surveyor of *The Castle* struggle to maintain autonomy and dignity as they climb the corporate ladder. This is still the psychic struggle for expert-bureaucrats.

REWARDS FROM WORK

Experts mention two kinds of rewards they want from their work: external recognition and inner satisfaction. Experts love medals, plaques, and awards, but payment and promotion are the highest forms of recognition. In companies where there is little chance for promotion, experts become extremely frustrated. But it is also important for them to be respected as professionals. A typical expert says, "I would like to be treated professionally, to have my decisions and opinions valued."

The inner reward comes from mastering a challenge, demonstrating competence. Some experts tend to seek the same challenge in sports.

A computer technician says: "I like most that my work is challenging, it's something new every day. I think that people should be given variety, but only after they have mastered the job." He reports that his "main satisfactions outside of work are boating, water skiing, scuba diving, hang gliding." These are challenging, individualistic sports. Many expert-executives love golf, a game in which one can continually measure one's response to challenge. Experts say they play not against another person but against the course. Competitive experts want not only to win, but also to measure their superiority as precisely as possible.

For experts, all challenges are tests and there is satisfaction in getting a good grade. A policeman says: "The police profession gives me a chance to deal with all types of people, mostly in time of extreme sorrow, rage, or difficulty. This tests me and my ability to handle people and I enjoy the challenge." A helper would have mentioned his satisfaction in helping people.

Another computer technician says: "Besides the money, the rewards I get from work are the fact that I have done a good job, and being smarter than the computer. It's a challenge to try to beat the system to get something done that the program says you can't do. I like having the freedom to do it. My boss is lenient, so we do things that aren't set up in the instructions."

Experts like to see the finished job and know it has been well done. The computer program works, the audit finding fits regulations, the patient got the right treatment, the sale was made, the case was won. "You like to see the dollar value of your job," says an expert-accountant. In contrast, the helpers measure their work in terms of its human impact.

THE EXPERT'S IDEAL BOSS

It follows that experts have an ideal of the kind of boss they want. Good bosses make their goals clear, have high standards, delegate, give you a lot of freedom, treat you with respect, listen to you, are there if you need help, and recognize accomplishment. But they are not around too much. An explanation for the success of the business best-seller *The One-Minute Manager*[1] is that it describes in dreamlike caricature the expert's model of minimal paternal management. The one-minute manager gives one minute's worth of directions and feedback, one minute's praising, and one minute's rebuke, all done respectfully and in such a way as to limit oppressive control. The image of the unexcitable one-minute manager sitting in his office, smoking his pipe, is like the good father the experts unconsciously yearn for.

Here are some verbatim descriptions of what experts want from managers:

The accountant from the big-eight firm says: "My ideal manager would just leave me alone and [here she begins to talk to the interviewer transferentially as though he were her ideal father-manager] I'll get the work done, and you should be there if I need you. You should recognize my accomplishments."

The air traffic controller says: "He gives us guidance when it is needed, otherwise leaves us alone."

A telephone company pricing and billing clerk describes her ideal: "A good supervisor should be seen and not heard except when necessary. You can't do without them, but they shouldn't stand over your shoulder."

Experts criticize managers who are either oppressive or weak. Their ideal is a manager who delegates responsibility. Experts want this autonomy, but on the other hand they want to control their own subordinates so they can feel they have mastery over ultimate performance.

A police officer complains about overcontrol. "You know that to leave a 20-by-20-block area, I have to ask two supervisors! They entrust to me a $10,000 car but I can't drive it beyond a particular block. I can arrest, take away a person's civil rights, or use a handgun, but when it requires going to a particular part of the city, I can't. I can tie up a helicopter, two canines, seven officers, and eight police cars for any length of time (yesterday I did that for one and one half hours), but to make a $2 phone call, I have to get the permission of a lieutenant, fill out a form, call through a district operator, and then wait five minutes for her to call me back while she puts the call through, even if the call is two minutes. Yesterday, it took one hour to arrest and process a burglar, and three hours to fill out all the paperwork."

Experts also resent managers who do not respect their expertise, and wound their sense of dignity. A nurse administrator of a county health facility says: "The thing that is really the hardest for me to take is that nurses were administrators of the health centers for years. And we know that they can do it. Now, what top management has done is brought in physicians as administrators. Their salaries are considerably higher and there is a tremendous amount of money spent on physicians' salaries which could be saved."

Experts also criticize managers who are uncertain, whose delegation expresses laissez-faire incompetence, and who lack goals and objectives. Experts also dislike matrix management, which requires them to report to managers in different departments. They want to know: Who is my boss? What does he want from me?

When experts have a relationship with a boss who is like a good father, they do not ask for formal feedback. One manager with this kind of relationship said, "It is clear what he thinks about my work. We understand each other." Where this relationship does not exist, the expert feels frustrated about the lack of paternal response and recognition, and wants a formal evaluation.

Experts also want the boss to hear their views, but they do not demand participation in decision-making. An auditor at the Government Accounting Office says: "I like leaders to tell me what they want accomplished, and what they want done. I don't want them to tell me how to do it. I like for them to be receptive to my questions of why. I want them to listen to me, and to listen with reason. And then after the decision is made, regardless of what the decision is, I will do it. Whoever is the boss is the boss, and I'll do it the way they want to do it."

Experts want a manager to consult them about their area of expertise. For them, this is participation. It indicates respect and efficiency. But a boss who asks everyone to share in making decisions is seen as a weakling who is afraid to take responsibility.

THE EXPERT AS MANAGER

The best expert-managers see the leadership role as taking charge. They believe in setting clear goals, letting competent subordinates do their thing, and following up to make sure things are done according to the plan.

A vice-president of a large company says: "This is what I believe about people. I believe people want to contribute and feel good about real contributions. I believe people like to win; they need wins. People like to be recognized. That doesn't come naturally to me. I have to push myself. People will rally to confident leadership, competent and knowledgeable. People need to respect leaders to function well. People need to know what to expect." This expert and others try to pick people like themselves who know them and what to expect. This expert has to push himself to take the father role because he is too concerned about pleasing his own boss.

It is difficult for expert-managers to give recognition, when they are themselves still unconsciously good children, seeking approval from a higher level. Others, including subordinates, may be seen as sibling-competitors. Only those experts who accept the paternal role can comfortably give the recognition subordinates need.

Expert-managers try to get rid of people who do not share their goals and are not good performers. They believe in giving everyone an opportunity, but they do not invest time in developing those who fail to measure up by themselves. For example, a medical administrator says: "How do I get my staff to accomplish their goals? I have chosen a staff, to the extent that I was able to have anything to do with the choice. I have pushed, prodded, and otherwise led people to have goals like mine when they didn't want them. We talk about quality patient care and quality of this and that quite a lot. Most of them share my goals. I had hoped that the others would leave, and I have done things so they might more likely make that choice."

Expert-managers tend to decide quickly whether people are good or bad in terms of whether or not they are similar to them. Subordinates who need more care, coaching, development complain they are ignored. Reflective experts admit they sometimes write people off too quickly.

125

Once expert-policemen become managers, they are sticklers for "complete, neat, and accurate" forms, and they see their challenge as getting subordinates to use the forms, follow the rules. Experts, as subordinate patrolmen, experience control systems as limiting their performance. As managers, these control systems *express* their performance.

Expert-managers feel they should know everything their subordinates know. Furthermore, they want to take responsibility for everything that happens in their organizations, and they hate making mistakes. So even though they want to delegate and give people freedom, they constantly demand to know everything and tend to second-guess, undermining subordinates' need for autonomy.

This behavior has been reinforced by traditional management training, which emphasizes control. Smart managers realize they cannot know everything and control everything by themselves. They must gain consensus and trust subordinates to make decisions. But when experts realize this, it makes them uncomfortable. "I've just come out of one of those damned Japanese-style management meetings," an expert—bank president told me. "I wish I didn't have to waste time listening to a lot of stupid opinions, but that is what my subordinates want."

Expert-managers don't realize that their style drives away competent people of the new generation. Such was one plant manager I visited in California. He was proud of his technology and work organization. He told me he had enriched the jobs and motivated his workforce. He was surprised when I asked if I could interview the workers. "What will you learn from that?" he asked. I said I would like to hear their views of work at the factory. He reluctantly agreed and suggested we meet afterward. The workers said they were frustrated. The younger ones were angry. The plant manager never asked for their views. Many had ideas for cutting costs, improving methods, but they had given up. Back in the manager's office, he asked me what I thought of the factory. I said he had a problem. "What is that?" he asked. I said, "It's a communication problem." "You are right there," he

126

said. "I keep trying to communicate the best ways to do things and they don't hear me." I said, "I mean two ways." "Of course I use two ways," he said. "I give speeches and I write memos."

The expert-executive has a hard time understanding the new-generation manager, who does not believe he must know everything and spend hours at home reading everything. In one large company, a new-generation vice-president spends his time with subordinates creating a common strategy and delegating assignments. He seldom takes work home. His results are always excellent, but the experts at the top of the company are skeptical of him. The new-generation manager doesn't know the answer to every question so they believe he must be superficial.

On the other hand, experts believe they can learn any new style, meet any challenge, exploit any new opportunity. All they need is a good book or a course in how to do it. But they can't change something if they are not aware of it. Experts do not know how deeply rooted are their unexamined assumptions that only people like themselves are reliable and most productive. Nor do they realize how the expert mind is programmed. Unlike the innovator, who treats organization as a tool which can be shaped differently to perform different tasks, the expert assumes bureaucratic structure and systems. Modifications are seen in terms of decentralization, which results in changing the number but not the shape of the organizational pyramid. If a big pyramid decentralizes into little pyramids, the only beneficiaries may be the ones at the various peaks, and then there is a new problem of integrating all the pyramids.

EXPERTS IN TECHNOSERVICE

Experts want to hold on to control at the top. It is difficult for the expert to adapt to the requirements of technoservice teams, interdependence, frontline decision-making, sharing information with everyone rather than up and down the ladder, no "one best way." Experts are reluctant team players. As one expert-manager said: "I prefer to work alone, because I prefer to do the work myself and be responsible for [read: have control over] my own work." Knowledge gives experts power and they do not share it easily.

But the design of organizations by experts often clashes with requirements of new technology. A study published by the International Institute of Applied Systems Analysts describes the same human cause of two major technical failures: the nuclear core overheat at Three Mile Island in 1979, and the North Sea Platform *Bravo* blowout in 1977. In each case, people close to the problem lacked the training and authority to close a valve and prevent a calamitous chain of events. The systems were organized by experts who retained authority at the top. The National Transportation Safety Board reports the same causes for the collapse of the mobile offshore drilling platform that took eighty lives in 1981.[2] A similar situation in the sense that those who knew most about the danger of the O-rings lacked authority to cancel the flight contributed to the ill-advised launching of the space shuttle *Challenger* in 1986, resulting in the deaths of seven astronauts.

The expert orientation also causes conflict with management and increased stress for air traffic controllers. One expert says, "You can't manage a controller's work. I'm there with a mike and a button. I do it the way I think is best. If I'm messing up, they're going to pull me out of there. That's the only management I need."

However, the supervisors feel it is the controllers who are uncooperative. What explains the conflict and the stress is that both controllers and supervisors are experts, and supervisors are trying to control the controllers. With a simpler technology and fewer flights, the individualistic orientation functioned well enough. These observations are reinforced by a study that describes the history of conflict: "A macho culture of hard-drinking risk-taking experts was formed. New recruits who didn't fit were rejected by the group. The union reinforced the controller's rights."[3] As the air traffic system becomes more complex, it requires a technoservice rather than expert orientation. Easy and clear communication between controllers, managers, pilots, and centers lubricates the system. An airline executive said to me, "One trouble is their name. Air traffic 'controllers.' They believe they control the air. They should be renamed something like air traffic facilitators or pilot helpers. That would describe their real function."

It is as managers that experts are the biggest roadblocks to technoservice. Not only are they overcontrolling, but their paternalism provokes sibling rivalry among subordinates, further undermining any impulse to cooperate. They try to solve organizational problems by increasing management control or instituting individual incentives, not by redesigning and developing relationships.

Some experts recognize they must better learn to understand people. They talk about taking courses to improve their "people skills," so they can communicate better. An AT&T middle manager says: "My biggest problem is communicating and getting along with people. I want to have a more open mind, understand people's ideas more. I'm too much 'My way is right and there isn't any other way.'" Companies present courses on techniques of listening which generally emphasize skill in explaining and rephrasing and try to sensitize the expert to recognize emotions that get in the way of rational analysis. However, even those who take the courses find it difficult to overcome their dislike of having to listen to other people's problems, of being forced into a messy world of emotions rather than the comfortable world of measureable facts.

The difficulty experts have with people stems in large part from their drive to master and control. To control another person's behavior, one must limit his autonomy, narrow his job. However, most experts are not hard-hearted. Beneath the armor of control, many are softies. When they treat people as predictable objects, they do so because they want not to have to deal with feelings. Furthermore, while bosses may be able to control behavior, they cannot control another person's feelings.

Some experts admit that people make them uncomfortable. The expert–government accountant says: "Don't tell me about the secretary's personal life, because I don't want to hear about it." Expert-policemen have no patience with the problems of people and little sympathy with those who have lost control. A policeman says: "I won't bullshit you. I'll tell you that when a citizen stops me and asks routine questions, he starts to become a pain in the ass."

The computer technician says: "I most dislike the politics about my work, having to be friendly to nasty people. A supervisor told me, 'Be sociable, learn to read the sports section.' This is a bunch of bull. Why should I try to snow someone? My work speaks for itself. If you don't like my results, let's discuss it. I will not be a yes-man just to get ahead."

When companies emphasize relationships, the experts get uneasy. Their confidence evaporates. They feel insecure. But development of experts is possible with good leadership and new organizational systems. In America, everyone, even the experts, shares an underlying suspicion of experts and an irreverence toward authority, or at least anyone else's authority. If they feel their knowledge is respected, many experts can become team players like the Hewlett-Packard engineer-salesmen who went out to their customers and learned what they needed. Nagel of Westinghouse puts experts to work finding ways to improve customer order forms, on-time delivery, and quality. However, experts must be taught that interdisciplinary project work and teaching are part of the expertise needed by organizations. The definition of expertise must include process as well as substance, teaching and facilitation as well as in-depth knowledge.

An element in the success of Japanese management is the redefinition of performance for experts. When a researcher asked Japanese middle managers whether their work included helping people, they were puzzled by the question. For them, the definition of work is helping co-workers, superiors and subordinates. That is how they are evaluated. They are cooperative not out of idealism or free choice but because an authoritarian system demands cooperation and shared responsibility. Japanese experts must balance intense individual ambition against responsibility to the company and their demanding superiors. They are expected to tell the truth, share information, and challenge authority in the interest of the company; listen carefully to each other yet gracefully subjugate themselves to the decisions made by authority. The balance causes intense stress but it produces successful results for the Japanese corporation.*

If individualistic Americans will not submit to this pressure of the Japanese corporations, we must find our own way of redefining work and motivating teamwork.

Experts can learn a participative approach to management, but the road may be rocky. The president of a well-known technology company introduced me to his vice-presidents in the following way: "Lately, I have been reading a lot of psychology," he told the VPs. "Participative management is good humanly, and it also makes an organization more effective. That may be hard for most of you to understand. Like you. I was trained to be an engineer and I know how rigidly you think. Why, you squareheads don't even know that without self-esteem, you can't be productive. Some of you may not want to work humanistically.

---

*Thirty-three successful Japanese managers in their thirties from elite companies were interviewed using the questionnaire I employed with American managers in *The Gamesman*. Questions probed approach to work, what managers found most satisfying and dissatisfying, relationships at work and outside, goals for self and society, and personal problems and symptoms. Seventy percent reported depression, and 40 percent, anxiety, particularly those who were the most self-affirmative and so most in conflict with traditional Japanese values of self-effacement. Roxana Moayedi, "A Comparative Study of Work, Character and Human Development Among Japanese and American Managers" (Tokyo: Social Research Institute of Japan, 1983).

This finding fits that of a ten-country international management survey that finds Japanese managers feeling more stressed than any others because of the demand for long work hours and the tension of interpersonal relationships. American managers felt somewhat less stress, and felt stressed for different reasons: lack of power and influence, and an incompetent boss. Report by Cary Cooper and Jules Arbose in *International Management*, May 1984.

You may be happier somewhere else. But here, we are going to participate. I'm sorry I can't stay to answer questions, but Dr. Maccoby will explain this approach and what it means." With that, he left the room. I asked the VPs to wait a minute and rushed after the president. I found him outside and said: "What you just did was a contradiction. You spoke about participation and self-esteem, but you did not let them participate and you put them all down as rigid experts. Will you go back and talk about it?" He said, "I can't. I've got to go to another meeting." I said, "If I go back in that room, I'll have to tell them that I don't want to cause you trouble, but there is no way to create trust without facing the contradiction. Should I continue or leave now?"

"OK," he said. "You can tell them."

I was not invited back again, but later I heard from one of the VPs that although angry at me, he has kept trying to change his style, to listen to others, and has fully supported participative management in his company.

Let me emphasize the point that expertise is not the problem: it is the expert value system. Leaders need a broader expertise that includes managing relationships and learning how to be educators, as well as knowing about strategy and technology.

Donald A. Schön, an educator at MIT, describes how an expert can develop into a "reflective practitioner" who can teach and learn with others.[4] Part of this requires seeking connections to the client's (or subordinate's) thoughts and feelings. Part is finding a sense of freedom, as a consequence of no longer needing to maintain a professional facade of omniscience. Schön adds that the experts will be more moved to change when clients (subordinates) renounce the comfort and danger of being treated as children for the satisfaction and the anxiety of becoming active participants in a process of shared inquiry.

By emphasizing quality and customer service and not just individualized performance measurements, the best innovators present experts with a new model to emulate, a vision that promises success, and an expanded sense of expertise.

CHAPTER 4

THE
HELPER

Helpers, both women and men, have taken the maternal role in the bureaucratic world. They tend the wounded, smooth conflicts, and build relationships. Without helpers, the autonomy-seeking experts would make organizational life unbearable for all but the winners.

Helpers care about people, especially those in need. They like to give assistance and support, and they try to bring a family spirit into the workplace. The best helpers respond to our needs with useful information and caring attention. The worst are well-meaning incompetents or smothering do-gooders. In business, competent helpers satisfy or gain clients by developing trusting relationships; for example, the successful telecommunications software company president who is considered like a mother by her clients, who call on her to solve their personal as well as business problems.

Helpers are a significant minority in the service sector. Combining the two kinds of helpers (those for whom helping people is most important—about 15 percent—and those whose first priority is helping the leaders of organizations—about 5 percent), one-fifth of service employees are helpers. The so-called "helping professions" have a much higher percentage—40 or 50 percent. But helpers can also be air traffic controllers, policemen, computer technicians, salespeople, even IRS agents.

THE APPROACH TO SERVICE

For helpers, the meaning of service is care. As doctors, helpers care about the patient as a whole person, not merely about solving the medical problem with medicine or surgery. Caring policemen prefer to prevent crime rather than apprehend criminals.

An example is this helper-policeman describing how he dealt with a disorderly, partially-dressed man. (Helpers tend to be descriptive. They like to tell the interviewer the whole story.) "When we got there, the fellow was in the middle of the street with his shorts and T-shirt on. We advised the dispatcher what we had and that there was no need for a scout car and an official to come. We would handle the case. Going through my mind was "What could be wrong with this fellow?" We departed the cruiser to approach the fellow and advise him who we were. [They were plainclothesmen.] The subject appeared to be intoxicated; he started crying and I wondered why. I advised him there was no need to cry. I asked him if he would step back to the car so everyone wouldn't see him without clothes. I gave him my jacket and we went back to the car. I asked the man what he was doing and told him he shouldn't be undressed. He expressed his anger and humiliation because his wife scolded him for drinking. My partner and I escorted the man up to his apartment and knocked on his door. His wife came to the door. We told her we were policemen and she asked us in, along with her husband.

"We sent him to put some clothes on while we talked to his wife. I explained to her his feelings. She began to tell me of the bills and things and how much they needed money, too much for him to be drinking it away. I then stopped her before she started crying. I told her some sad stories that happened to others in the same manner. Then I told her that she and her husband should talk things over, or maybe go to a bank and discuss it with them, they might help with a loan. She agreed. I then found he had gone to sleep. I told the wife that when he awakened don't try to talk with him about money and try to take my advice. She agreed and thanked me for being so kind. I gave her my name and number at the office, and told her if I can be of more service to give me a call. We departed and advised the dispatcher of no report other than saying the subject had family problems along with being intoxicated, and was now sleeping it off. We went back to patrolling." Rather than being interested in the man or trying to help, the expert would have likely arrested the man for drunkenness and indecent exposure, and in the process, gotten credit for an arrest.

Secretaries or staff assistants who are helpers to leaders speak about doing things for the boss to "lighten his workload." A few helping IRS agents want to give the taxpayer a break, and when they audit, they explain the tax laws. An IRS agent says: "My job is negative because I play the heavy, but if the taxpayers cooperate with me, I work to make it as painless as possible."

In contrast, expert-auditors monitor by the book and the more aggressive defender-auditors do not mind making the auditee uncomfortable to provoke admissions of guilt.

A head nurse sums up the helper's view of service as "having to do with caring for other people. You can't be a good manager if you don't really care for other people: caring what happens to them, helping them to get better from an illness. Medicine is too technical and scientific. Many of the physicians have become technical experts."

HELPERS VERSUS EXPERTS

The typical helper dislikes the experts and their world of hierarchy, status, and measurable performance. A helper-auditor says: "The experts are report-oriented and like to work with paper. I like to interact with people. They say the report is the most important thing, but it is very frustrating for me.

"*Professionalism* is a word that means a lot to them. For me, it is a nothing word. For most of them, it is doing a job, not getting emotionally involved. It has a snobbish feel to me, like it's a code word for 'white collar,' not a ditch digger or something like that. I don't like the word." This helper doesn't like the experts' lack of interest in people.

A helper-pediatrician speaks out against the medical model of expert control of health care. She says: "I think we've created excuses when we set up the medical model. I remember an argument with a nurse at the pediatric hospital. We had a core team and a nurse was describing the job for her child-health nurses, as she called them. And she said certain things were beneath the level of a nurse. And I said, 'That's silly.' As a physician, I don't think anything is beneath my level if it helps the patient. If a child spits up in the room while I'm examining her, I'll wipe it up. I don't call some other person to do it. It's part of my job description to be a helping person." This helper emphasizes the sense of equality and teamwork among co-workers. She speaks of learning from others, including those lower in job status. Experts are threatened when subordinates know more than they do.

Helpers are opposed not to expertise, but to the expert mentality that treats people without sufficient care.

CHARACTER FORMATION

Helpers often come from mother-oriented families, and in a sense, they try to recreate them in the workplace. If the paternal demand is for performance, the maternal value is unconditional care for all members of the family. The helper's ideal is acceptance based on common humanity within the extended family, rather than on performance. The mother-oriented approach provides an ameliorating haven from the paternal world with its admiration of success and contempt for losers.

The backgrounds of helpers suggest two different dynamics, one from a childhood of scarcity, and the other from a background of abundance. Many helpers come from a poor background, one in which the father did not achieve and the mother and grandmother kept the family together. These families survived and members got ahead because they helped each other. There was a strong religious belief in doing for others what you would have others do for you.

The helper-auditor expresses his admiration for the maternal values of his mother. "She is super, an incredible person, and the women in my life—daughter, wife, mother, sister, and grandmother—those five women have had so much impact on my life. Mother is at the intersection of it all. She will do anything for anybody. I talk to my mother every day. She never interferes but will do anything she can." He expresses his orientation to work: "I feel others give me so much, and it's not material things necessarily. I want to give them so much because they have given me so much." This man is going to graduate school evenings, taking advanced courses in psychology, and does volunteer work with the elderly.

The dynamic of abundance includes people from well-off families with values of service, influenced by a strong, liberated mother. A staff assistant to the head of a government agency comes from such a family. She typically admires "Eleanor

137

Roosevelt, not only because she was a risk-taker and an innovator, but also because she cared about people. She had loyalty and honesty that I like. I'm like that. She really stuck by Franklin through a lot of stuff. My mother was the greatest influence on my life. She's a saint, an enabler. She empowered other people to bring out the best. She set high standards, but never by withdrawing love or approval."

This category also includes women with successful husbands and grown children, who do volunteer work, a shrinking group as women of this class pursue careers. (For example, one IRS agent says she doesn't have to work because her husband supports her, but since she was doing a lot of volunteer work anyway, why not be paid for it?)

Helpers admire those they have known personally who help and public figures like Martin Luther King, Jr., Gandhi, Mother Teresa, Abraham Lincoln (for freeing the slaves), John F. Kennedy ("for his call to service," "for his attitude that problems could be resolved, you could make the world better just by putting in a lot of effort and caring"), and Hubert Humphrey ("for his honesty," "for his human concern").

WORK RELATIONSHIPS

Relationships at work are extremely important to helpers. The auditor says: "Even if the work is boring, if you get along with people and help each other out, it makes it better. I place more importance on the people and relationships than on the work itself. When I worked in a warehouse and when I really didn't feel too well and they had to cover for me, they knew that on other days I would cover for them. You need help and understanding and compassion for people."

Helpers want to work with people who are lively, enthusiastic, and caring. They want to be with cooperative, trusting, loyal people who are "warm, outgoing, dependable, with an accepting attitude," and who are not "supercompetitive." The negative of this is that helpers sometimes spend too much time chatting or "schmoozing" with co-workers and clients. Relationships at work can get in the way of productive service.

Helpers are often frustrated by management systems which they feel are made by and for experts. Helpers who are policemen and auditors complain that the system rewards performance in quantitative, not qualitative, terms.

The government auditors who are helpers complain that they are rated on the number of errors or criminal defalcations they catch. If they try to help someone who gets in trouble later on, they are blamed. And they gain no credit if their help is effective.

A social worker claims that an agency encourages caseworkers to push welfare clients into jobs to get credit for a case, when in fact they know the person is unskilled and untrained, and likely to lose the job, be back needing help from the agency, and fall into deeper despair.

One of the helper-policemen points out that not only is it difficult to measure helping, but helping can actually hurt your job rating. He says, "According to the general orders of the police department, the most important purpose of every member of the police department is the prevention of crime. A policeman standing on the corner may or may not be preventing a crime at any given moment. This is something that is unmeasurable. In other words, there is no way of telling if a policeman is fulfilling his most important function. A policeman is usually judged by the number of good arrests he makes. But if a man is diligent in his coverage of an assigned beat, crime will be low and his chance for an arrest will be lessened. Therefore he will go down in the eyes of his superiors."

Another policeman says: "Patrolmen are under the constant strain of 'quotas' in apprehending law violators, competing with other officers for top evaluations to achieve promotions, which are accompanied by substantial monetary and status increases.... One possible solution would be to lessen the salary differences between the ranks, thereby eliminating officers who are looking only to monetary gain....Many times the officer must compromise his own ideals and standards, possibly severing a good working relationship with his fellow officers, in following a course of action designed to please his superiors. Current supervisor requirements consist of memorizing department rules and regulations and obtaining a good evaluation from supervisors who have obtained their rank through the same process. Both requirements overlook the most essential elements in supervisory personnel, the ability to help and work with subordinates and to inspire people to do quality work and not just what is required."

A third policeman says: "Once I had a partner who was a great talker. He really liked people and had received many commendations from various community groups. In 1965, he received an award from the chief of police for collecting the most money for the Police Boys' Club. This man just had a great personality. He made few arrests, and generally tried to talk to people about the law violation or situation. But in serious criminal situations he knew what had to be done and he did it. When he took the promotional test for sergeant he was among the twenty-one men to pass the written test. But he was given a very low efficiency rating. He appealed and was told that he just did not make enough cases. This officer retired a private."

Thus, helpers see their strengths which benefit people unrewarded by bureaucracies. The experts design objective, measurable standards which do not reward helping, even when it achieves the organizational goals.

REWARDS FROM WORK

Helpers seek good relationships, the opportunity to see people benefit and, ideally, grow. They feel more rewarded by being needed and appreciated than by receiving money and promotion.

A corporate secretary says: "Money is not the reward. I consider myself well paid. I am fortunate and pleased; for what I do I am overpaid. My father in construction doesn't make that much. My reward is self-satisfaction, of doing a job well and knowing that I am helping. I enjoy contact with people."

One of the policemen says: "It is a reward to know you have helped someone. If I can prevent one juvenile from becoming involved with drugs, I feel I have done a good job that day." Note again that he is more likely to be rewarded for arresting a drug seller than for preventing sales from taking place.

The pediatrician says: "I guess I'm just an Indian, I don't want to be a chief. I just want to be a good pediatrician. Nobody knows me and I don't care. When I leave the office, I don't care if people know I'm a doctor. But I do know that the children I took care of and their parents know that I did a good job."

Sometimes she complains that people do not appreciate the help she gives. "You don't get feedback from the administration. You don't get very many strokes in what you're doing. You get complaints. Compared to private-practice medicine, you seldom get good feedback. And the patients don't say 'Thank you' when you help their child get healthy. A thank-you would be enough."

Some helpers turn off at work when they are not appreciated. In one office at the Commerce Department, expert-managers asked me to help them deal with a secretary who they said was unmotivated and unproductive. They suspected she was incapable of doing the job, but because she was black they were hesitant to confront her. They were afraid she would accuse them of racism. It turned out that she was a competent helper to the needy, a leader of her church who felt demeaned at the office. With little respect or appreciation from managers, she did the minimum. Many helpers, frustrated by their paid work, express themselves in volunteer work. Another government secretary says: "I'm involved in church activities and do lots of missionary work, visit the sick, shut-ins, those confined to a hospital. There's hardly a week when I don't make a hospital visit. I oversee a woman who is 104 years old. I make sure that her basic needs are met. She gets food stamps and groceries. I am also president of the deaconesses and I work with the Board of Education for Sunday school teachers." This helpful enthusiasm could find expression at work if managers respected and encouraged it.

One helper in a large company is resentful of unappreciative management and her low status. She says: "A clerk's job is largely helping. Managers delegate the detail work. Some are chiefs, some the braves. It is necessary to have workers, so how can it be demeaning to be one? Sure, everybody would like to make fifty grand, but who is going to carry out the trash? Our society says, 'Oh, couldn't you get a better job than that?' What happened to the days when a guy was proud to be a streetcar conductor and supported his family that way? America needs to reprioritize its values. How can I be proud of what I contribute if no one really values helping?"

At AT&T, half the operators I have surveyed see themselves as helpers. A generation ago, operators took pride in helping people complete calls. Then, advances in technology made them feel like appendages. Today, the company is reinterpreting their job so that they again have more freedom to help customers complete calls that contribute to profitability. Furthermore, through the Quality of Worklife process, operators in Columbus, Ohio, Salt Lake City, and elsewhere have initiated projects to help old people who cannot get to the phone easily. The operators call in regularly and make calls for them. Of course, when they feel they are helping people in need, work becomes more meaningful for helpers and they are motivated to help the company succeed. Many of these operators have contributed their evenings and weekends to sign up subscribers for AT&T long distance.

HELPERS AND MANAGEMENT

As employees, helpers want managers who care about them, their growth and sense of dignity, and who listen to their ideas. They resent the expert-managers who don't help. A twenty-eight-year-old telephone company clerk says: "The supervisors are not helpful, they're worthless. I don't like the tiers, the class structure. My current manager sees us as a temporary bother! There is no warmth or communication. You either feel stupid and awkward, or you get discouraged. It becomes boring and you get apathetic. But as long as you spend a third of your life working, why not make it fun and helpful?"

As managers, the best helpers are teachers and developers. Weaker helpers fail as managers because they can't deal with conflict. They want to be liked and appreciated, and hesitate to give unpleasant feedback. They want people to succeed and are slow to discipline.

The best helper-managers practice individualized coaching. A manager of information services: "I had an employee once who wasn't showing up for work and whose work quality was poor. The supervisor said he was incompetent and didn't know what to do with him. When I talked with him, he said his supervisor was the problem. I worked with him defining the problem, how he saw it, and developed a way to let the employee make more decisions. I worked with the supervisor too, to develop a software package and some training for this employee, and things improved. I heard of another case of a woman who just wasn't turning up for work, but did good work when she came in. The supervisor took the time to talk to her and find out what was wrong. It turned out she was an ex-actress who was really suffering from having to do 'ordinary' work. The supervisor was sympathetic, helped her get involved with a community theater group, and her attendance improved immediately. But that goes even beyond work, and it takes the commitment of the supervi-

143

sor to sit down and talk with the person to find out the real reasons for what is going on." Expert-managers would likely not solve these motivational problems because they lack the helper's interest in understanding people.

One of the most respected leaders in the Foreign Service is a strong helper, an institutional helper and a developer of people and policy. She combines qualities of helping, institutional loyalty, and expertise. She sees her strength as creating openness and developing people so that she can delegate responsibility.

She says: "As an ambassador, you have to create relationships to be sure you are not cut off. I did a series of things. I was a regular at the Marine house Friday-night parties. I found that over a beer, people would bring up things that were bothering them. Along with three secretaries, I was a member of a pinball team. I maintained a very close relationship with the deputy chief of mission (DCM) and administrative counselor. I encouraged my secretary to be receptive to complaints or opposing views and not to be afraid to bring them to me. I told her to do this unless she was personally uncomfortable in that role, and she became the regular spokesperson for different points of view. I encouraged the DCM to be visible throughout the mission....I couldn't have done my job without the DCM. He visited everyone in the mission regularly to sound out their opinions, and I occasionally dropped in."

She adds: "I have an enormous respect for institutions and for structure. I prefer the risk of openness to the loneliness of singleness. I want to have fun and have others share in my work." Like the best helpers, she emphasizes values of integrity and honesty as essential to creating the trust fundamental to an open embassy. "We are not playing a game," she says, with an implied rebuke to the gamesmen of diplomacy. "Our work and careers are not a game. We must do a good job. I want and value good character."

The Foreign Service is the elite of government, where the dominant style is that of elegant experts whose highest value is expertise at political analysis, crafting a cable to Washington, and negotiating a treaty. Helpers are more likely to thrive in the helping agencies, like ACTION, which includes the Peace Corps, VISTA, and volunteer programs for the elderly.

In a Midwestern city, a woman in her early fifties runs the ACTION Agency's volunteer programs to help unemployed youth and old people. A survey of ACTION employees named her one of the three most effective managers in the agency. She is a helper with enough of the defender in her so that she is a strong team-builder and a developer of both institutions and people. For her, that means helping, mothering, and protecting.

She went to the Deep South at the height of the civil rights movement there and founded the Congress of Racial Equality chapter in her city. Her mother was a "very religious, churchy lady," but she moved away from the church when the pastor did not support civil rights work. Later she went back to college, got a degree in community organizing, and worked with a union. Eventually, she got into government work at ACTION, where she tries to hire other helpers:

"First I look for someone who has been a volunteer, and not just a formal volunteer, but has done something in their community. It could be a mother who has tried to do something in the schools. Secondly, I would look for some interpersonal skills, people who don't take themselves too seriously, are not pompous, and don't get upset at what the community says about them. They have to enjoy seeing other people grow, and not be too materialistic. They don't have to agree with people, but they have to like them." Her management philosophy expresses the helper's emphasis on building one-on-one relationships, and understanding the strengths and weaknesses of individuals.

"I have to treat employees all the same, but different. My philosophy is that people can do, if you help them and keep a positive attitude. I have to know them as people, and how they work. Gary is a hard worker, but he is new and is still learning, so I have to go by and give him a few strokes rather regularly to keep him going. Norma is meticulous. I have to push her to keep doing the bigger things. I have to slow Domingo down. He really likes to work hard, and is always out in the field rushing around. I sometimes have to give him some detailed desk work to get him to slow down or remind him to take some time off and take a vacation with his family. Cathy is hypertensive and very nervous. Sometimes I have to let her blow and then say, 'Okay, let's look at what's happened and try to put the pieces back together.' Dennis is new and is not very aggressive. I have to put him on training Vista volunteers to help him learn to be more outgoing.

"That's the way I treat my employees differently. Working with people is the thing I like most about my work. I really like seeing people grow, not only the staff, but also people in the projects. For example, before my people do a site visit, we talk. We go over the problems and discuss a possible approach. Then when they come back, they have a debriefing with me. Then they write up the site visit report. I try to get them to make a recommendation. That's hard. They would rather that I did it. They don't want to have to make the hard decisions like terminating a project or getting rid of a supervisor. If we have to make those kinds of decisions, I write the letter and sign it. This puts them in a position where they can negotiate and they don't have to take all the heat."

It happens that the two outstanding helper-developers quoted here are women. This would appear to confirm the findings of Carol Gilligan, a psychologist, that women, more than men, think of moral issues in terms of relationships rather than abstract principles, and envision an ideal of community rather than of autonomy.[1]

There are male helper-developers, like the ones I described in my book *The Leader*, who also are innovators, but the purest helper types are women. Perhaps helping and team-building is a style of management where women have a distinctive competence, especially when combined with the courage of the defender. As work increasingly requires an attitude of service to internal and external clients and customers, the positive qualities of helpers become a valuable asset to organizations.

WEAKNESSES OF HELPERS

The strength of helpers lies in their care for people, idealism, and cooperative spirit. Their weaknesses stem from overestimation of their ability to help and reluctance to defend their views.

Some helpers recognize that they run the danger of making people dependent on them. Trying to help without sufficient understanding and knowledge about people, their motives and capabilities, can weaken the client. The impulse to help can foster dependency, become oppressive rather than developmental.

A California social worker says: "They get dependent on me because I tend to take over and do things for them. You cannot spoon-feed everyone and expect them to feed themselves if you do not teach them. I think many of us, and I am from the old school, are more likely to do *for* people. I think this is necessary, but in addition you must do *with* people. With all the diagnoses and follow-ups, you keep doing for the patient. You make arrangements with them for going to Dr. Jones, for going for laboratory tests, you find out how they can get money to pay for it, you arrange for the transportation, you do all this for them.

"In a way, many of us enjoy doing it because you have a sense of accomplishment—like I said earlier, I am appreciated, I am needed, I have done something. But from a larger perspective, if you keep on doing for Mrs. Smith all these things, Mrs. Smith will never learn, Mrs. Smith will expect this to be done. So I am saying that sharing the responsibility is important. Like, 'Mrs. Smith, I know you have no transportation, do you have anyone at home? Well, maybe my brother-in-law. Well, ask him. Instead of me calling someone, you call your brother-in-law.' Or, 'Do you know what to do if Johnny has a temperature? Will you get a thermometer? Go out and buy it today so next time when you need it you'll have it.'

"Sometimes the person has to learn gradually to take responsibility. I think this is one of my frustrations with the social system. We do *for* people. For a certain segment of our population, we have to do it because they have not been taught, they do not know, but by and large, people should do things for themselves."

Helpers also suffer from gullibility. They want to believe people are good. They think they can get along with everybody. They also expect appreciation, and when disappointed, they become disillusioned. Some burn out or become hard.

Helpers try to avoid conflict and that keeps them from standing up for their principles, or protecting the people they are trying to help, or improving service by resolving conflicts within the organization. One manager at the State Department was pushed into a role that demanded telling people what to do. He was uncomfortable and felt incompetent. "I'm a very human-oriented type of person, as you can tell. Management above me made it necessary for me to be the typical authoritarian manager. Whatever I tried to do to humanize the situation even a little turned out to be a disaster, and I mean a disaster. I don't have the skills to do that. I was constantly forced into an adversary role. I don't do well in an adversary role. It was terrible, I don't even want to talk about it."

A helper generally admired for his achievements is criticized by his subordinates because he doesn't enjoy fighting. Another subordinate adds, "He has clarity of communication, but a reluctance to enter the fray, avoiding the unpleasant side of management such as criticizing people." Still another: "He is too much for the underdog. It's hard for him to be tough. He lets people get away with too much, gives them too many chances." He rationalized his unwillingness to defend his views: "If those bastards are too dumb to understand, forget it."

Some helper-managers naively believe that through participation, a consensus of good ideas will emerge. They pay insufficient attention to conflicting interests. They underestimate the need for tough-minded analysis and lack the courage to attempt new organizational approaches and to defend them.

A helpful manager at ACTION says: "My husband and I have a personal philosophy—you never do anything to hurt anyone. But people hurt us all the time. I don't know why—am I a sissy, do I have no backbone to stand up to people?"

She continues: "Often supervisors must protect employees, and I don't mean in a mothering way, but I know I need to stand up to my boss when he takes away space or moves people without asking first." But she lacks the courage to do so.

ADAPTING TO TECHNOSERVICE

Helpers try to humanize the system, to create a team, even a family, within bureaucracy. They make narrow roles bearable by humanizing relationships. They concentrate on dyadic, one-to-one relationships, rather than questioning whether the organization's existing structures and systems might be redesigned to better accomplish its service goals, and develop and motivate employees. For helpers, morale and motivation result from good relationships. In contrast, new-generation self-developers, who share the helper's dislike of bureaucracy, are not necessarily motivated by, good relationships. They require new organizational forms and a more businesslike, less emotionally involved approach. As managers in technoservice, helpers must balance coaching and care with expertise about strategy and organization.

Fortunately, many helpers welcome the opportunity to learn new skills, especially in management, and they recognize their shortcomings. They welcome technoservice leadership that develops their skills and focuses on satisfying customers.

CHAPTER 5

THE
DEFENDER

Defenders define service in two ways. One is advocacy for customers, clients, or subordinates, including defense and protection. The other is defense of larger institutions, companies, and nations from cheats, subversives, and enemies.

Organization breaks down when no one takes responsibility for defending values against the few who flout them. An essential element of leadership is to articulate and defend values. Thucydides describes the greatness of Pericles in forcing the Athenians to see that they could not maintain the freedom and luxury they so highly valued unless they were willing to defend it. And the American Revolution was led by men who called on farmers, craftsmen, and small businessmen to put aside immediate self-interest to defend the common value of liberty. The most admired political leaders have been defenders.

Among those we interviewed are social workers who defend the poor, the handicapped, and the victims of injustice; whistle-blowers outraged at the excessive harm, cost, or poor quality produced by people who squander the taxpayer's dollars; and policemen and prosecutors in search of criminals. They are angry, indignant at the cheaters, contemptuous of the expert-bureaucrats, who remain detached and objective, and impatient with the peace-loving helpers, who don't confront injustice.

However, in the technoservice organization, defenders can polarize people into "we" and "they." Unless they are in charge, they act like loose cannons on the organizational deck. As long as they feel they are the only ones who represent justice, they make life difficult for everyone else.

Only a small percentage of employees see the most important meaning of their work as defending against those who do not respect the law, who do harm, or who undermine values necessary to good organization. Only 1 percent of the Service-Sector and High-Tech samples check this orientation as most important, 2 percent of Telecommunications, and 6 percent of the IRS.

Americans are ambivalent about defenders, and the new generation, oriented to tolerance and positive experience, dislikes the role of policeman or protector. None of the people—mostly in their thirties—selected as Young Leaders by the Kellogg Foundation checked the defender as most important, and only 9 percent considered that it described them very well. When I asked them why, they said things like: "I don't want to be a cop." "I don't like to judge people." "Why should I defend institutional values, when I had no say in forming them?"

However, unless the new generation accepts responsibility for organizational values, defenders will take leadership roles and block the teamwork and delegation essential to productive technoservice organization.

We studied forty cases of defenders to distinguish patterns in relationships with clients, managers, subordinates, and co-workers, the rewards they seek in their work, the development of their character in childhood.

THE APPROACH TO SERVICE

The defender-helper, the tough institutional helper who can be called a protector, is perhaps the only bureaucrat who is portrayed favorably by the media and is the hero of novels and movies: Bumper, the cop on the beat, in Joseph Wambaugh's *The Blue Knight;* Georges Simenon's Inspector Jules Maigret; the Swedish detective Martin Beck in the novels of Maj Sjöwall and Per Wahlöö; and countless others. Maigret is the prototypic protector: suspicious of authority, but a fatherly coach to his assistants, contemptuous of the snobbish, sympathetic to the victims of society, even to the criminals he so relentlessly pursues. Bumper and Beck fit the same mold. However, this mold is the exception, not the rule. Most policemen are in fact experts, and defenders can be found in all kinds of jobs, not just the police department. Disproportionately, they move to the top, especially in organizations where there is little trust, because they build loyal teams, are effective bureaucratic jungle fighters, and protect their people.

Here are some defenders describing their views of service:

A California social welfare worker says: "I went to bat with the idea that the deserving should be helped, and those that cheated should get kicked off the rolls. It's a fair and square system and should be defended. I wanted to save the taxpayers of California money. I wanted to protect little children from abusive parents and protect the welfare system from clients who would take advantage of it."

A manager of volunteer programs for the elderly says: "What I like most about my work is the fact that I'm dealing with older people. I feel I'm an advocate, a friend. I'm helping people, a quarter of a million older people." How did he become interested in the elderly? "I became interested in forced retirement and ageism. People talk about racism and sexism; there's ageism, too. Old people need defenders."

A Commerce Department manager speaks of effectiveness by creating a loyal team: "You must believe in your staff, but more important, you must support your people down to the lowest working level, because without them you would be nowhere. I insist upon loyalty, but I believe you must earn their loyalty." This manager thinks of effectiveness more in terms of maintaining power than of cost-effective service, and he supports incompetents who are loyal to him.

A telephone company secretary and union shop steward sees herself as defending and helping fellow employees. She helped form a Quality of Worklife committee that trains a team to innovate and solve problems. She says: "I have a deep commitment to what I believe in. I'd go to bat for anyone who is overlooked. I love this QWL committee. I fought so much for the girls. We are one. We are together. I've often thought, if I went to my grave today, what would I want people to say about me? I'd like them to say, 'If it wouldn't have been for Cheryl, I wouldn't be able to do this, or be where I am today.'"

Some emphasize defense of institutions and laws rather than people. An IRS agent says: "We serve by enforcing against the people who don't pay their taxes. We serve the many by enforcing against the few. We don't serve the people we enforce against."

A Commerce Department auditor says: "We are fighting program people, fighting contractors. The auditor is the enemy of those who cheat."

A civil rights prosecutor for the Justice Department says: "I'm not sure I'm serving the public, because my work goes against the mainstream of the public, the majority's view. But by doing that, I'm serving the public in a way they don't appreciate, because my work fosters a system that permits the tremendous freedom we have. By championing the minority view, making the system available to everyone, there's a benefit to the public, although they don't necessarily perceive it as that.

"What I do causes certain individuals a lot of pain and hardship. They could lose their jobs or be incarcerated if convicted. And sometimes, investigating unpopular things, forcing people to be witnesses, causes hardship to them. For example, they can lose their jobs or be ostracized by the community or their peer association. But there's no solution to a problem without sacrifice."

A medical administrator states: "I owe it to the Health Department to see that it's getting something for the money it's putting out. I believe that. You know, I'm responsible to them, for those management things. I wouldn't let them get cheated. If it weren't going well, it would be my job to do something about it or let people know."

An administrator who also publishes a whistle-blowing newsletter says: "I feel I'm helping to inform the taxpayers—exposing waste and mismanagement."

A Nuclear Regulatory Commission (NRC) engineer who blew the whistle about safety problems, hidden from the public, sees his service as bringing "truth in government." He testified to Congress: "The agency has forced us into widespread deception of the public, and that includes Congress."

An auditor who sees himself as the "taxpayer's watchdog" examined a government-funded training program for the disadvantaged. He says: "They decided they wanted us to take a look at the program, actually go out and interview some of the people being trained. And I was finding out it was a lot of fiction. They were taking people, putting them on a payroll, and giving them a nothing job to do until the money ran out and then they let them go. And I started reporting this.

"I said, 'It's a whitewash.' Back in Washington, top management put the best face on it and said, 'Well, they made their best efforts.' I wouldn't accept that. And I fought and I fought and I said, 'Dammit, you've got to address the issue.'"

CHARACTER FORMATION

The central theme in the childhood of defenders is the struggle for justice—to be treated with respect and to triumph over humiliation.

We can distinguish two variations of defender backgrounds, although they may also be combined. One is the child who is unjustly picked on because he is weaker or different, and who reacts with courage and becomes acutely sensitive to humiliation and injustice. The second is the child from an intact family with strong standards which has struggled against adversity, poverty, or prejudice.

Some defenders lost their fathers when they were young. The father of one had a mental and physical breakdown. Another's father was an alcoholic. They felt unprotected. They see themselves as people who are weak, vulnerable to humiliation, or at a disadvantage, and became strong because they fought back. The strongest defenders seem to have had mothers who taught them to fight for their dignity.

The role of President of the United States calls for someone who, if not dominantly a defender—FDR and JFK were gamesmen-defenders—must at least have a strong identification with that orientation. The President takes an oath to defend the Constitution of the United States. Recent presidents, LBJ, Richard Nixon, and Ronald Reagan all share some of the family dynamics we find in the defenders we interviewed: a strong mother who emphasized pride and self-respect; a family where the father was ethical but not a success; a mother-generated drive to rise above failure, yet a touchiness about wounded dignity.[1] Defenders are quick to see slights and insults, and in a profound way, an attack on their dignity is felt as a threat to survival.

Defenders feel they would rather be bloodied than oppressed

and humiliated without a fight. They seek those who share their values. The new generation is not comfortable with the defender's intense view of relationships demanding total loyalty and ideological agreement. Reagan's attractive style, the professional actor's detachment, a graceful sense of humor, and profound optimism mitigate the defender qualities of aggressive self-righteousness disliked by the new generation.

In poor families where there is a strong father and mother, we find defenders like the consumer advocate Ralph Nader, whose parents were Lebanese immigrants in a predominantly white, Anglo-Saxon, Protestant Connecticut town. Some of the defenders we studied recall being outcasts because they were from immigrant families, or families with different religious or cultural backgrounds. These children became alert to attacks on their dignity. They were constantly challenged to prove their worth. This, of course, has also been the situation for many black families in America.

It is also true for some poor white families. The government auditor says: "People talk about ghettos and all that. I lived in one, too, in Albany, New York. We were looked on as outcasts. We didn't have anything. And we worked to get it. My mother was tough. She was a wheeler-dealer. She knew exactly what direction she wanted me to go. She pushed me. I knew what I wanted. We lived on a farm for a while behind the university, and I knew damn well I wasn't going to the public high school. I was going to prep, and then I was going to the university. Mother told me, 'We can't pay for it, we don't have the money.' I said, 'I'll get it, I'll work for it.' I said, 'I don't need any help from anybody. I can do it.' And she and my father told me, 'Well, as long as you are going to school, you get free room and board, but you are going to have to do the rest of it on your own.' So from the time I was twelve years old, every piece of clothing on my back and all the tuition I spent for school was paid for by me. You name it, I did it. I was delivering milk forty hours a week when I was ten. Delivering newspapers, door-to-door salesman..."

A State Department official who is known as a defender of ethics and a protector of those who share his standards says: "It was the Depression years when I was growing up, in the thirties. We had no money, had to scramble for every speck of education. Our background was not only ethical, but there was a sense that you could rise above it and manage."

Defenders are survivors who have toughened themselves to cope with and rise above threats to their life, livelihood, and dignity. The State Department official says: "The Depression experience was topped off by going into war for four years. By the time you get through combat, with friends wounded and killed, you have your values redistilled, your character is molded. You either go to pot or you don't. I tell my wife we are the last of the nineteenth century. After us came the Pill and everything else."

A social worker in her forties whose mother was a migrant worker, grew up traveling in camps in California, had five step-fathers. She never knew her father, but thinks he was a gambler. She married a soldier, had a son, and "he left me with all the bills." She became a country-western singer, then married a well-off manufacturer who agreed to support her schooling. "I wanted to be a social worker, because I remember they were the only ones who came out in the fields and cared about us. Coming from where I did, it's sometimes hard to realize that not everyone is as strong inside as I am." She admires her mother because "she never gave up and still hasn't."

Defenders admire heroic qualities: courage, bravery, integrity. In contrast to experts, who admire father figures who are teachers or models of mastery, defenders admire models of courage and ethics. Some of the same people a helper would cite for their care, a defender admires for their moral strength. Many admire Winston Churchill (for his tenacity, courage), Abraham Lincoln, and Martin Luther King, Jr. (for his bravery and determination, and because he stood for human dignity).

A manager of VISTA volunteer programs says: "I like Ralph Nader, but I think he's a bit too radical at times. I admire him because he really took on a big task and didn't buckle under the pressures; and I admire the courage, I guess, and the fact that he was trying to fight for something that wasn't very popular. In most cases he was right. I think after he got there, he was a little bit more extreme than I expected him to be. Not everything has to do with people getting cheated. Yet probably you need somebody who is fanatical about what he is doing to get the attention."

It is worth adding a quote from an interview with Dan Burt, the tough lawyer who took on CBS in defense of General William Westmoreland. His ideal is Captain Carpenter, a mythical superdefender in a John Crowe Ransom poem: "If you went and looked up 'Captain Carpenter,' you'd get a better sense of what I respect. It's an allegory. Captain Carpenter is a Don Quixote type. He goes out day after day over the course of some unspecified span, apparently it's his life. And he keeps meeting with various evils, and they keep beating the hell out of him till finally they've cut off his arms and legs and he still goes rolling on. Finally they cut off his head and as his head rolls down the road in the dust and gravel and pebbles and mud and dirt, his tongue is still going. He's still fighting, he's still doing what he thinks is right. With a measure of spirit and a measure of élan."[2]

REWARDS FROM WORK

The rewards most important to defenders have to do with getting results, seeing their efforts make a difference, achieving a sense of justice and triumph over enemies.

The auditor for the Commerce Department says: "One joy is seeing someone take my finished product, and I'm not looking for praise. In fact, if they accept it, and take action, and it works, that to me is a joy. I don't want a reward for it. That's my reward—the action taken."

To achieve these goals, power is important, and defenders think about it more than do other types, with the exception of innovators. While for defenders power means direct control, for innovators power is the ability to create wealth by organizing and motivating people.

A union leader and activist for AFSCME (American Federation of State, County, and Municipal Employees) says: "You must recognize that everything is done on the basis of power. There are other things too, of course. Power doesn't necessarily mean competition and things like that, but if you are dealing with two people, you are dealing with influence. Therefore, you're dealing with power of one over the other."

Defenders consider money and promotion as their right, not as a reward. They demand what they believe they deserve. The defender wants to be treated with dignity and to be heard. If this does not occur, he feels exploited and gets angry.

DEFENDERS AND MANAGEMENT

Defenders want courageous bosses they can trust to defend principles and a sense of dignity. They dislike those they consider unjust, weak, and detached.

An IRS defender describes an ideal manager: "They all (subordinates) respected him. Some didn't like him, because he was very hard, but he was kind of fair, too. Very fair, a very *just* person."

Union leaders also want to deal with strong managers. One says: "I want to be able to sit down with my boss and discuss the solution of problems. At the same time, it has to be a guy with a strong backbone, who can pound his fist on the table when needed. It must be someone with whom you can discuss something, and who sticks to his word. Then we can trust each other."

A social worker in San Francisco complains about weak, unsupportive management. He caught a welfare mother with a man's clothes in her closet, but he lost the case in court. "I had her, I took her to court. In court she got her pastor and neighbors to testify for her that the man didn't live there. I was put through the third degree in court and lost the case. What bothered me was that I didn't get any backup from my superiors. They said it wasn't worth tying up the courts. It costs money."

Defenders are more indignant than other types about being ill-used, exploited. The Justice Department prosecutor says, "My manager uses me when he sees he has the opportunity, and kicks my ass when he has the opportunity to do so."

The chief medical officer is angry that top management doesn't listen to her. "Yes, I don't want them to get a fucking thing from me. What can I say? No, they never used me fully. But they're using me even less fully than they were. All they had to do was listen."

No one likes manager who are not just. But defenders are more outspoken then other types against those who play favorites, such as the manager who "places value on people who defer to him, particularly to anyone who kisses his ass. So brown-nosers are considered good employees worthy of praise."

More than other types, defenders describe their refusal to cooperate with managers they consider unethical. A defender working for a real estate firm: "They found their costs were going to go up. They wanted me to try to talk people into pulling out on their contracts. In order to do that, I had to lie. I wouldn't do it. My boss fired me because I wouldn't obey."

Since defenders demand the truth and push management to confront risky or politically delicate issues, they often become pariahs. The whistle-blower says: "They don't really trust me. They withhold routine information; they hold meetings without including me. But I insist on having the information."

As managers, the best defenders in fact do express the philosophy and behavior that defenders look for in a manager. A manager at IRS says, "I have a keen sense of respecting the dignity and worth of somebody else." The nursing supervisor describes her management philosophy: "First, the dignity of the individual." And these defender-managers want subordinates who share their values.

The State Department official describes his management philosophy: "A few simple rules. Try to use common sense, try to delegate, and trust the people who work for you, always back them up." How does he bring his principles into his managerial philosophy? "I look for a reflection of my own priorities and principles in the people who work for me. People who are not straight, or are self-serving, apple-polishing—I help them get another job. If you are trying to build a team, you need people in whom you have confidence. Else it's not a compatible team of your own."

Do his subordinates understand principles? "It's hard to speak about people, but I think they do. I've had the feeling that the guys who work for me know I want honesty, fairness—that I don't like and wouldn't approve apple-polishing, slyness, deviousness. I have the feeling this fundamental attitude is recognized at the office level."

His subordinates recognize these values and respect the boss. It's been said that when then Secretary of State Henry A. Kissinger asked this official to be his spokesman, he refused, saying, "I can't take the job, Mr. Secretary, because I don't trust you to tell the truth." When I asked him about the story, he confirmed it and said he had expected to be fired, but Kissinger promoted him.

Defenders talk about having their own loyal team, in contrast to the gamesmen, who are concerned with competence and don't think much about loyalty or character as long as the team wins.

Defenders also demand openness from subordinates. Just as they want the truth from superiors, they allow no secrets to be kept from them. The supervisor of nurses talks about staff problems that preceded her arrival: "Anyway, they were unhappy, and so they did the whispering and they decided they were going to have a meeting without the supervisor, and they did that. And when I came, they were still having meetings from which the supervisors were barred. Staff-nurse meetings once a month. Well, to me that's totally useless. Even if you are pissed as hell at me, how in the hell am I going to do anything about it if you're going to sit back there in the room and talk about what a bitch I am? Somebody's got to tell me. So I eliminated these meetings."

Defenders make tough bosses. They demand compliance and loyalty, and they run a tight ship. Though they boast that they care about their people, they are the type least bothered by firing those who don't measure up. They feel justified. Even in government, where this is exceptionally hard to do, they do not hesitate to bite the bullet. While most government managers fear firing subordinates and facing the possibility of a time-consuming court case, a manager at ACTION says: "I guarantee I can fire any employee in four months if he doesn't continue to perform and refuses to do so. You set up the criteria. What is required is that the senior manager know how to do that. You write everything as if for a court record."

He says: "There is just enough flexibility built into bureaucracy that the extraordinary needs are manageable. It means you have to spend a little time fighting the good fight."

Defenders believe, with Harry S. Truman, who made his reputation as chairman of a Senate committee investigating war profiteers, "If you can't stand the heat, stay out of the kitchen." They are willing to fight.

WEAKNESSES OF DEFENDERS

The most effective defenders are the courageous institutional loyalists, protectors of people and principles. But even the more productive defenders can cause conflict in organizations by di-

163

viding people into loyal friends and potential enemies. The we-they mentality overpersonalizes and fragments a technoservice network.

For the less productive defenders, legitimate in-fighting can become power-driven jungle fighting; the demand for loyalty can become oppressive domination; the demand for trust and openness can become paranoid suspiciousness. Defense of dignity can become a touchy unwillingness to accept criticism or admit mistakes, resulting in carelessness about the dignity of others. A zeal for justice can become identification of self with the law.

Speaking of defenders, a policeman says: "A man can be driven by the pressures of police work from enforcing the law to being the law. He will accept this as natural and there will be no remorse for his actions. He has accepted a new reality, the type that he has tried to prevent in others."

When I was hired in 1978 as a consultant to improve work in the Commerce Department, I held a series of meetings with top managers. One manager, a defender, aggressively challenged my credentials, assumptions, ideas. I took him aside after a meeting and asked him why he was so hostile. He said it was true that he was testing and baiting me. "The question is: Can I trust you? You are entering a family I care about—to change people I care for."

Yet, he was the least cooperative of the bunch. He was unwilling to delegate to his own staff, who were frightened of him. He was not a protector but a bully who thought of himself as a defender. But he had made a career by persuading insecure political appointees that he could get results.

The suspiciousness of the defender can turn into paranoia when possibilities of attack are treated as though they were probabilities. Explaining his suspiciousness, a Justice Department defender says: "I'm not a do-gooder. I'm not a bleeding heart. I don't immediately trust people. I don't just give them an open hand and say, 'I like you.' I'm suspicious—that's my nature. I think it's healthy."

Paranoia is fed by anger and hostility, which are projected onto others. Others respond angrily to the hostility and thus confirm the paranoid suspicions. A patient once asked me if the fact that he had put four locks on his door indicated that he was paranoid. Half-jokingly, I said, "Even paranoics have enemies." "Especially paranoics," he said.

The civil rights prosecutor had recurring dreams "about a black pick-up truck with wooden side panels, an old truck, which would run me over in the dreams. In some I'd cross a street and it would run me over. In others, I'd be trying to do something so it wouldn't run me over, even running up a wall of a building, but it would run me over. There was a man driving the truck, a male, it was like an albatross to me." This man is always expecting that his enemies are out to get him. But he continually creates enemies so that his fear will not make him feel crazy.

A telecommunications marketer, a defender who criticizes his boss as unjust and weak, says: "I've had nightmares related to my ratings. I'd be doing very bad things to my boss. I couldn't sleep. In one, I was driving out somewhere and came upon him on the road. He was in need of help. I tried to hit him."

The danger for defenders is that their strong defense against the hardships, slights, and injustices of childhood begins to dominate their personalities, that their anger, suspicion, and self-righteousness isolate them and make them ineffectual.

ADAPTING TO TECHNOSERVICE

The greater the incidence of injustice in an organization, the more likely that defenders will take positions of leadership. In impersonal hierarchies, where people are treated as a mass, someone is needed to defend the rights of the powerless. People without power seek protectors.

When people at the front line are empowered, there is less

need for defenders, because everyone has reason to defend organizational values. Members of the new generation say they will not defend these values unless they have been involved in developing them. In technoservice companies like American Transtech and Westinghouse Furniture Systems, where employees are respected and have freedom to improve their work, there is no constituency for paranoid-style defenders.

As long as there are injustices and powerless people, there will always be a role for defenders. In the technoservice world, defenders must relax their defenses and invest in the skills of dialogue and facilitation. They must trust more in the good faith of people. At the top, organizations will always need leaders with the courage to defend the organization against its enemies. There will always be a place for principled institutional loyalists to support leaders and stand up for organizational values. But those leaders will do best who balance the values of the defender with expertise, care, and innovation.

CHAPTER 6

THE SELF-DEVELOPER

The people who respond most enthusiastically to innovators like Lemasters, Nagel, and Carlzon are self-developers. They are the type best adapted to the technoservice mode of production, the flux and uncertainty of the new competitive world. This type will shape the workplace of the future. Although innovators will design the new organizational models, the self-developers will make them work.

Like the other types, self-developers are defined by the values that determine their approach to work. They focus on self-development to maintain a sense of authority, self-esteem, and security by upgrading marketable skills, integrating usable information, facilitating effective teams, and understanding customer needs. Brought up in an environment of change, they have learned to adapt to new people and situations, and to trust their own abilities rather than parents or institutions. They value independence, and they accept responsibility for themselves. They try to stay in competitive condition, physically as well as mentally, to grasp opportunities, and enjoy life to the fullest. Their weakness is the reverse of their strength: detachment, reluctance to commit themselves and to take parental-type leadership roles.

Self-developers dislike bureaucracies. They want organization based on shared responsibility, reciprocity, and continual learning. Unlike father-oriented experts, they are not motivated to please the boss in order to get promoted. Unlike mother-oriented helpers, they do not value relationships for their own sake. Unlike defenders, they are not driven to protect people or uphold justice against cheaters and bullies.

Self-developers want to be business people, not bureaucrats. They look for work that develops business and social skills, but if the job does not meet their needs, they express themselves outside. Some establish entrepreneurial businesses on the side, reinforcing their sense of independence within the workplace where they are employed.

Self-development is a traditional American value reinterpreted by each generation and social character. The Founding Fathers believed that our representative democracy requires a commitment to public education so that people can participate in government and understand their larger common self-interest. Benjamin Franklin, spokesman for the craft ethic, preached self-development as a means toward prosperity and a rich cultural life. Ralph Waldo Emerson, Henry David Thoreau, and William James expressed the New England version of developing a strong independent character. In the age of Horatio Alger, development became oriented to making money. In the twentieth century, it focused on moving up the corporate hierarchy through training in administrative expertise and in how to win friends and influence people.

Each of the character types—except defenders, who rarely express the need—has a partial vision of self-development. Experts speak of "increasing intellectual knowledge and becoming an expert in my field," and "improving skills that management says need improvement." Helpers speak of "learning to help people more effectively," and "growing" in confidence. Innovators talk about self-development in terms of new careers, finding new challenges, experimenting, risk-taking (a gameswoman: "I love risk-taking because that's where the fun and excitement come from"). For them, self-development means testing themselves and breaking boudaries.

For the new generation, all these definitions are attractive but incomplete. Self-developers want competence and knowledge so they can progress in their careers. They like helping people do things better, not because they want to form a relationship, but because it is good business, or because teaching is a good way of learning. They enjoy new people, experiences, and challenges because learning is fun and expands their sense of competence.

Self-developers are searching for meaning beyond success, or success beyond money and status, and this includes the meaning of self-development itself. They seek a sense of wholeness and of power as ability to live well. This includes learning to get along with different kinds of people and to understand them. It includes "developing the ability to be content with what I have." There is a search for a sense of being: learning to listen to oneself, to concentrate on one thing, to gain control over one's body in order to look and feel good. It includes courage to become more independent. A twenty-year-old secretary with a high school education said: "I'd like to be a more independent person, to accept, learn and realize the uniqueness and differences in all kinds of people. And not be stifled by social traditions and trappings. There are a lot of things I don't do because it's not done. I'd like to grow around that. I know I'm young and inexperienced. It will take time and patience; it will take initiative and guts to go out there and live."

THE APPROACH TO SERVICE

Self-developers enjoy meeting new people, solving problems, facilitating teamwork, and sharing information. Unlike the helper, who sees the client as dependent, the self-developer sees help-seekers as equals, or potential equals, customers with a purpose toward which the self-developer can contribute.

Although self-developers are more interested in people than are experts, this interest is more gamelike and detached than that of the caring helpers. They want to read people, understand what makes them tick, because it is interesting and useful for problem-solving or making a sale. They don't feel responsible for dependent people. They want people to treat others as independent adults, as they would like to be treated themselves.

Self-developers define service in terms of productive relationships:

1. Facilitating a team, so that each member contributes knowledge to arrive at good, consensual decisions.

2. Providing information, so that people can achieve their goals, make more informed choices.

3. Offering advice, or constructive criticism, so that people can do a better job.

4. Educating, teaching others so that they can do it themselves.

5. Participating with others to understand and solve problems, or to try new approaches.

A management consultant from a big-eight accounting firm, age twenty-eight, says: "We do a lot of consulting on information systems. I help people say what they need, trace information flow, and so on." She goes into firms where she must gain trust and develop solutions with her clients. She likes her current assignment because she is "picking up a good technical background which I figure has good resale value."

An IRS agent, age forty-six, says: "I try to look at the taxpayer as a whole person, to find out why they have a problem, and what to do to correct it....I find the people fascinating, how they react to you. They don't like us all the time. Some shade the truth, some hide it. Some give you nothing. We're sizing each other up. It's a game of wits."

An AT&T middle manager, age twenty-eight, says: "I like the interface with people. I need to deal with programmers, head-quarters, technical people, making sure the machines work. I like finding ways to get around hard-nosed people. I like deal-ing with people, solving problems, research."

A Communications Workers of America (CWA) union stew-ard, age thirty, says: "A steward should be a problem-solver, not a grievance-filer. You try to find the fastest, quickest method to meet the employee's goals....I make it easy for people to be open."

A thirty-eight-year-old entrepreneur develops data systems for business and government. He hires people who want self-de-veloping work and asks them to design their jobs. "I ask them what kind of service they would like to provide, and although I can't promise we will move into that business immediately, we always succeed within a year or so." Does he like to help peo-ple? "Helping is too personal. It is more development for our mutual interest."

In each case, the service relationship adds value for everyone involved.

REWARDS FROM WORK

Money is necessary for independence and a good life. Self-de-velopers believe in value for value and they are not afraid to negotiate. Although they are less interested in recognition and medals from authority than experts, they expect their fair share. A partner in a large Washington law firm, in his fifties, contrasts the new-generation lawyers with his colleagues of twenty years ago: "Then the senior partners made even more proportionately than we do now. But we never thought of complaining. We were disgustingly grateful when they gave us a bonus of $1,500. The self-developers demand a fairer distribution. But even more, they want to participate in the process of dividing up the profits. They want to know the criteria, and have no wish to please the old men."

Self-developers are disappointed by jobs where money is the only reward. In that case, as one telephone company clerk, age thirty, says: "I feel I'm prostituting myself really, doing the routine. It's dull. I'd like more technical thinking, decision-making work. Now my work is repetitious and doesn't require any brains."

Those who feel most rewarded have jobs that allow development and exercise of their skills and abilities. A thirty-five-year-old lawyer considers his job "a lab of self-study and self-improvement. I need friction. How can I work on how I relate to people if I don't work with people?"

Self-developers are rewarded by a sense of responsibility, creativity, and stimulation. They like to use all of themselves. A thirty-two-year-old supervisor of sales at AT&T says: "What I like about my work is that I have complete responsibility for my own actions. I can develop something out of my own belief, implement it, see if it works."

A twenty-nine-year-old financial systems consultant from a big-eight accounting firm says: "What I like is that you get to be very independent. You have to pull your weight, and people you are working for have to delegate to you. You have a lot of demands put on you, often of a conflicting nature, so there is a high stress level. It's very stimulating."

Conversely, they are also rewarded by the sense of being needed, of having a unique, necessary, meaningful role. An auditor for an accounting firm, age twenty-nine, says: "I've got to know that what I'm doing is meaningful. It's extremely important. The job you do has to be special, special to you."

A thirty-one-year-old Library of Congress manager who provides information to senators and congressmen says: "A psychic reward is that you see words you wrote written into laws, reports, used in speeches. I have a role but no real power, but the role is enjoyable. I do feel I'm giving the great leaders of the country their good ideas."

WHEN THE WORKPLACE IS FRUSTRATING

If stuck in dead-end or dissatisfying jobs, self-developers look for better work and, meanwhile, find new ways to express themselves inside or outside the company. They switch jobs more easily than other types. Sometimes they stay in the job only to finance their real vocations as struggling entrepreneurs, jazz musicians, artists, and artisans.

The telephone company clerk who has given up on her job is sharpening her writing skills at a local community college. Her goal is to write and be able to support herself from her writing.

Another example of a frustrated self-developer is a woman of forty who works as a statistical assistant to two economists in a federal agency. At age twenty-nine she was extremely motivated to learn on the job. She says: "I went to work as a clerk so we could afford a house. At that point I didn't have any goals—just to earn money to buy a home. But as time passed I thought I could sharpen my skills. I asked my supervisors if I could take some courses. I took one in statistics and one in keypunch. The problem was not being able to use what I'd learned and rise up. It was a dead-end job. It wasn't my major interest, but it could have been. Since it was a job I was already in, I could have developed it, but when I saw this wasn't possible, I said, 'What else can I do to develop myself?' So I switched from business to writing and drama. Maybe there's a chance to develop there. I went to school part-time and got my degree. Now I'm involved with a group of graduates who are trying to start a production group. I acted in a play to raise money for the department....

173

This position here is at a dead end. Just knowing that I have something else that could materialize at any time gives me hope.

"They come by now and then to check the numbers. I don't even know what they plan to do with my work. If we knew why, we would feel more a part of it. I've asked, but my question wasn't answered."

She keeps the job for the benefits in unemployment insurance, health insurance, and pension. She does the minimum in the office and takes night courses at a university where she writes plays, helps produce them, and acts. She identifies herself with the new generation: "My creative juices are always going, trying to fantasize how that can be put on paper. I'm observant of people, and describe them in my mind. I'm anxious to get to know them. I believe in opening up America to our young and letting the sky be the limit. My favorite people are the young ones. They are so candid, frank, and genuine. Older people get fixed in a mold. Younger people today are more flexible, and I love it."

In contrast to the woman whose creativity finds expression outside the office, a telephone company manager has been surprised to find his workplace so interesting. On the side, he owns his own jewelry business; he designs the pieces and cuts the stones. He also plays the jazz saxophone and has toured the country with a jazz group. Two years ago, he joined the company, he thought for a year, to make some money and get the medical benefits, but the job has become interesting. "I never did quit. I like the security; you don't have that with music." He enjoyed the excitement of "tracking down a problem on new computer systems, then deciding how to solve the problem." He also liked supervising five people and wanted to move into higher management. But a year ago, he was again thinking of quitting. There was "too much bureaucracy."

A BALANCED LIFE

More than other types, self-developers say that work shouldn't be the most important thing in life. The ones with families want to keep a balance. They want "to be happy, both professionally and personally." Men don't want work to separate them from family; women don't want family to undermine career possibilities. A highly competent and motivated executive, age thirty-eight, says: "I work fifty hours a week. I come in early and go home late, but I leave it at the office. I am not going to push my little son off my lap because he is messing up papers from work."

For self-developers, both family and work require attention. So does physical well-being. Good diet and frequent exercise are essential to maintain the competitive work pace. They also help one to feel well. Sometimes self-developers skip lunch to work out or run. A twenty-nine-year-old manager says: "We watch the things we eat. We run. If you're a workaholic, after a while you're not really productive. You may work seventy-five hours, but how much work are you really getting done in seventy-five hours?"

A technician, age twenty-eight, says: "I'm family-oriented. If the phone rang and my wife said I was needed at home, I'd go. Even if my supervisor said I shouldn't. I can always get another job, but I only have one family."

A manager at the Commerce Department, age thirty-three, says: "My overall philosophy is: Work comes second to family. Keep the harmony going at home, take care of those needs. Sometimes work does take precedence, but overall, the family gets the primary attention."

The manager turned down a promotion that meant traveling, which would interfere with family life: "I don't really want the money. I'd rather have less pressures so I can live a long and full life than have a lot of pressures and live five more years and die with that....I know I'm not at my maximum pressure level. When I get to my maximum pressure level, I don't want to go over that regardless of the money. A job that would demand travel 80 percent of the time would not have fit into my situation....My outside life and inside life with my job are both important to me, and too much travel would mess up my outside life with my family."

An IRS agent, age twenty-seven, expecting her first child, says: "I take the attitude that I can only do what can be done in eight hours. Right now I'm caught between being a wife and being a careerperson. Now I'm expecting my first child. I want to be so organized that I can achieve a balance between the things I want to do. I'm still very young. Some concentrate on their career and then later their family, but I wanted to taste a little of it all. It's harder to adjust to being a wife and mother, but I have the determination to know that I won't give up on wanting to be a careerperson. It wouldn't have worked as well, I think, if I'd been a wife first."

A computer technician, age thirty, sums up the new generation's concern: "At one time, I was concerned with my work being good, and then it was. And then I was concerned with my personal life, and then I got that in shape. The problem now is getting the two coordinated."

This coordination is not an easy task for self-developers seeking success in the competitive workplace. Many find that their resolve to achieve balance cannot withstand their drive to succeed.

CHARACTER FORMATION

If we consider the traditional family as one in which the father is the sole wage-earner and the children grow up in one place, then self-developers come from nontraditional backgrounds. We analyzed forty-five interviews of self-developers. What this group shares is a background of continual change, mobility, lack of clear norms other than the value of continually learning to adapt to new conditions. Over half the self-developers came from dual-career families, another 20 percent from families broken up by death or divorce; only 30 percent came from families where the father was the sole breadwinner. In some of these families, mothers had semi-careers as volunteers. In others, the father's work was all-consuming, or kept him traveling constantly, so that the children didn't see much of him. About one-quarter of the mothers had high-level jobs as managers or entrepreneurs. The others were teachers, nurses, secretaries in large corporations. These percentages are different from those of the expert, who was raised in a family with a sole male wage-earner. They are closer to the average for American society of the eighties, rather than the fifties or sixties, when these self-developers were children. The sense of balance of mother-father authority and lack of paternal dominance free the child from strong bonds of dependency and facilitate peer relationships. Frequent parental disappearance may also cause self-protective detachment.

Unlike experts, self-developers do not need to please the father and copy his model of success. They do not have the expert's transferential relationship to bosses as father-figures. On the contrary, some criticize fathers as too driven by work. Although they lack a clear model of authority for themselves, they have grown up in families where authorities negotiate decisions and share authority. This becomes natural for them.

The self-developer does not have the maternal orientation of the helper, does not want to create a family at work. Self-developers value friendly, helpful relationships, but they are uneasy with intimacy; it makes them feel trapped. They like the interaction of the team that plays together but splits at the end of the working day.

Thus, the self-developers have been less overtly programmed for traditional work and family by childhood than the experts, helpers, or defenders. They see themselves as needing to create their own style of work and authority which combines traditional male and female values. This means husband and wife both work, cook, clean the house, and care for the children. Rejecting both the paternal and maternal emotional attitudes of protective authority and unconditional care, what is emphasized is equality of rights and responsibilities, and tolerance.

ROLE MODELS

Self-developers admire people who have helped them along the way or who are models for their own development. These admired people are seen more as colleagues than as parental figures.

A computer programmer in his late twenties: "One of my high school teachers had a great influence in my career, how it was started. He used to say, 'Set your goal and don't let anything turn you away.' He was more a buddy with adult wisdom than a teacher."

A probation officer in her thirties: "I admire my therapist, because she is sixty-five years old and continues to grow as a person. And she's helped me a lot."

An AT&T salesman in his early thirties: "I admire Bill, my boss. He operates like I would like to. The way he handles people. He's able to communicate with people well enough so that he doesn't offend them when he says, 'No way.'"

Self-developers admire people who have changed careers, taken nontraditional paths. One mentions Albert Schweitzer, who had a career before age thirty as a successful musician, then went to medical school and theological seminary, eventually earning a total of four doctorates.

But they can also be critical of the people they admire. A thirty-three-year-old manager of research admires Marie Curie, Eleanor Roosevelt, and Albert Einstein, but her admiration for the latter two is qualified: "Eleanor Roosevelt...she was more problematic. A woman who achieved great things. Had broad interests. But she was not universally loved. Her personal life wasn't what I'd like my personal life to be...she didn't have a happy marriage. I value that a great deal." Einstein "was a difficult person to live with. He didn't devote too much attention to his personal relationships."

Self-developers want to learn from but not copy models. Their ideal is to be "themselves," and to learn effective practice from good models but also what to avoid from bad models.

THE SELF-DEVELOPER'S IDEAL BOSS

Because they expect less from bosses than do experts, helpers, and defenders, self-developers can be more objective about them, more understanding of bosses' strengths, limitations, and constraints. However, they are clear about what they want from management: freedom to express their views; respect as adults; authority to make decisions; open information; a clear contract as to expectations; competent leadership and coaching so that they can develop their potential.

The telephone clerk says: "I want to be treated like an adult, make my own decisions whether right or wrong, because that's the only way I can learn." The computer technician says: "I like supervisors who will work with you in a give-and-take relationship. As grown-up human beings we learn how to get along." An air traffic controller, age twenty-seven, says: "Managers must become more sensitive; some have not accustomed themselves to dealing with new employees who are forcing them to grow. Being more sensitive produces more. There is a need to instill confidence. Many managers are old Marine types; they don't want a bilateral relationship." What he and others want is sensitivity to the individual's sense of dignity and more responsiveness to their need for information.

Self-developers describe a good manager as a value-added resource when needed, a facilitator of teamwork, and a developer of people. They don't need managers to do for them what they can do for themselves.

The twenty-eight-year-old AT&T manager is pleased with his boss: "I'm given flexibility to change my job the way I want. I'm mechanizing the whole thing, with advanced office systems. It's a credit to my boss and district manager. They tell me, 'Here's the ball of wax, go for it.' I mold my job, I make major changes."

Self-developers appreciate real leadership. Like experts, they are contemptuous of laissez-faire management. Where they differ is their emphasis on sharing information and its meaning, and facilitating teamwork. In contrast, the expert wants autonomy.

The young manager at the Commerce Department complains: "I'd like a few more deadlines, even if they're arbitrary, just to keep me chugging along. My boss is too laissez-faire. I work better under pressure, as do many. We could benefit from regular meetings to keep us informed of all the issues before us and what needs to be pushed along."

Self-developers also complain about management that does not develop employees but leaves them in dead-end jobs without opportunities to advance and learn.

A secretary at the Department of Agriculture, age twenty-seven, says: "I wanted to be given an opportunity to see what my limitations are. If I do a good job, then I should be given added responsibilities, but that doesn't happen here."

A telecommunications manager, age twenty-nine, says: "Management isn't developing people here. There's a lot of potential. If they were, maybe there would be more turnover, but people would also have incentive. Now, there's an overabundance of management. We lost a lot and it was a good thing. How many more are here that we don't need? At least twenty-five percent." (Since we talked, about that many have left.)

Sometimes new-generation self-developers learn to manage their bureaucratic-expert bosses. I was invited to speak to managers at a large company by a thirty-year-old self-developer who was near the bottom of the management hierarchy. I asked how he was able to organize the meeting of top managers and invite me. He said: "I know what makes my boss run. I let him know how he will gain from my project. He's the kind of guy, if you wind him up and point him in the right direction, he goes straight ahead."

While self-developers criticize bureaucratic management roles, they do not necessarily blame the individual manager. Rather, they are more likely to blame the system and see many management jobs as poorly designed or unnecessary because they involve paperwork or monitoring people who can manage themselves.

An IRS agent, age thirty-seven, says: "I'd like to see management a facilitator, in a helping role to the revenue officer. They're given so much shit to do, it directs them in the opposite way. When they're doing those reports, they can't manage the employees."

Self-developers want managers who "have frequent meetings," are "always available for consultations," "work with you in a give-and-take relationship," and provide constructive criticism and coaching. They want managers who tell it like it is. They not only want information, but also want to know what it means.

Self-developers want feedback from managers, co-workers, therapists (six out of forty-five mention seeking psychotherapy or psychologically-oriented workshops as a means to self-development). But they prefer to be measured by the market, because it is real and protects them from subjective evaluations by superiors who make them feel small. They are also disgusted by bureaucratic make-work and meaningless measurements.

A high-level Washington bureaucrat, age forty-five, who works in the White House, says: "I once headed a federal internal consulting agency which provided services to agencies on a reimbursable basis. This was lots of fun, a fascinating period really. Very entrepreneurial; feedback was from the outside. The goodies were to get contracts, and we did $600,000 on the books for that year. A very rewarding way to work, at least for me individually. The idea of the challenge, of having an outside opinion, getting outside appraisal. If we weren't attractive to an agency, we got no business. I like that, it just turns me on. I liked also that the only obstacles to doing a good job were those I put forward myself, such as not knowing how to do it. I like the enterprising feeling." Self-developers rarely find this kind of work in government or in large businesses. That is one reason they are drawn to professions, and to starting their own businesses.

WORK RELATIONSHIPS

In contrast to hierarchically-oriented experts, egalitarian self-developers appreciate help from co-workers. They are natural team players. They grow up learning the importance of cooperative peer relationships, and they recognize that without cooperation, technoservice becomes ineffective.

The research service manager at the Library of Congress says: "I need the cooperation of a lot of people, a lot of inputs on time. You need their help and ideas. I get help from other divisions a lot. When we have interdivisional projects, people really can say no; mostly they cooperate. If they say no, we end up with egg on our face, with a lesser-quality report."

The IRS agent says: "You can't know all the aspects of tax law. If we didn't help each other we wouldn't be able to do it. And it involves interpretation, so we compare notes, how to research something, how to get something out of the computer. There's a lot of gray areas and you need help researching the manual. People have complex problems and you can't get it all in class. I've gotten a lot of help; I wouldn't have gotten as far as I did without people showing me an easier way to do things."

A public health doctor, age forty, says: "I'm very strong on the team concept. I've learned as much about public health from the public health nurse and public health social worker as from any doctor. I really believe in teamwork. And I don't necessarily believe the doctor's always in charge of the team."

But teamwork requires trust based on respect and competence. The government auditor: "What we do is an opinion based on what we dig up. I can bounce things off them if I have respect for the other person. If I don't like you or trust you I can't bounce anything off. It makes all the difference in the world. You need to work with people whom you're comfortable with. And who are comfortable with you. Respect is important. If you can't really like somebody, you *can* respect them and work with them, and you can learn from them."

Self-developers value work relations that facilitate business. They dislike those they consider heavy with emotion or sticky with sentiment. They want relationships to be freer and less attached than those of the familial helpers, more equal and less threatening to self-esteem than those of the hierarchical experts, more independent and less concerned with power than those of the suspicious defenders, and more down-to-earth and matter-of-fact than those of the ideological innovators.

An AT&T systems analyst, age thirty, says: "I think it's unhealthy sometimes to socialize with people you work with. It causes conflicts at work."

An ACTION manager, age thirty-five, says: "I'm a very private person. There's a difference between working with people and really being their friend. When I leave work, I like to get out of work. I try to leave it when I leave the building." She adds, "I think people need to be *friendly*, but you don't have to be friends, close friends, to work together."

SELF-DEVELOPERS AS MANAGERS

Self-developers are natural facilitators. They are egalitarian and interested in other people's views and ideas. As one new-gener-

183

ation manager says: "I think of people working under me as working *with* me. I try to set the example." By avoiding the parental role, they diffuse transferential emotions, but they frustrate the experts and helpers who want a caring leader.

Self-developers often mention fun as a valued ingredient of work. Like the gamesmen, they use humor as a managerial tool when they feel it necessary to lighten up the atmosphere. The twenty-eight-year-old AT&T manager says: "I'm people-oriented. I like to joke around a lot. I approach things seriously, work hard, but also have the sense when things get tight, let's joke around." Self-developers not only want to relieve tension, but also create a playful spirit that supports intense competitive work.

Self-developer-managers provide opportunities for subordinates by involving them in organizational goals and letting them develop their own roles. Since their need for information is so great, they are sensitive to the need in others. All this is not necessarily altruistic. Self-developers believe they create organizational power by providing opportunity, using more human potential.

A TV executive, age thirty, a former high-school teacher, describes how she manages: "I like to give people responsibility. From teaching I've learned you have to structure for success, give steps for results. Then you must follow up. I'm motivated internally. I won't say I can do something unless I can do it perfectly. Most people say yes, even when they don't know how. There is a need to evaluate ongoing activity, to give feedback. People must feel they are important. But I like people who like to work and take pride in their work. Who don't need to be told fifteen times a month they are terrific. You can't go overboard so they think they're wonderful and don't need to grow."

What all self-developer-managers do believe is that to succeed, they must create a motivated team. For them, being a team player does not mean group thinking. It means playing a special role on a team where each player has a say in how to implement strategy.

The service manager for a computer company says: "I'm moving from a management to a leadership role. Leadership requires greater delegation and accountability to others—being willing to compromise, greater sensitivity to support staff; but the best way to get the staff to do the policy is to get their participation. The best productivity comes if we have initial agreement on the way to do business. The challenge is to get the staff to buy into a policy, or figuring out how to improve the quality of life of the people in the office as well as improving the effectiveness of the work we do.

"I had been questioning the management of power, but in fact, the more you share, the more you gain. Some people really operate by selling and trading information only for personal gain, giving out information only when you get something in return, really selling it. I didn't like that 'power-coercive' style, but in many ways it seemed to be the way to do business. But it's only through the sharing of power, the group participation, that you can really go farther; the old style will get you only so far. Participation is required if you are going to take another step."

Self-developers naturally move toward the technoservice mode of production. The research manager at the Library of Congress says: "I'd like to do away with all secretaries. During one of the spells when we didn't have a typist, I started doing my own stuff on a word processor. It eliminates a lot of paper drafts and I could see my ideas taking shape on the screen and in my head at the same time. If you put control of correspondence in the hands of policy-makers, you have a different organizational structure. Then do you just drop out the lower half of the organization? In 1980, we introduced word processors and reduced staff through attrition. We used to have 600 people, now we have 200."

A self-developer can even run a government agency in the technoservice mode. Here is a thirty-two-year-old manager of volunteer programs for ACTION. He is exceptional in that he combines the self-developer's objectivity, respect, and playfulness with the helper's caring and idealism.

He says: "I have a really great staff. They need little supervision. What I like most is getting people to work together to get the task done, to set priorities and procedures. I like being a manager. My philosophy is getting people to work together as a team, to get them participating, and letting them do it, rather than dictating it. When there is a problem or a task I present it to them, and let them figure out how to do it. We usually do this as a group, and I try to include the clerks.

"Openness and honesty in the office is very important. It inspires them to do their job. A manager must trust employees to get the job done. Otherwise he tries to do it himself, and therefore he's not managing, or he's a dictator.

"I share just about everything with my staff. First, I have a weekly circulating file where I circulate almost everything that comes in, but not everything, because I throw some stuff out. Second, we have a meeting about once a week. They know also that they can ask to have a meeting if they want. Then, and this is one of the advantages of being in a big, open room, I can make announcements immediately. If I have just talked to someone on the phone and heard some news, I just immediately tell them. I prefer to tell them before they hear something by rumor. But I don't tell them about personal individual cases. They try to get me to, but I don't.

"The main quality I look for in an employee is a person who will fit into our office. This means someone who is loose and relaxed, a person who is willing to do all the functions, including answering the phones. Someone who is not hung up on 'That's not my job.' Someone who is not hierarchical or status-oriented. I look for idealism, the desire to be of service.... I'm going to continue hiring the kinds of people who have a background in volunteerism, but not those who are just here for a job. I want people with a basic liking and trust of people, an ability to create that atmosphere of trust and respect in the way they do business or in their lifestyle, and the ability to get people to work together.

"Evaluations I handle by having a one-to-one discussion with them about any problems they may have, and I try to do that at least once every six months. But if something is changing either from outside or in the internal process, I might have sessions with them more often. And they can also talk to me at any time, and sometimes do. I usually have one of these one-to-one sessions in a private office, or we go for a cup of coffee, and it can last from five minutes to one or two hours, depending on the individual. I try to develop a mutual exchange of feedback, how they're doing and how I'm doing. Are there any personal problems? It's pretty open.

"In the past, when I have had individual sessions with employees, I asked them, 'What do you want beyond your job?' And if they said they wanted to become a manager, and some of them do, I've made sure to appoint them acting manager when I wasn't here, so they could get experience. I've tried to get them some visibility with others and to discuss their interests in the informal network. I've also tried to get them to take some courses when there was money. Actually, two people from this office have become placement managers and two have become area managers."

He learned management not from books and courses but from experience. "I learned to be a manager from my other jobs. My first job as supervisor was awkward because I was managing friends and peers. Then when they left and we got new people, I managed mainly as technician, saying, 'I have done this work before and so I know it and I can help you learn it.'"

"I try to give public credit for work. If someone has come up with an idea and I write it up, I say, 'Harriet had this idea.'"

While many self-developers believe in providing an open team atmosphere and opportunity, they are less likely than this manager to take a paternal-like coaching role. They are not comfortable with getting too personal. They don't have the expert's transferential need for father-son/daughter monitoring. On the other hand, they lack the expert's need to know more than subordinates. They expect and want to learn from subordinates, clients, and customers. They succeed best when, like this manager, they institute good practice: frequent evaluations, team meetings, and training in group process and problem-solving.

In *The Leader*, I described the ideal leader for the new generation as a developer of organizations, products and services, and people. Since 1981, when that book was written, I have found no reason to discard that ideal. I have seen, however, that managers approach it differently, according to their dominant character style. Those most likely to reach the ideal combine values of innovator, expert, helper, defender, and self-developer. Those least likely are the ones dominated by a single orientation.

WEAKNESSES OF SELF-DEVELOPERS

The weaknesses of self-developers, like their strengths, are rooted in their childhood adaptation to insecurity and continual change. More than any other type, they describe their strengths as intellectual, rather than moral or emotional. They sometimes rely on intellectual flexibility too much.

Typically, they describe themselves in terms like these: "I am considered intelligent." "I am open and eager to learn." They have learned to be quick studies, fast learners, flexible team players. But compared to traditional types, this can make them superficial and shallow. They tend to overestimate their strengths and underestimate the importance of judgment, experience, caring, extensive and in-depth knowledge, commitment to and defense of values.

Some feel they have unlimited possibilities and are consequently unrealistic about what they can achieve and how much work achievement demands. Critics of the new generation focus on their pathology: narcissism, lack of loyalty and commitment.*

---

*The most dramatic is Christopher Lasch, who, in *The Culture of Narcissism*

The critics have a point. Without a purpose beyond the self, without a larger meaning, self-development becomes an unfocused search for self-realization. For some, compulsive self-development seems an anxious drive for elusive self-esteem.

A thirty-five-year-old IRS agent expresses the compulsive quality of self-development: "Self-development is very important to me. It means reaching a point in your life where your self-esteem is at a level that's admirable. That you feel good about yourself. That you owe it to yourself to go on and make progress. If you stopped self-development, you'd be vegetating, you wouldn't be living. You owe it to yourself."

A lawyer, age thirty-five, describes the underlying anxiety: "My only goal is that I become everything I have the potential to become. My big anxiety is that I could be missing out in developing a potential in me." This man's father died when he was six. He had to act a mature role in the family before he was ready and without a paternal model. He became extremely self-critical and self-demanding. "As a lawyer, a logician, I'm brilliant. I'm very critical of myself first, then others. Mine is a critical approach rather than accepting. I always think, here's what's wrong rather than what's right." He seeks self-acceptance through psychotherapy and feels he has begun to understand himself better. "My character is unfolding. The more secure I get, the more solid I become, the less criticial."

Some self-developers seek meaning in compulsive unfocused activities, "forcing myself not to stand still," be dependent or "stagnate."

A financial consultant, age thirty-six, divorced, with an MBA, is running away from boredom and meaninglessness into a frenetic life of achievement and uncoordinated "learning experiences." She describes the self-developer's inability to commit herself to projects. She says, "I'm what you call achievement-oriented. It drives me crazy not to get things done. An industrial

(New York: W. W. Norton, 1979), excoriates the new social character from the point of view of the moralistic expert.

psychologist told me I'd be happier if I just failed at something. I guess I'm afraid of failure. . . . I guess I'm too other-directed. I should have a life plan. I never figured out where I want to be. . . . You can't plan in a vacuum. I'm just a normal healthy girl. I'm fairly intelligent. Have an active mind. I'm continually frustrated because I don't have enough time to do what I want to do. I try to balance things, you have to in this business; if you don't, it becomes dull."

What is self-development to her? "Forcing yourself not to stay still. To learn and do new things. Anything, I guess. Like if I go through with my resolution of today, it would be to get a copy of the *Iliad* and read it, or my resolution in Hawaii was to learn wind-surfing.

"I assume I'm more interested in self-development than the average person. I watch maybe two hours of TV a week. You have to not allow yourself to vegetate. Particularly if you have a challenging job. Life is too short. I love to cook gourmet meals. It depends on how you define self-development. It's more important to keep moving and growing, learning more. It makes you more interesting and your life is more interesting.

"I don't have a great plan. This year I've been reading a lot of technical computer journals. I started taking aerobic dancing. I should stop smoking. What does my poor body think, when I go from aerobic dancing to smoking? Going to Hawaii was self-development. Going to a new place and exploring.

"I still don't know what I want to do when I grow up. Part of me would like to have my own business, but I don't know what that business would be. I'd like to learn more about data processing. It never hurts to develop expertise at anything. And it's our most salable product and it enhances my career path, if you want to call it that—if there is a career path.

"I regret not reading more than I do. At the end of my day, I'm too mentally tired. I do well analytically and it's intellectual, but I'm not so good at creating something. It's the difference between playing scales and writing a symphony like Beethoven. I've always shied away from abstract thought. Work does get you to think about things like 'Why is this important?' I'm afraid of getting mentally lazy."

I believe she is afraid to face her sense of meaninglessness. As a compulsive performer and experience-seeker, she avoids listening to herself, to her deeper needs for intimacy and commitment. Her response to people is shallow. Her interests are diffuse and confused. Without commitment to meaningful projects, her energies are wasted in a search for information and experiences that seems more self-indulgent than developmental.

Some of these compulsive self-developers seem like neglected, hyperactive children. An accountant at a big-eight firm, age twenty-eight, says: "I can't stand to wait, to hold on a phone, wait in a line or for a check in a restaurant. I'm just hyper. I always like to be doing something. In the first grade, the teacher wanted to put glue on my seat. There's been no change."

A twenty-four-year-old account executive appreciates her husband because he helps her to be "more accepting, easygoing, patient, and to just enjoy life." Otherwise, she can't stay still. She enjoyed painting, but gave it up because "it keeps you by yourself in a room," not out making contacts.

Even though some of the most successful self-developers have disciplined their drive and gained a sense of independence, they still remain detached and lonely.

This is the story of a highly successful woman, a self-developer, age thirty-eight, the vice-president of a data services company in Chicago. Her parents were both businesspeople in a small city; both believed in education. In college in 1968, she became involved in the antiwar movement and joined protests. As the New Left sputtered to a halt, she and her husband began a series of successful businesses, starting with restoring inner city houses and reselling them for big profits. She remained liberal in terms of foreign policy and antinuclear politics, but economically she moved toward the neoliberal view that government must be concerned with creating wealth, not just distributing it. She points out that many of her friends became extreme Republican libertarians. All of them shared a critique of bureaucracy and big government.

As their business grew, her husband wanted her to stay at home and raise their child. She felt he neither understood nor appreciated her, so she took their daughter and left him, went back to school, got an MBA, then joined a large company for the experience. Today, her second husband runs their five jointly-owned businesses, including a trailer park, a car wash, and a beauty salon, while she operates at the top of a major corporation.

I watched her in action for three days. She gets to the point, demands concrete examples, is flexible and open. But she seems all intellect. There is little human resonance. She does not get emotionally involved with people at work.

I asked her what self-development meant to her. "I call it 'working on myself.' It includes education. I'm taking philosophy courses. It includes health, running. It includes team experiences, like Outward Bound, where you get feedback on your interaction with people."

Don't subordinates find her tough? "Yes, they say they are sometimes frightened of me. They don't know where I am coming from." Her boss, a sixty-four-year-old paternal expert, feels she is too driven. Is there any meaning for her beyond constant self-development? She values the creation of wealth. She enjoys the excitement of the game, and the support of the team. She has money enough so that she feels she can turn down a job without fear. Beyond self, she supports a vital society, improved education and health care. But something is missing, a sense of caring. One feels she could leave everything, her husband as well as her job, and start a new adventure without missing a beat. She does not seem happy. Is there a happy person who does not care about people? I have not met one.

Some self-developers seem to be struggling for deeper spiritual meaning, to transcend the self, to reach the state of mystical, pure being.

The member of the White House staff who comes from a broken home says: "Some of the more difficult parts of myself are that I'm a person who has a tendency to be self-centered and who probably has a fragile sense of self-esteem. I can be compulsive and a perfectionist.

"St. Francis is a model for me. He talks about 'self-dying'; it's the burden, it's the dealing with the 'me,' this thing which I carry around—this 'self' and 'I.' I seek this because my happiest moments are when I have forgotten myself. His prayer is very beautiful, he asks the power to understand, rather than being understood, 'for it is in self-forgetting that we become true persons ... and become alive in dying of self.' "

The air traffic controller also compares his quests for spiritual, physical, and mental development with St. Francis, whom he admires "because he had a controlled mind and purifying thought."

But neither of these self-developers practices St. Francis's style of life or discipline of the heart. They leave out love, serving God by giving even when it is not a good deal. They are too isolated in their own struggle for self-esteem to respond deeply to others.

Commitment and intimacy are problems for self-developers. Of the people we interviewed who see themselves as self-developers, a high percentage (25 percent) have been divorced and fewer than half are in their first marriage (48 percent); 22 percent are single; 2 percent are widowed. This compares to only 6 percent ever divorced in the *Gamesman* sample of high-tech managers in elite companies, 16 percent divorced for experts, and 9 percent for helpers. Given that self-developers are on the average younger than the other types, the differences may become even greater in the future, as more self-developer marriages break up.

Self-developers' describe their marriage in terms of doing things together, traveling, sailing, going out to dinner, taking courses. Few speak of trust, caring, or deepening knowledge of each other. Some, as we have mentioned, do look for a parental kind of support in spouses. This is the kind of unconditional love they yearned for in childhood.

Based on self-developers' backgrounds and my clinical experience with the new generation, I can speculate about the cause of this problem. Some self-developers as children lacked consistent, caring parental experiences. Insecure about their own worth, they doubt others can really care for them. Needs for love and acceptance are suppressed, hidden by the compulsive quest to prove their worth. Intimacy is threatening, not only because one may be rejected, but also because one may be too needy, dependent, and trapped. One rejects and represses needs that make one feel vulnerable and weak.

Describing the breakup of his first marriage, a forty-year-old manager says: "I could not say no to anything. That sort of thing destroyed my first marriage. When you can demonstrate real feeling and not worry about the other person skipping out on you, the relationship grows."

The lawyer describes his anxiety-reducing mechanisms for avoiding intimacy: "I withdraw. I get into a neutral experience —movies, hanging around with safe people, drinking too much."

Much attention is focused on the weakness of the new generation by disapproving traditional types. Self-developers are caricatured as Yuppies and "gold-collar workers," materialistic, demanding, unconcerned about society's losers, contemptuous of people who are poor, undeveloped, or flabby. They are lectured to be more committed, caring, and altruistic.

Self-developers are not insensitive to social problems but they are suspicious of solutions that increase bureaucracy and helping that keeps people dependent. Many are idealistic and struggle with materialism. They want their work to help make the world a better place. But rejecting traditional paternal and maternal roles, faced with the freedom to choose, they have not found a model of maturity.

A self-developer manager in his mid-thirties says: "The main thing wrong with our society is that the nuclear family and extended family have disappeared and we haven't developed a new contract or learned how to behave. Our values were a by-product of the extended family. We have to learn to help other people and to get help from other people in new ways."

Commitment for the self-developer, whether at work or in relationships, will come not from moralistic pressure, a sense of loyalty, or a desire to please the boss, but by free choice based on reciprocal self-interest. Self-developers will commit themselves to meaningful projects rather than to institutions, which they distrust. Their commitment is not just to material goals, but to emotional and intellectual development as well. They must have unambiguous contracts at work which describe mutual expectations in terms of both rights and responsibilities. The rules of the game must be made clear. Leaders like Lemasters, Carlzon, and Nagel, who expound freedom and provide opportunities for learning at work, create highly motivated followers among self-developers. Beyond this, self-developers need knowledge of what is required to gain their goal of wholeness and happiness. They must be willing to invest in emotional as well as intellectual development.

If they are to become leaders, they must also understand the needs of traditional types. They must learn to find meaning in taking responsibility for larger enterprises. The next chapter addresses the question of how self-developers can work at this.

CHAPTER 7

STRATEGIC INDIVIDUAL DEVELOPMENT

This chapter is addressed to all those who recognize they must develop themselves to adapt to a changing economy, and especially to the new generation: the self-developers, a generation defined by values, not age. Their influence is greater than their numbers. According to our survey, for 30 percent of employees under the age of thirty the most important meaning of work is self-development, and this percentage rises for college students. Over 50 percent of all age groups identify strongly with this value of self-development. Among young leaders, 90 percent describe themselves as self-developers.

The influence of self-developers is even stronger because the world of work is moving in their direction. The loyal traditional types can no longer trust organizations to take care of them. Given global competition and changing technology, neither companies nor people can predict the future or guarantee employment. Technoservice demands different attitudes and competencies from those that fit the industrial bureaucracies. To maintain employment security, experts and helpers as well as self-developers must sharpen their skills and prepare themselves for continual change.

Few companies or government agencies are dedicated to developing people at work. Few managers are innovators or coaches. A recently promoted clerk, age twenty-eight, defines self-development as "taking responsibility to train yourself." He said: "For six months I was getting frustrated. These guys aren't developing me like they told me they would. Then I thought, 'Hey, I've got to do it myself,' so I went to my supervisor and asked, 'What courses should I take? How should I change?' It's up to you to do it." But taking courses is not enough, and managers may not know how to advise an ambitious self-developer.

Self-developers will not move ahead by modeling themselves on experts who made it in the past, who were taught to define development in terms of success in passing exams, being promoted, achieving status. Such a narrow model is neither appealing nor effective for technoservice. Effectiveness requires knowledge and inner authority not measured by traditional tests.

Self-developers aspire to more than economic success. Broad knowledge of history, literature, the arts and sciences, increases their sense of authority. The dual-career family increases their sense of freedom. Dual-career partners resist sacrificing the other's career for their own promotion, believing that each has equally legitimate demands. A double income allows you to take more risks at work.

Members of the new generation know more clearly what they do not want at work than what they do want. They dislike having power over people, but rightly fear powerlessness and stagnation. They believe that power corrupts, but are also learning that powerlessness perverts. It causes anger, regressive narcissistic self-protectiveness, and inflexibility. This is more obvious in the violence of Palestinian terrorists or unemployed black teenagers from city ghettos, less obvious in the passivity and helplessness of the middle class, made powerless by their own inability to take advantage of their affluence.

How should the new generation envision self-development? When I raise this question, I am aware that some young people despair of envisioning a future in the thermonuclear age. But such hopelessness paralyzes. To live productively, we must make the leap of faith that there will be a future. It is a rational gamble. One loses nothing by planning a productive life, and risks a sense of powerlessness by not doing so.

WHOLENESS AND POWER

Just as the innovator creates strategies for organizational development, so can a person create strategies for his or her own self-development. Each individual must begin by asking, "What are my goals?" Not just in terms of traditional external goals of success, but also the internal goals of successful development of one's value drives in a creative and meaningful way. Many young people tend to view their lives in terms of vague and sketchy plans, not serious strategies. Strategy requires understanding one's values and goals. "What is my vision of self-development? And what precisely must I do to achieve it?"

The new generation speaks of a new aesthetic, moral, and religious ideal: wholeness. Each person frames this ideal differently, according to individual talent, temperament, and beliefs. For most people, it is easier to define the feeling of the absence of wholeness in their inner lives, rather than its positive development. Wholeness, which comes from the old English *hal* (as in *hale*), is the root of health. It is the opposite of feeling like a partial person in a narrow work role. It includes integrity, which has to do with being faithful to one's commitments. But it is more than this. It is the expression of creative potential at work. It is the goal of employees who feel they are stagnating, not developing. Furthermore, people do not feel whole who let their bodies disintegrate due to poor diet and lack of exercise. People do not feel whole if they passively accept the disintegration of mind and body, if they give in and do not fight for themselves. Nor do people feel whole if they are lonely, afraid of intimacy, unwilling to reach out to others. The state of wholeness is a changing one, requiring continual development.

I believe the new generation's aspirations can be summarized as a striving for power to master self, understand, create, love, enjoy; power to gain respect from others, to maintain meaningful relationships and a sense of dignity and integrity. This kind of power is not the same as power over people. Where the new generation seems to me most confused is in understanding how to gain the kind of power it needs at work and in intimate relationships.

POWER VERSUS PERVERSION

What is known about the conditions necessary for development as whole persons? Values expressed at work are formed in the family and in school. As I said in Chapter 1, I've come to believe that we can view human development in terms of the eight value drives that all human beings share across culture and time. From Stone Age tribes to twentieth-century civilizations, these drives—survival, relatedness, pleasure, information, mastery, play, dignity, and meaning—have directed human development. What are the conditions that lead people to channel these drives for their personal development and not their destruction, to realize their brightest potential, to achieve a sense of wholeness and potency instead of internal conflict, stagnation, perversion, and addiction? In behavioral terms, what are the conditions that transform drives into developmental instead of addictive needs?

In every society, five conditions must be met for human development. Each condition implies both good human relationships and conscious individual decision-making. Family, school, and work organizations either succeed or fail in satisfying each of these conditions. Remember, the opposite of each condition causes perversion, which is defined as channeling the drives into addictive needs rather than the developmental needs that strengthen us. The conditions are:

> care vs. neglect
> freedom vs. oppression
> discipline vs. indulgence
> balance vs. excessiveness
> commitment vs. diffusion

The first two conditions, care and freedom, are created in a positive family environment, and recreated in good schools and places of work. The third condition, discipline, is strongly influenced by family, school, and workplace, but also by individual understanding and choice. The final two conditions, balance and commitment, are largely determined by informed free choice, especially in a society like ours.

CARE

The first condition for development as a whole person is care. Childhood builds the foundation of care. To gain a sense of trust, infants must have a secure, nurturing adult who helps them express drives with satisfying results.* Infants cannot survive, gain pleasure, affection, and a sense of security all by themselves. The caring parent helps them master their bodies, contain strong feelings. Satisfying this first condition is one requirement for positive expression of drives. Without this experience of being able to count on help, a child is damaged in the ability to trust and create relationships essential for develop-

---

*Erik H. Erikson, in *Childhood and Society* (New York: W. W. Norton, 1963), has described the stages of development from a psychoanalytic standpoint. The above explanation builds on his work, that of Anna Freud in *Normality and Pathology in Childhood: Assessment of Development* (New York: International Universities Press, 1965), and that of Jean Piaget (see Chapter 2).

ment. For adults who have lacked this experience, psychotherapists try to provide in a healing encounter a basis for building caring, trusting relationships.

Neglect, especially in the first year of life, causes drives to turn back on the self. Frustration when no one responds creates rage, and social drives are perverted into narcissism, which is an addictive need for self-care. Narcissists are typically hypochondriacs whose attention focuses on their bodies rather than on the world of other people. When I use the term neglect, I do not mean just giving infants too little food, shelter, and playthings. Neglect is much more a psychological problem of absent child care. Rene A. Spitz, a psychiatrist, studied abandoned children and found that even when well fed, institutionalized infants who were not hugged and talked to became autistic and uninterested in the world, aimlessly playing with their own feces. Preoccupied with their own bodies, their drives become increasingly directed toward themselves, not the world. In contrast, babies in a nearby hospital with less food but more cuddling were healthier, physically and emotionally.[1]

Less severe emotional neglect of children by inadequate, infantile parents or uncaring guardians can produce a semi-schizoid character, seemingly devoid of feeling, because the drive for relatedness is repressed. That is why some seemingly cool and detached new-generation people are shocked by the intensity of their needs and dependency once they move close to another person. For such people, intimacy is understandably frightening, and they feel safer maintaining minimal contact.

The importance of care in childhood makes it imperative to provide good day care for the young children of parents who work. People who have received good care as children respond positively to caring teachers, managers, co-workers. There is a feeling of reciprocity, of wanting to respond to care with care.

Neglect in the workplace, an uncaring management, provokes egotistical strategies of self-interest. Employees feel unprotected ("If they don't care, why should I?"), like the director of nursing who described the lack of caring about nurses on the part of doctors and administrators: "People do not feel good about each other.... There is a feeling of stagnation.... The nurses have not kept up with advances and changes in the way nursing is delivered. Some of these areas are technical, some are management.... There is a feeling of worthlessness, individually and collectively. Powerlessness."

FREEDOM

The second condition for development of wholeness is freedom. At about the age of two in our culture, the issue of freedom arises in a child's struggles with parents. The child must master bowels and limbs to avoid shame, gain social approval, and maintain a sense of dignity. Notice how two-year-olds express dignity and a growing wish for independence through negativism. They demand to choose the clothes they wear, the stories they hear. They enjoy saying no, to the despair of uncomprehending parents. By five or six, if not before, the child must learn to leave home for the day, act with initiative toward strangers, and master the symbols necessary for knowledge— reading, writing, and arithmetic. The parents or teacher helps motivate a child toward mastery by setting goals that are challenging but attainable. Goals that are too low bore children; goals that are too high discourage them.

To gain a sense of initiative and develop a need for achievement, the child must be free of overcontrol and have time to experiment through play. The children who become most cooperative are those who feel secure enough to criticize authority, but also protected enough to leave an oppressive peer group. Adult approaches to work reveal the importance of these early experiences and resulting attitudes. The future expert is too impressed by adult authority, while the future helper withdraws from the contest into protective relationships.

Neglect and oppression can deform and distort character and self-perception. British psychoanalysts W. R. D. Fairburn and Harry Guntrip describe cases of parents whose oppressive behavior causes a splitting of the child's self.[2] What results in the child is an inauthentic conforming self that hides feelings of humiliation and anger. My clinical experience supports these observations. Rather than blame parents, patients who have been neglected and oppressed will blame their condition on their own "bad" drives, accepting the parents' view that they had impossible, selfish demands. Otherwise, the rage they feel against their oppressors threatens to break the fragile ties that bind them to their parents.

Oppression takes forms of domination, control, and seduction. Historically, whole groups or classes have been oppressed as slaves or exploited workers, children of bondage brought up to submit, to repress their drive for dignity. Submission is not the perversion; submission may be necessary for survival. The perversion of dignity is servility and sadomasochism. Fromm's analysis of sadomasochism describes this perversion in the authoritarian character who compensates for submission and humiliation by identifying with a powerful and punishing organization or leader in order to maintain a sense of dignity.[3] The masochistic child may later gain mastery, a sense of relatedness, and pseudo-dignity through sadism, expressing power over those who are weaker.

The destructive effects of oppressive control extend to the workplace. For example, oppression in the workplace can cause angry sabotage by those unable to quit their jobs. It can also bring out the sadomasochistic tendencies in bureaucrats. Studies of government workers show that some sadomasochists rise in the civil service because they flatter insecure, inexperienced political appointees and promise to get results by "kicking ass."[4] What they get is either servility or sullen compliance.

Members of the new generation want independence and opportunity at work. To maintain independence in the unstable organizations of today, they must maintain marketable skills, but also the willingness to quit their jobs if these jobs become oppressive. The dual-career family helps to fan the spirit of independence. So does money in the bank, or secondary entrepreneurial ventures.

DISCIPLINE

The third condition for development of wholeness is discipline. To develop a sense of power as potency, children must learn to manage themselves and master various disciplines. In common language, we use the term *discipline* in two ways. One meaning refers to punishment. Either an oppressive authority demands unquestioning obedience, or a benevolent authority sets limits, thus expressing indignation toward bad behavior that transgresses the rights of others. Parents who understand the feelings of children, and especially their need for dignity, find that the child responds more positively to reasonable discipline, and learns early to understand the difference between just and unjust punishment. The second meaning of *discipline* refers to the training or development of individual skills. The disciplines required for our open, high-tech society with its limitless opportunities and distractions include more than those that are intellectual, physical, or even artistic. The term *discipline* also includes the trained power to resist the seductiveness of a consumer society, to concentrate despite distractions, to listen carefully, and to discriminate among claims, propaganda, and sales pitches. Discipline for freedom requires critical thinking, and discipline for success requires self-restraint and good habits that keep the mind sharp and the body in shape for long hours and frequent travel.

The opposite of discipline, indulgence, can cause perversion. This I have observed most dramatically in patients who were brought up in very rich families without sufficient discipline. Easy satisfaction by servants feeds limitless, addictive needs; mastery becomes too easy. Without discipline, they fear tests of competence and avoid them, thus causing a vicious circle of avoidance and failure to develop competence. The drive for effortless pleasure comes to dominate their existence, weakening their will and causing self-contempt.

Indulgence is not limited to the very rich, and of course, some rich people (like John D. Rockefeller and Joseph Kennedy) create a disciplined family culture with strong values of public service. There are different causes of indulgence. Neglectful parents may indulge children to compensate for their own sense of a deprived childhood, mistakenly believing this will make the child happy. Liberal parents may indulge because of a vague Rousseauean belief that the "natural needs" of the child should be met. Busy parents may indulge to salve their consciences for not giving more real attention.

Parents may also indulge children to try and keep them dependent and close, a form of oppression and seduction. Parents can pervert the child's drive for mastery by manipulating with extravagant praise and attention, inflating self-esteem, and making greater demands for performance that tighten the bonds of dependency. Positive reinforcement has its value, but it may feed an addictive need. To get a quick fix of adulation, children are driven to achieve not for themselves, but for the parent. The child has been robbed of an authentic sense of dignity, which has been replaced by a grandiose self-image.

BALANCE

The fourth condition for wholeness is balance between work and love, mastery and play, mind and body, head and heart. The popular phrase of the young in the eighties, being "in touch with myself," expresses their deeper goal to realize and develop all of their value drives and become a "whole person." When a single value directs the personality, one drive then dominates at the expense of the whole person, and the individual loses the capacity for growth. Other drives do not disappear, but are repressed or undeveloped. Experts intent on mastery lose the ability to play, innovate, and create. Gamesmen obsessed with winning lose the capacity for human understanding, caring, and loyalty. They may be daring but lack courage: the knowledge of the heart, the quality essential to a sense of integrity.

We shall see in the next chapter that balance of values is also a key to successful entrepreneurial leadership.

COMMITMENT

The fifth condition is commitment. The new generation struggles against the limits that commitment implies. Both the search for and the escape from commitment dominate discussions of work, family, and relationships. "How much of myself am I willing to commit?" is a popular phrase for a new generation. Our potentialities are greater than we can realize in a lifetime. We must focus our energies, commit ourselves to projects and people. When these commitments integrate value drives, they allow for satisfying self-expression and development, rather than a sense of diffusion, superficiality, and meaninglessness.

Of course, self-developers fear commitments that are entrapping, freezing development in oppressive relationships or rigid ideologies. They guard their flexibility at the cost of superficiality and diffusion of energy.

They struggle against self-indulgence through exercise and diet. They seek balance in mind and body, work and family. They are used to negotiations and trade-offs and, when necessary, cutting their losses. They are less clear about the discipline of the heart, the courage to fully experience oneself and others, and to act on the basis of felt conviction. They lack the sense of hope generated by commitment to projects that improve life, that develop not only the self, but also the larger world.

TOWARD BALANCE AND COMMITMENT

The new generation is sensitive to conditions at work that further development. While skittish about intimacy, they want people in the workplace to treat each other with respect. They resent overcontrol and refuse to submit; rather, they fake compliance, do the minimum, and start looking for better opportunities. Where they seem most in need of guidance is in understanding the developmental issues of discipline, balance, and commitment.

Poor adult choices cannot all be blamed on childhood. Self-development is less a matter of satisfying needs than forming good ones. Young people with many opportunities make bad choices. They avoid the hard work and self-restraint necessary for mastery and achievement. They pursue pleasure at the expense of mastery and dignity. Alternately, they become addicted to one-dimensional mastery at the expense of relationships. They marshal all their energies toward success at any cost.

Self-development today calls for an inner dialogue based on strategic questions about one's life: "How can I balance my drive for self-expression with a commitment to meaningful projects and satisfying human relationships? How can I gain a sense of security and at the same time experience a sense of creativity at work?" To answer questions such as these, it is necessary to become aware of one's value drives and understand the conditions—care, freedom, discipline, balance, and commitment—that support the ideals of wholeness and effective power.

1. Caring relationships establish a sense of emotional security. They are most successful when based on mutual understanding of each person's values. Relationships which include shared meanings and concern for dignity are the basis of the trust which is essential to building good developmental friendship. In such relationships, caring and empathy are balanced by support for each other's positive values and developmental needs, and intolerance of each other's addictive needs. One's closest relationships should be evaluated in these terms.

2. To maintain a sense of freedom, people must develop their marketable skills, learn how to run their own businesses. In avoiding addictive dependency, they must guard against the illusion that they can do it all by themselves. A certain amount of dependency can be developmental if one is helped by trustworthy people who share ethical values and common goals. However, only with a sense of independence can one challenge the corporate experts. Each person can test the workplace, and in the process, join with others in transforming it.

3. Self-discipline is never-ending. Self-control requires self-understanding. To frustrate addictive needs, one must recognize them and admit they rob one of potency. To reinforce developmental needs, one must commit oneself to challenging goals and push oneself to practice good habits. Without intellectual and artistic discipline, self-expression remains primitive and unsatisfying. Few of us are blessed with great talent, but we can all practice disciplines that enhance self-expression throughout life. Once a technique has been mastered, we can express ourselves spontaneously. Mastering academic technique in their youth, painters like Turner and Monet, composers like Scarlatti and Verdi, expressed themselves in old age with an exciting sense of freedom. Those of us who are less gifted can still gain satisfaction in disciplining intellectual, musical, and artistic talents, writing, learning to speak in front of others, even cooking and gardening.

4. We can all reflect on the balance in our lives by charting our values. Which of our "needs" and values are developmental and which addictive? To become whole, hale, healthy, potent, and powerful, in the sense of capacity and energy, we must frustrate the addictive needs, reach for higher values.

Do not forget fun. If there is none in work and love, a person is in the wrong place, with the wrong people. But fun itself, linked with playful experiment and dialogue, is developmental.

Those who want to become enterpreneurs might benefit from comparing themselves with the leadership styles described in Chapter 8. "Am I an expert, protector, facilitator, or innovator? What are my strengths? How can I build on them? How can I compensate for my weaknesses by working with others who have strengths I lack?"

5. Energy is generated when projects connect with value drives. It is spent and drained when there is conflict, unresponsiveness, deadness at work. Some of the most effective leaders in business and government today are the entrepreneurs who followed their own interests rather than someone else's prescription.

Development requires commitment to meaningful projects that integrate values, develop skills, and make common cause with people who share one's values. It is unwise to invest all one's hope in promotion; no one can predict the future of any company. Rather, one can envision the competencies one wants to acquire and develop them, envision the life one wants to lead and plan to create it. We should all ask ourselves what kind of environment, community, society we want to live in. How will it be created? If we don't participate in building the future for ourselves and our children, who will? Through our work, we are forming ourselves. By our work, we are creating the world.

In a sense, each of our lives is a project. Either it may just happen, and be over before we know it, or we can plan to make it meaningful and adventurous. This requires not only living well and developing skills when one is young, but also continuing mature development by accepting responsibility, authority, power to influence others, even power over others. The new generation rejects the older models of authority but has not yet found one that is meaningful for itself. This it cannot do without willingness to defend the values of freedom and dignity, which are essential to self-development. Nor can it gain authority in the minds of others without commitment to projects and people. To become technoservice leaders, self-developers must also become educators, and developers of others.

TECHNOSERVICE AND SELF-DEVELOPMENT

The technoservice organization needs people who can continually learn and adapt to changing conditions. Managements should welcome those who want to be whole persons, as opposed to narrow experts. Continual development requires a corporate culture balancing care, freedom, discipline, and mutual commitment to meaningful projects. No company or government agency will ever fully succeed in achieving this ideal, but there are some, which come much closer than the average, where the meaning of work includes self-development and creating useful services. The problem for America is that so many workplaces are closer to the opposite—cultures that cause powerlessness rather than creating power.

CHAPTER 8

LEADERSHIP FOR OUR TIME

History and experience teach us that leadership is an essential ingredient for the success of human activity. A group without leadership is a collection of different interests. The function of leadership is to motivate—persuade, force, inspire, manipulate, or bribe—followers to work for common goals. But the kind of leadership needed depends on the challenges of the historical moment and particularly on the values of the led.

We yearn for great leaders and at the same time fear them. A great leader gives us a vision that realizes our shared values and sparks a motivating sense of hope. However, the leader also asks much of us: that we abandon narrow self-interest for the good of the group and to live up to our higher ideals. When George Washington took command of the Continental Army in 1775, he noted that: "Such a dearth of public spirit and want of virtue, such...fertility in all the low arts to obtain advantage...such a dirty mercenary spirit pervades the whole." He saw his task as inspiring and persuading unruly, self-seeking individualists that the freedom they so highly prized required discipline and risk of life and fortune. We rightly fear the brilliant, charismatic leader who may seduce us into self-destructiveness, as Adolf Hitler did the German people. It is not surprising that we Americans have both revered great leaders like Washington and watched them with fierce suspicion when they held power. We are a nation that prizes liberty second only to life. And while we recognize that we need leadership to preserve liberty and to create wealth, we guard against the misuse of power by leaders.

In recent years, there has been a new emphasis on the importance of leadership within government and business. In government, we are coming to recognize that we must elect a president on the basis not only of the policies he proposes, but also of his managerial competence, which is as much a matter of personal values and style as it is skill. Richard M. Nixon, a brilliant political strategist, strengthened enemies and undermined support by a conspiratorial style of leadership. Even those who supported Jimmy Carter's policies and admired his idealism despaired of his nit-picking, overcontrolling approach to management. In retrospect, historians admire Dwight D. Eisenhower's bureaucratic skills in resolving conflicts; however, at the time, many Americans criticized what they considered his inactivity, and his successor, John F. Kennedy, was elected on a slogan of getting America moving again.

Today, there is great concern about getting America competitive again, but this will not be achieved by massive government spending as in the missile and space programs of the 1960s. Indeed, the Japanese and Germans have succeeded with relatively little of such spending by directing research and development directly to commercial products that compete in the international marketplace.

We are learning that national strength depends not only on military preparedness, but also on the global competitiveness of our industries. Much of American industry is not competitive in global markets. We are mired in wasteful inefficiencies that result from lack of competition in the period after the Second World War, when the United States was unchallenged in world

214

markets. Then the strategic goal was output: mass production that would cut cost and increase demand for standard products. Today the winners produce high quality at relatively low cost through automation and organization, and gain new markets by customizing products and services. Global competition requires continual innovation and tough decisions about investment. The old-style planning by extrapolation, what GM calls "rear-mirror planning," is over. What happened last year does not predict what next year's market and competition will do. Success requires new competencies from leaders who can make companies competitive.

ADMINISTRATORS VERSUS ENTREPRENEURS

Before the breakup of the Bell System, a group of AT&T executives invited me to help them change their management style. Eighty percent agreed that the style that had propelled them to the top when AT&T was a regulated monopoly would not succeed in the new competitive telecommunications market. Like most managers during the period when American industry dominated world markets, these executives had learned to be administrators of industrial bureaucracies. They had reached the top because their superiors had felt comfortable with them and had trusted their judgment. They had maintained a good track record and they knew how to play the role of leader. They represented the company and not just their own interests, and they spoke in terms of "we" rather than "I." They exuded an aura of optimism, confidence, and toughness. At best, they were coordinators of experts, fair scorers, responsible gatekeepers, judicious arbitrators, intrepid fire-fighters, and conservative policy-makers, advocates of high standards of conduct, and protectors of the public interest. At worst, they were monitors and martinets, jungle fighters who jealously guarded their turf; or alternatively, loose, laissez-faire figureheads, pleasing their bosses and showing up to represent the company in community affairs. They all saw that the future would require from them a new approach to management, new attitudes and skills. In the competitive world, they believed they would have to be entrepreneurs and leaders.

I have listened to the same conversation in other large American companies, forced to change because of global competition and deregulation. Executives are rethinking management style. Administrators believe they should become entrepreneurs, but they are not clear what that means. By *entrepreneur*, they do not necessarily mean assuming the risk and management of new business, and they rightly fear handing the company over to hip-shooting gamblers who cause needless crisis. By *entrepreneur* they do mean enterprising managers who respond to new customer opportunities, develop competitive strategies, and at the same time, motivate organizations. Without such leaders, organizations cannot adapt to change; there will be no new ventures or initiatives that force people out of comfortable roles and demand that they stretch themselves.

THE FUNCTIONS OF ENTREPRENEURIAL LEADERSHIP

In large organizations, entrepreneurial leaders administer the still-existing bureaucracy at the same time that they lead the way into entrepreneurial ventures, including joint activities with other companies. The chief planner of one major multinational company suggests that executives must be schizophrenic-like to operate in such different organizational worlds. The most effective leaders can think as expert strategists, using formulas like the ones popularized by the Boston Consulting Group to manage a portfolio of companies in terms of market share and growth potential: milk the cash cows, feed the stars, watch the question marks, unload the dogs. But they should also be able to function as turnaround leaders, like Lemasters, Nagel and Carlzon, who have transformed dogs into stars. They do this not only by understanding that a new approach to business strategy is needed, but also by understanding what it takes to be a successful leader—that is, *to lead well*. Their approach to leadership can be described in terms of four broad interrelated functions: *strategic thinking, implementing policy, building teams and alliances*, and *creating a motivating corporate culture*.

IMPLEMENTATION

Implementation is essential to all the rest. Any definition of a leader must include taking actions that cause people to work toward common goals, including making decisions, communicating their meaning, and making sure they are carried out. It requires a sense of timing and courage to act when reason and intuition call for decisiveness. Lemasters involved his whole organization in change, but at a certain point, he decided to go ahead and put pressure on managers who lagged behind. Carlzon took time to get input and criticism from his managers before implementing the new strategy. In that way, he established their ownership, and gained their commitment to making it work. Nagel continually involves his organization in developing customer-oriented strategy and taking responsibility for followthrough. How the leader decides, the process of decision-making, including the role of consultation and participation, shapes the culture and can be a form of team-building and teaching. The leader who creates an ongoing dialogue about strategy forms a learning organization. Such strategic dialogues reveal the values that determine decisions. Such conversations build trust and a common sense of meaning. How the leader implements decisions demonstrates knowledge of people, ability to trust, and concern for their dignity and development. While making and implementing decisions, the leader inevitably models human values. By paying attention to the behavior of subordinates, giving praise, showing enthusiasm or displeasure, the leader demonstrates what is important to make a strategy succeed.

STRATEGIC THINKING

Business uses the term *strategy* rather loosely. It comes from the Greek *strategos,* meaning *general.* It is used to speak of specific goals ("Our strategy is to increase market share"), visions ("The Businessman's Airline"), and even tactics ("Our strategy is to be the lowest-cost producer"). The most complete strategies are systemic and include a broad vision of goals and tactics.

As we have seen with Lemasters, Carlzon, and Nagel, a technoservice strategy means integrating all the factors that make a company successful: products and services, capital investment, financing, technology, and organization, including information systems, rewards, and responsibilities. These factors are conceived, even felt, as driving forces that must be harnessed for success. A holistic approach integrates external strategy and internal organizational-change strategy to create a competitive advantage. The strategist studies customer and competition, scans the environment for change in technologies and public policies, and invests in those products and services that will meet the customer's needs better than those of the competition. But this is not all. The strategist develops not just a formal structure, but also the informal organization of work relationships that will make the external strategy succeed and build an innovative company.

The holistic strategist understands that organizational design and personnel or "human resource" policies (selection of employees, training, measurement and reward systems) will also determine success or failure because these influence employee motivation, the use of technology, and the quality of service provided. The industrial bureaucracy operated with a relatively stable organizational structure. Technoservice requires continually changing the organization to fit new technology, customer demands, and alliances with other companies.

FROM INDUSTRIAL BUREAUCRACY to TECHNOSERVICE
Automation and Customization As Determinants of Organization Strategy

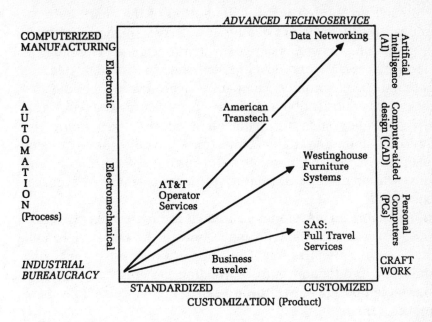

CUSTOMIZATION (Product)

This chart roughly indicates two factors that necessitate the transformation from industrial bureaucracy to technoservice organization: The *vertical dimension* describes the *process* of producing goods and services, from electromechanical to automated computerized processes. On the *horizontal dimension*, the producer tries to meet customer needs with standardized or customized *products and services*.

In the lower lefthand corner, a traditional industrial bureaucracy can produce standardized products with electromechanical processes. Jobs can be simplified and specialized. To be sure, management can, within limits, improve motivation and efficiency of standardized production by educating workers to take greater responsibility for quality (as do the Japanese), since this translates into less need for quality inspectors and less loss from defective products. In these standardized businesses, the factor that spurs organizational change is automation of the

219

most routine work, leaving craft, maintenance, and administrative functions that cannot be precisely formatted.

Moving up the left vertical dimension of the chart, automation can result in higher quality, lower costs, and greater flexibility, but only if workers are educated to use the technology as a tool. As research and development shorten product cycles, as in consumer electronics, companies need flexible manufacturing systems and flexible employees who can manage continual change. Unless such an organization decentralizes control on the shop floor and trains employees broadly, these systems break down. Furthermore, the flexible manufacturing system allows differentiation of product for large customers or market segments.

Organizational development allows industries like Westinghouse Furniture Systems to move toward the upper right and technoservice organization. The company succeeds by focusing automated production and information systems such as computer-aided design (CAD) toward satisfying the special needs of large customers.

On the right vertical dimension, we find the office workers, professionals such as engineers, scientists, accountants, and marketers, who learn to use the computerized tools to solve problems for both internal and external customers. These tools, properly used, flatten hierarchy, eliminating the need for lower-level technicians and managerial monitors.

During the rise of the industrial bureaucracy, customized craft products were standardized for mass production. Now, in the age of technoservice, companies must customize standardized products and services. AT&T, which replaced operators with electronic switches, now sees customized operator service as a form of product differentiation. Standardized air travel has been customized by SAS for international business travelers, so that front-line employees—operators, cabin attendants—are free to respond to the customer's special needs. So it is also for American Transtech employees who answer customer requests for specialized information. To function efficiently, employees must internalize corporate strategy and values, as opposed to following a rulebook.

The most complex of AT&T's services, data networking, requires the packaging of customized advanced technology products and programming. To sell, design, create, and maintain a data network, teams of employees, salesmen, engineers, programmers, systems architects, lawyers, and technicians must work together and with the customer. Each system is customized, built to fit the particular customer's needs and business strategy. Team members may use an array of tools, ranging from paper and pencil to computerized design and artificial intelligence. The systems they create are continually evolving as their customers require new functions, so that technical consultants from AT&T and other data network providers remain on the customer's premises. How these systems are employed depends on the strategy of the customer, which may use the data networks either to standardize services within an industrial bureaucracy or, like SAS, with its plans for a reservation system, to customize them for technoservice. Success at selling data networking requires organizational as well as technical knowledge and skills. The provider needs to understand the customer's business and build the system with input from those who will use it.

In a number of business areas, market competition pushes companies with traditional standardized production toward combinations of standardized and customized service. This is the case for banking and insurance companies dealing with large customers and specialized needs, and for medical services as affluent customers demand the newest technology and customized treatment.

In banking, low-level services formerly customized by a teller have become automated, while bankers use data networking to provide large clients with customized international transfers. Many large companies find themselves faced with the need for integrating different types of organizational design to produce different products and services for different customers or market segments.

In the auto industry, the complexity of production and service requires a mix of organizations. Three-fourths of the value added is from engineers, technicians, and finance and marketing personnel, who are moving up the right vertical dimension of the chart. Much of the component manufacture, such as stamping body parts, is automated, near the top of the left vertical dimension, and requires teams of self-managed workers. Although final assembly can be organized according to bureaucratic-industrial principles, high quality requires organizing work to increase responsibility and improve motivation. A challenge for leadership is to create a common culture that integrates different organizational solutions. This same challenge exists in large banks, supermarkets, and medical facilities.

In terms of these dimensions, most government services remain standardized and are organized by bureaucratic-industrial rules. Some, like air traffic control, require more automation and customization to serve pilots. They suffer because management is still patterned on the industrial-bureaucratic model. Others, like auditing and policing, would improve with techno-service management.

If government leaders thought more strategically about service, they could strengthen our economy, but there are three constraints to achieving this goal. The first is the attitude of political leaders who bad-mouth the civil service when running for office and then once elected pay little attention to good management and sometimes try to undermine its integrity. Political appointees, many of whom are gamesmen and jungle fighters, enter government with a short time frame. They try to push their agenda through a civil service dominated by experts, even if this means ignoring regulations and destroying efficiency. The experts defend themselves with red tape and the system is inefficient.

The second constraint is that the measurement systems of

government emphasize control over service. The helpers and new-generation self-developers complain that they are rewarded for catching criminals and serving their bosses, but not for helping the public.

Third, the civil service is overregulated, which makes it impossible or extremely difficult to improve government organizations. Too much needless paperwork is required by regulation, and there is no incentive to improve efficiency. Those managers who achieve more with fewer people are likely to be downgraded because rank is determined by the number of people one manages.

To improve government we need leaders who balance the values of democracy, which rightly set the goals and priorities of government, with the values of technocracy, which ensure efficiency, fairness, and the development of competent civil servants. We shall have such leaders only when an informed electorate demands managerial competence from its leaders.

THE BOTTOM LINE: DEVELOPMENT OF TEAMWORK AND MOTIVATION

For the strategic leader of a competitive organization, the bottom line should be measured not only in dollars, but in developing competent and motivated people who can adapt rapidly to changing technology and markets, work together and create synergies, and interact with customers as though they were speaking for the company.

Robert H. Hayes of the Harvard Business School has written an incisive article on the weaknesses of strategic planning by American executives. According to Hayes, their goals are too short-term and quantitative. They put too much emphasis on strategic leaps as opposed to incremental steps. Strategic leaps are directed from the top: large investments in plant and technology. Incremental steps are generated by employees at middle and lower levels with the knowledge and freedom to innovate.[1] In Hayes's terms, Lemasters, Carlzon, and Nagel balance leaps and steps by creating organizational processes that make use of incremental innovation.

No individual alone can develop strategy for a large company. Nor can strategy be formed by putting together the forecasts of isolated experts. Information must be shared. All must understand the corporate values so that the strategy moves toward realizing them. As we have seen from the innovators, transformation from bureaucracy to technoservice requires the continual development of competitive services, people, technology, and organizational systems. The seeds of strategic change come from experience with customers and technology.

The great danger for executives of large companies, especially for experts, is that as they move in a Wall Street world driven by numbers, they become alienated from productive values essential to corporate success. Isolated from the front-line managers and workers who must make any strategy work, they assume people can be motivated by partial-man theories and inspiring speeches. Unaware of changes in the front line, some top executives think of technology as what it was when they were operational managers. Others, who have come through business school, finance, or law, are experts in transactions with little knowledge of technology. Their top-down strategy does not integrate the possibilities of information technology, the needs of customers, or the values of employees. It is not enough to wander around and observe the troops. Traditional administrators would like their staffs to present them with polished plans they can implement. These seldom work the way they are envisioned. Entrepreneurial leaders develop innovative strategies by posing the right questions and seeking answers from people, both staff and front-line, with appropriate knowledge. They initiate strategic dialogue that begins with partially formed ideas. The knowledge and experience of the organization are integrated into plans that implement themselves, because the participants believe in them.

Building Teams and Alliances   Successful organizational leaders must manage downward, upward, and sideways. In the industrial bureaucracies, administrators learned to please their bosses, control subordinates, and negotiate with peers. In the world of technoservice, leaders gain support of superiors, including boards of directors, and create teamwork with subordinates and alliances with other leaders who can help or hurt them.

In one company, an expert-style CEO was pressured by his subordinates to build a top-management team. They complained that the CEO did not trust them but only his own large staff, which continually demanded information from them. They considered this a waste of both their time and company resources, and believed that the CEO would make better decisions if he organized the vice-presidents into a team to replace the staff. In this way he could make better use of their knowledge and model a style that would strengthen the company at all levels. The CEO was willing to try, but he was skeptical. He told me: "Each VP represents his division. Each wants to maximize his group's gain in competition with the others. That is natural. I am the only one responsible for all the divisions and accountable to the owners. Therefore I must make independent decisions, and I need a staff to inform me."

This viewpoint feels rational to the expert, but as the CEO conceded, it would be more efficient if the VPs could work as a team and trust each other to put the good of the whole company ahead of their divisional interests. A bureaucratic-industrial monopoly can afford large staffs and internal competition at all levels. But in the technoservice world, entrepreneurial companies need teamwork at all levels, and lower-level managers model themselves on their bosses.

Business leaders often speak about the value of teamwork, but like the concept of participation, teamwork means different things in different cultures. In Japan, teamwork is achieved by a combination of training, leadership, and strong values that push ambitious individuals to conform. Japanese teamwork suggests the harmony of a family headed by a patriarchal leader. In the Confucian tradition, leaders are responsible for the education of subordinates, who in turn are expected to be loyal and obedient.[2] Most Americans find this model too authoritarian or paternalistic. The American ideal of teamwork suggests a sports analogy, with clear goals, rules, and roles, but also lots of room for autonomous expert improvisation and fun. The leader is a playmaker, and at best, a team-building coach and educator.

My experience with effective business teams in the United States and Scandinavia fits neither the metaphor of family nor that of sports. To be sure, business requires clear goals, rules, and roles, and fun is motivating, but in the technoservice organization, people must solve problems together. There is little room for autonomous improvisation. Business teams can innovate and learn together through *strategic dialogue*, led by entrepreneurial leaders who take the role of activating teachers.

Facilitating Strategic Dialogue   A word about dialogue, which has become another popular managerial concept. *Webster's New Collegiate Dictionary* defines *dialogue* as no more than "a conversation between two or more persons." But conversations do not necessarily educate. They may merely be exchanges of opinions or prejudices.

A strategic dialogue is neither a conversation nor a series of monologues. Nor is it a democratic process. It poses questions about *how* to develop a vision and implement it. It requires leadership that sets priorities, chooses the right people, maintains the values of honest inquiry, and takes responsibility for the outcome.

A strategic dialogue starts with the leader posing a *strategic question*: for example, "How can we satisfy the business customer's needs?" or "How can we design rewards to improve overall quality and customer satisfaction?" or "How can we create an assembly plant where highly motivated employees will produce a high-quality product at the lowest possible cost?" (This latter was the question recently given to a design team at Volvo, including managers, engineers, psychologists, and union representatives.) The second step *explores alternatives*. There is an analysis of the strategic issue from both "the outside in," focusing on market, competition, and technology, and "the inside out," focusing on employee goals and values. Then everyone on the team is responsible for presenting a viewpoint that expresses his own values and knowledge. The third step requires *engagement*. Alternatives are criticized, questions of fact explored.[3]

Strategic dialogue does not dampen conflict, but uses it to raise issues that may require study and experimentation. It transforms information into knowledge. Good dialogue also requires a spirit of disciplined play: the dialogue is fun. Members of the Volvo team built a workshop where they could play with different designs. For a few months, the project leader rejected the vision, passionately proposed by project members, that the assembly line be thrown out and that work teams build a whole car. It seemed technically impractical. It appeared that costs would increase since all the materials would have to be delivered to each team. But the designers played with ideas and began to find a brilliant solution. They figured out new ways to package parts for ease of assembly and deliver them when needed by the workers. They suggested ways they could assemble more efficiently by allowing workers to take the car apart and group pieces for easy assembly. Instead of changing technology, engineers were designing a choreography of work. By putting emphasis on both better pre-assembly and more efficient craftsmanship, they found a workable and motivating compromise that left open possibilities for workers to continue learning and for engineers to discover better ways to design the car for ease of assembly.

A good strategic dialogue stimulates innovation. The final step of dialogue is *decision* for action. Although there may or may not be a clear consensus, the leader takes responsibility for the decision and for explaining the reasons for it.

This kind of strategic dialogue is much easier to create at the middle or bottom than at the top of organizations. At the bottom, people just speak for themselves and there is little competition among them. At companies like Ford, AT&T, General Motors, Xerox, and Alcoa, EI (employee involvement) and QWL (quality of worklife) teams solve business problems and suggest ways of making work more satisfying. At the top, it is harder. Executives represent their divisions or subsidiaries. Political maneuvering interferes with open conversation. The executive "team" may be riven by rivalries so that teamwork is more like negotiation than problem-solving or strategic dialogue. The most effective leaders in the industrial bureaucracies have understood the personalities and politics and, through a combination of power, persuasion, good process, persistence, and a sense of partnership, created an executive team. In the techno-service world, this is not enough. Like Nagel, Lemasters, and Carlzon, leaders must be able to facilitate a continual strategic dialogue that creates a learning organization. Managers and workers must learn and invent, not in courses isolated from the workplace, but on-line in teams to solve real customer problems and to experiment with new ways of measuring and rewarding achievement. The results of good strategic dialogues are solutions that not only solve problems but also engage and motivate the problem-solvers.*

---

*This approach to leadership also works for unions, which are, after all, in the business of service. In 1984, to strengthen the Bricklayers and Allied Craftsmen (BAC) and stem the decline in its membership, Jack Joyce, an innovative president, established Project 2000. He brought together twenty-seven union business agents representing all regions of the country to determine what strategy was needed to build the union for the year 2000. The group discovered that union membership depends on the competitiveness of their industry as well as their own ability to organize and serve members.

American masonry is a 15-billion-dollar-a-year industry made up of thousands of small contractors. BAC is the integrative organization. By interviewing contractors, manufacturers, architects, and leaders from other unions, the local business agents learned that unless they support market research and R&D, masonry loses out to competing materials. The process of a strategic dialogue stimulated these expert craftsmen to go beyond their local problems in order to understand how all of them depend on a strong union and growing

Creating and Maintaining a Motivating Corporate Culture
Now we come to the task of creating and maintaining a corporate culture that supports the strategy and reinforces the teamwork and the focus on customer satisfaction. The term *vision* is much used in discussions of leadership and corporate culture, but, I suspect, is seldom defined. Lemasters, Nagel, and Carlzon present a compelling picture of strategy that drives behavior and also sparks hope by describing a future in which both owners and employees can see opportunities for themselves. Their strategic service vision focuses the organization on ensuring that the quality of the customer's total experience with the company—people, products, and services—measures up to or exceeds expectations. But even these technoservice visions are incomplete. They do not fully describe the shared values necessary for success in the technoservice economy.

When I think of a powerful shared vision, what comes to mind are the deliberations in 1787 over the Constitution of the United States, the prospect of a political system that would balance plural interests with the overarching value of individual liberty. There is a much-debated view that the ideal for a corporation is democracy. This is, I believe, a confused ideal. Direct democracy was not even the ideal for the United States of America. As James Madison argued in *Federalist Paper No. 10*, direct democracy stands for rule by majority and the triumph of the larger interest groups, sometimes at the expense of minorities. The aim of the Founding Fathers of the United States was to promote individual liberty, and to this end they devised a government of checks and balances based on representative democracy.

A corporation, of course, is not a country. It is a subculture that seeks to attract some of the most gifted, motivated, and highly trained members of the society, and organizes them to

---

industry. Using the results of Project 2000, Joyce sponsored a study circle program to educate union members and develop local leadership. And he has initiated successful experiments in organizing, based on surveys of potential members' needs and radio, TV, and newspaper advertising.

create wealth. To do this, it must respect the values these people bring with them. It must also compensate for skills that are not developed so strongly outside a corporation, particularly so-called skills of communication: writing and reading, speaking and listening, dialogue and problem-solving.

The aim of the corporation is not to guarantee individual liberty to pursue happiness, but to satisfy customers in such a way that generates a competitive return on investment compared to alternative uses of capital, within the boundaries of law and national custom. Most of us join a corporation not because it is a right we are born to, but because we see it to be in our interest.

The corporation requires that people support its strategy. It demands more discipline than does the general society, more precision, and a greater concern for excellence. It demands that highly ambitious individuals temper their drives and work together for common goals. It requires that workers who might be happier doing something else see their own futures as involved in the company's success.

The corporate vision must engage the values of its members. In the past, it might have been enough to feel part of a powerful army, to identify with the elite, to feel protected, well rewarded, and highly regarded. Doubtless, this is still part of corporate appeal. However, the most independent and creative of the new generation do not find it sufficient. In increasing numbers, the young seek to develop themselves at work intellectually and emotionally, to feel more secure not because they are protected, but because they become more capable and marketable. Their aspirations fit the needs of companies for innovative projects and profit centers, for general managers instead of functional specialists.

Representatives of the owners select a chief executive officer to lead the corporation. This is the case even in worker-owned firms. CEOs have broad mandates and the power to influence strategy, vision, and corporate culture, although they are restrained by practical considerations. To keep their jobs, they must be successful. Their strategy must be in tune with the historical forces of the market and the rules as defined by government. To gain effective power in an era that so values free speech and due process, they cannot rule like Machiavellian princes. In a period of cutbacks and takeovers, it would be naive to say that there is no fear in American corporations. But in a free society, the style that spreads terror instead of trust drives away the best people. Leaders must focus fear on outside threats rather than internal power games. They must share power and create power to gain authority and influence. They must turn conflict into constructive dialogue. They must be able, at the same time, to think like raiders and like creators, to make the best possible use of human as well as financial assets.

Although leaders cannot democratize the corporation, as they succeed in humanizing it they will attract the new generation. Ideally, this means demonstrating values of both head and heart —intellectual excellence, analysis, innovation, and flexibility as well as critical thinking, fairness, integrity, perseverence, and respect for individual dignity. And, above all, they must demonstrate the courage to defend these values against the pressures of expediency and fear of failure. Leaders who control valuable resources must sometimes resist heart-tugging appeals for help from individuals in order to defend the good of the larger group. They must be able to balance receptiveness and toughness, honesty and responsibility, responsiveness and accountability. While caring about people may make them more appealing, integrity, defined as meeting commitments and acting with consistency, is what creates trust.

Styles of Entrepreneurial Leadership

Even when they understand intellectually that these functions of entrepreneurial leadership require a new style, few executives can practice it. Their values get in the way of learning.

Through interviews with sixty top executives at AT&T, vice-presidents and above, about their leadership practices, I have distinguished four distinct styles of entrepreneurial leadership. (See the AT&T management questionnaire, reproduced in Appendix D.) Subsequently, I have used these questions to interview ten executives at a conglomerate and seven at a chain of supermarkets. These interviews, given as part of a process to improve management, show that these differences in style can be generalized to other companies. I started with the dichotomy suggested by executives at AT&T of *administrator versus entrepreneur*, and together with them expanded and refined it. The leadership styles are rooted in the different value orientations: *expert, protector* (helper-defender), *facilitator* (self-developer), and *innovator*. Each has strengths and weaknesses. The best entrepreneurial leaders combine and balance styles; those who are more easily stereotyped are less effective.

Expert-entrepreneurs are decisive, competitive risk-takers who invest in products and services based on market research and sometimes on their own hunches. They want in-depth knowledge so they can extrapolate what has worked in one market and enhance it for another. Then they can establish managerial processes they feel they control. They are fervent salesmen and take pride in performing in meetings. They value their skill at cutting deals. They are no-nonsense cost-slashers. They pick good people, usually experts just like themselves, set demanding goals, and try to delegate, but it is hard for them to keep their noses out of everything. Sometimes they are hipshooters, overvaluing their knowledge as they make too-quick decisions. They tend to be poor at listening, unless they are sucking up information for their own purposes. They are impatient and overly controlling. They are unaware of how they bruise dignity and turn people off, especially those who do not relate to them paternally or share their values.

Typically, expert-entrepreneurs who start their own businesses get into trouble when their companies start to grow and significant delegation is required. They tend to fragment functions and interdependent lines of business, second-guess subordinates, and cause a sense of insecurity.

Protector-entrepreneurs believe they will gain organizational strength not only by sharing power but by creating it. They do not merely delegate. Protectors encourage people to expand their functions and take risks. They share information freely and explain its meaning, thus creating a common understanding of goals. They care about their people, and coach and protect those subordinates who share their values. People are motivated not only by responsibilities and opportunities but by their trust in the leader.

One such top executive defines his managerial philosophy: "Most people will not give their best because they feel you don't care. We need to send a message that we do care. Most work relationships are like cool business transactions at best. Usually there is not even much trust. I motivate and encourage by creating big jobs with clear role definitions, and then by getting out of the way. But I am there when I am needed. I see myself as a coach, counselor, and barrier-remover so that my people can do their best."

The weaknesses of protectors are softness and loose management. People tend to become too dependent on them. Protectors may become overprotective and lose their objectivity about subordinates, because they want them to do well. They may avoid facing necessary conflict within the team and fail to maintain discipline because they want to be loved by everyone. However, to defend their own people, they may cause conflict with other parts of the organization.

Facilitator-entrepreneurs avoid these weaknesses. They work for consensus on strategy and action, but they are not coaches or protectors. They like to solve problems with subordinates, and are skillful in making sure that everyone contributes knowledge and experience. More than other types, they are egalitarian. Used to seeing things from different points of view, they work easily and effectively with different types of people. Their weakness as leaders lies in a tendency to believe that consensus guarantees good decisions and that harmony is always better than conflict. While they are more objective about people than are the protectors, they remain more emotionally distant from subordinates. While they are tolerant of value differences and like to try new approaches, they do not take responsibility for coaching those subordinates who cannot take advantage of the opportunities they offer. In contrast to the entrepreneurial expert or protector, they are uncomfortable in a parental-type role. Goal-oriented, they measure success in profitability, not esteem or applause, but in so doing, they deprive people of reassurance and inspiration.

Innovator-entrepreneurs offer strategic visions that integrate customer service and participation. They have an intuitive sense of workable wholes, and they take risks to prove their theories. They energize the organization with their enthusiasm. As their vision creates hope, they may become charismatic leaders: as people respond with trust and put their hopes in the leader, this injects the leader with a sense of certainty and spontaneity; this glow, ease, and self-confidence further strengthen people's trust, and correspondingly, the leader's charisma.

Their weaknesses are the other side of their strengths: utopianism, seductive promises, intolerance of other visions and value orientations. They need help in team-building and maintaining trust. Real participation brings them down to earth and improves their vision. It is notable that many successful innovators, like Lemasters and Carlzon, use subordinates and consultants to teach these skills to the organization. Unlike the experts, they recognize that they need to employ complementary styles.

Each entrepreneurial type must beware of its own characteristic tendencies to sabotage good intentions in moments of stress. Experts become autocratic and unsympathetic to the weaknesses of others. When things go wrong, they grab back authority. They make decisions too quickly and pay for them later because subordinates do not buy in and decisions are not implemented. Protectors risk the opposite failing: taking too long to gain everyone's buy-in, procrastinating until it is too late to solve problems, rationalizing their unwillingness to make tough decisions that will hurt some people. Facilitators work well with project and marketing teams, but lack the inspirational leadership that pulls an organization together. In a crisis, they appear uncommitted and uncertain, and they may settle for a superficial consensus. The weakness of innovators is falling in love with their creations, becoming true believers in their visions, and losing their experimental playfulness and flexibility. Instead of engaging people in rethinking the strategy and perhaps compromising with approaches that are less pure and more pragmatic, they exhort and preach the true faith as the ship goes under.

With the help of the AT&T executives, I constructed the Management Style Matrix (page 236). I asked each of them to first circle the behaviors that most characterized them. These could be in any of the lists of entrepreneurial types or under the heading "administrator."* Then I asked them to circle the behaviors they would like to develop. This became the basis of a strategic dialogue about how to change themselves and their organization. I invite the reader to do the same.

The majority of executives I've interviewed see themselves as administrators and expert-entrepreneurs, but believe business goals require them to become better team-builders and innovators. Most experts can imagine themselves learning the skills of the facilitators, but not the behavior of the protectors. They see the need to create strategic dialogues but not to become more understanding and supportive.

The best organizational leaders are not pure types, but combine the positive values of expert, protector, facilitator, and in-

---

*To be complete, the category of administrator could be separated into expert, helper, and facilitator-administrator (the innovators are invariably entrepreneurs). In fact, managers resolve this problem by circling "administrator" plus some of the behaviors from the entrepreneurial side (e.g., an administrator-helper would circle "coaches").

MANAGEMENT STYLE MATRIX

POSITIVE (+)

Administrator	Expert	Entrepreneur		Innovator
		Protector	Facilitator	
Functional expert	Extrapolates	Empowers	Creates consensus	Holistic strategist
Coordinator	Enhances	Shares meaning of information	Open—learns from coworkers and customers	Experimental designer
Gatekeeper	Delegates	Defends values	Tolerant	Visionary
Scorekeeper	Risk-taker	Coaches	Egalitarian	Enthusiastic
Arbitrator	Quick decision-maker	Creates loyalty	Adventurous	
Represents organization	Sells aggressively	Supports and develops		
	Deal-maker	Removes roadblocks		
	Cost-cutter			

NEGATIVE (−)

Administrator	Expert	Entrepreneur		Innovator
		Protector	Facilitator	
Autocrat	Hip-shooter	Avoids conflict within team	Diffuse	Utopian
Turf-defender	Fragmenter	Creates we-they	Uninspiring	Intolerant
Laissez-faire	Know-it-all	Soft on loyal subordinates	Superficial	Manipulator
Figurehead	Power-grabber		Uncommitted	Grandiose

236

novator along with administrative skills. These orientations are so integrated that the leader can change behavior, yet still present a style that is consistent over time and has proclaimed values. The best leaders are decisive experts who take control in a crisis, but develop policy through participative teamwork and encourage continual learning and innovation. They gain loyalty by their faithfulness and dedication to shared values.

BECOMING A LEADER FOR OUR TIME

Of course, it is easier for researchers to describe the ideal than for leaders to practice it. Entrepreneurial leadership is messy and uncomfortable. While elation and satisfaction are the rewards of success, there are also times of weary self-doubt. Often, leaders must push themselves to the limits of competence and physical endurance. Leaders today will succeed by mobilizing and directing value-driven energy that has been frustrated by outmoded bureaucracies. But inevitably, they will also provoke resistance in experts and helpers who were comfortable doing things in the traditional way. There is always the danger that leaders will protect themselves from anger and hostility by retreating behind omniscient, narcissistic self-images that cloud perception. The developmental need for achievement and knowledge can become perverted into the defensive addiction to applause and reassurance.

It is cleaner and more comfortable to be an expert-administrator than an entrepreneurial leader thrust into the hurly-burly of continual change. It is safer and clearer to be a professional self-developer than to commit oneself to risky projects and the education of others. Can the experts change? Will the self-developers commit themselves to a larger project? Only if they are convinced that change and commitment are necessary. This conviction is growing as American managers realize that to compete in the global market, to satisfy demanding customers, they must motivate the troops, and this requires more than is indicated by the partial-man theories.

My hope is that *Why Work* will help would-be leaders to reflect on their values and experiment with new approaches. Competence in entrepreneurial leadership is developed through practice in organizational innovation. As the Japanese have shown us, one does not have to be a pioneering innovator like Lemasters, Nagel, or Carlzon to learn from innovations. In the process of changing an organization, the leader must forge new relationships, create supporting networks, and define personal values. By practicing new styles, expert-leaders show their determination and encourage their followers to take risks. By stimulating helpers and self-developers to express their visions, and integrating these in the organizational strategy, leaders gain both useful ideas and motivated followers. The leader needed for our time will not be the expert—father figure or the charismatic innovator, but rather one who balances higher values—integrity, expert knowledge, innovation, responsiveness, equity—with pragmatic toughness and skill in facilitation and dialogue. These are the values that will motivate the new generation. Without such leadership, the American economy will stumble and flounder into the technoservice age. With it, the new generation may find meaning in the workplace, creating new solutions to human problems.

FOLLOW-UP INTERVIEW QUESTIONNAIRE ON VALUES AT WORK

Date and place of interview:

Name:

Age:

Marital status and children:

Please describe where you grew up (city, suburb, rural—probe to understand the social background).

Education:

Parent's education and occupations:

Brief family history:

Job history (explore to understand changes in interests or motivations):

THE JOB

1. What is your work? (Include: How does your work relate to technology and management? How does your work relate to the goals of your office or department?)

2. What do you like most about your work?

3. What do you most dislike about your work?

4. How would you like your work to be changed?

5. How would you like to be managed?

6. What rewards do you get from your work besides money? (For example, career development, personal development, friendships, sociability, sense of service.)

7. What is your definition of service? How do you serve the public, or customers?

8. Does your work require helping? Do you help customers or clients? The public? The organization? Is there anyone at work who needs your help?

9. Describe an example of when you have helped someone. If not at work, where?

10. Do you need help from anyone at work?

11. Describe yourself. What are you like?

12. What are your main satisfactions in life outside of work?

13. Name three people, living or dead, you most admire, and state why.

14. Can you remember a dream related to work?

15. What does self-development mean to you?

16. What have you done to develop yourself?

17. Do you get any help in developing yourself?

18. Can you recall how you got interested in self-development?

19. How would you like to develop yourself at work and outside of work? Do you believe your present work could further your goals of self-development? Please explain.

20. What is your vision of the kind of person you would like to become?

A NOTE ON VALUE DRIVES

There is no ideal word to use when talking about the forces that move us. We cannot see them or directly measure them. We experience them. If *need* is a misleading term, because it implies the lack of something, so is *instinct*, which is too biological. The inner forces that drive us are both inborn and shaped by culture. We might call them desires or passions, but these terms are too hot, too suggestive of sex or irrational drives. To speak of a passion for mastery or play suggests abnormal complusiveness. The term *want* is an alternative, but it is commonly used to indicate conscious acceptance of one's impulses, when in fact, once irrational strivings become conscious, they are often rejected as dangerous, inappropriate, or inconvenient. We might just call the forces that move us *values*, but by itself, the term *value* does not suggest emotional strivings or intense appetites, even though these express values. Deep values, or emotionally driven values, would be more precise. The concept of *value drives* seems to be useful, because it combines the commonly used term *drives*, suggesting force and energy that can be either conscious ("I am driving toward the goal") or unconscious ("I feel driven to repeat these relationships), with *value*, a cognitive word used to define culture. We commonly speak of motivated people as "driven," as people with "drive," and this always implies that they have aims and values.

APPENDIX B

In the nineteenth century, William James postulated the existence of human instincts and described them as inborn reflexes or impulses that become drives through early learning. He described social drives as rooted in man's instincts to imitate and to love, but he also described how other "instincts" like anger, acquisitiveness, and fear can conflict with sociability, forcing us to make choices. There were problems in James's approach, particularly in distinguishing instinctual from learned behavior. Unlike the fully patterned instinctual behavior of insects, fish, birds, and reptiles, and even of some mammals, human instinctual reflexes in large part become shaped by learning, and are eventually largely controlled by the neocortex.

Freud used the concept of drives (trieb) to describe the dynamic, intense nature of behavior, the expression of passionate impulses in symptoms and dreams. His concept of drive as directed psychic energy connects seemingly unconnected strivings and usefully explains development and perversion, intensity of feeling, and emotional attitude. The problem with Freud's theory of drives is that he makes them too biological and reduces too much, finally subsuming them under two forces, Eros (love) and destructiveness.

Of course, drives are rooted in biology, but the mechanisms are more complex than Freud was able to show, particularly since dynamic human strivings combine the lower and higher brain, the autonomic nervous system, and the neocortex. Although we can infer the connection, no one has traced precisely how the reflexes and purposeful activities of infants become human drives.

From a biological point of view, we can observe the following: although each of us is born with different constitutional levels of energy, different intensities of dynamic tendencies, intensity also varies with age, and all value drives are affected by cycles of ebb and flow, excitation and satiation. The intensity of value drives also depends on exciting stimuli, such as sexual arousal. Threats to life trigger flight or fight with strong infusions of adrenaline or noradrenaline, and good-tasting food excites appetite.

As we mature, intensity varies not only because of the aging process which erodes drive, but according to whether we strengthen or weaken value drives through good or bad habits, skills and competencies, activating or addictive needs, and good or bad fit with other people and the environment, especially work and intimate relationships, both of which engage all of our drives. Value drives expressed with productive results are strengthened. Those invested in dissatisfying activities or relationships deplete energy, causing, as it were, emotional bankruptcy. Value drives that are continually frustrated and suppressed, because of either the environment or conflicting drives, may eventually weaken, although they may maintain their force through perversion.

Parsimony is a criterion for usable theory, and the human brain cannot easily remember more than seven or eight categories. I have grouped the value drives into eight categories: *survival, relatedness, pleasure, information, mastery, play, dignity,* and *meaning.* I made separate categories only when it was necessary to maintain a causal distinction, keeping in mind the rule from typal analysis that each concept in a category should be more like each other than like one in any of the other categories. The end result is still arguable. I debated the idea of considering self-expression or individuation as a separate value drive. After all, babies show a dynamic tendency to express self through speech, singing, making marks. With discipline this develops into speaking, art, writing. However, this not only adds a category, but separates self-expression from mastery, play, and dignity, when the expression of these is in fact self-expression. In the process of development, disciplined self-expression is what individuates human beings.

I recognize also that the value drive to reproduce the species has been left out. This drive affects motivation to work in complex ways, depending on cultural factors. Men have traditionally been driven to provide for their children, while having and caring for children have been women's work. In every society, as women gain independence and enter the workforce, they limit their childbearing. There are two reasons for this, egotistical and altruistic. Children tie them down, and by having fewer children, they can provide each child with better opportunities.

I have grouped value drives according to concepts that can be experienced and understood by people in every culture. In discussing this grouping, I have tried to follow good English usage, avoid technical language where possible, and yet include the best evidence from psychology and anthropology.

STATISTICAL RESULTS FROM THE VALUES AT WORK QUESTIONNAIRE

OVERALL RESULTS

MOST IMPORTANT APPROACH TO WORK

	SERVICE SECTOR	TELECOM.	HIGH-TECH	GOVT.	NASA	YOUNG LEADERS	COLLEGE INTERNS
Expert	47%	48%	59%	64%	70%	20%	43%
Helper	15	13	10	9	4	24	3
Defender	1	2	1	6	1	0	1
Institutional helper	7	7	4	2	6	4	7
Innovator	5	8	12	0	4	17	5
Self-developer	20	20	12	19	12	35	41
No choice	5	2	2	0	3	0	0
	100%	100%	100%	100%	100%	100%	100%

245

RESULTS FROM SAMPLE GROUPS

TELECOMMUNICATIONS SAMPLE   N = 295*
(This describes me)

	Very well	Somewhat	A little	Not at all	Total
Expert	76%	22%	2%	0%	100%
Helper	55	38	7	0	100
Defender	25	31	32	12	100
Institutional helper	44	40	14	2	100
Innovator	30	41	22	7	100
Self-developer	51	35	12	2	100

*N is the sample size, the number of people who answered the questionnaire.

HIGH-TECH SAMPLE   N = 180*
(This describes me)

	Very well	Somewhat	A little	Not at all	Total
Expert	75%	23%	2%	0%	100%
Helper	36	49	15	0	100
Defender	7	19	35	39	100
Institutional helper	23	48	26	3	100
Innovator	26	46	20	8	100
Self-developer	36	46	16	2	100

*N is the sample size, the number of people who answered the questionnaire.

GOVERNMENT SAMPLE   N = 135*
(This describes me)

	Very well	Somewhat	A little	Not at all	Total
Expert	88%	12%	0%	0%	100%
Helper	51	36	10	3	100
Defender	44	31	14	11	100
Institutional helper	30	35	25	10	100

	Very well	Somewhat	A little	Not at all	Total
Innovator	10	31	26	33	100
Self-developer	48	38	10	4	100

*N is the sample size, the number of people who answered the questionnaire.

NASA SAMPLE N = 706*
(This describes me)

	Very well	Somewhat	A little	Not at all	[Missing]+	Total
Expert	92%	6%	1%	1%	0	100%
Helper	51	34	9	3	3	100
Defender	28	22	23	22	5	100
Institutional helper	61	28	6	2	3	100
Innovator	31	35	19	11	4	100
Self-developer	58	26	10	3	3	100

*N is the sample size, the number of people who answered the questionnaire.
+For the other tables, missing questionnaires were taken out in calculating percentages.
This table was prepared by a task force sponsored by the Academy of Public Administration. "Equal Opportunity and Management Practices in NASA Headquarters" (Washington, D.C.: National Academy of Public Administration Report, January 1987).

YOUNG LEADERS SAMPLE N = 46*
(This describes me)

	Very well	Somewhat	A little	Not at all	Total
Expert	85%	11%	4%	0%	100%
Helper	60	29	11	0	100
Defender	9	29	27	35	100
Institutional helper	36	34	23	7	100
Innovator	35	30	30	5	100
Self-developer	91	6	6	0	100

*N is the sample size, the number of people who answered the questionnaire.

COLLEGE INTERNS SAMPLE   N = 106*
(This describes me)

	Very well	Somewhat	A little	Not at all	Total
Expert	84%	14%	2%	0%	100%
Helper	40	42	18	0	100
Defender	10	37	34	19	100
Institutional helper	34	52	12	2	100
Innovator	40	42	15	3	100
Self-developer	73	21	5	1	100

*N is the sample size, the number of people who answered the questionnaire.

SERVICE SECTOR SAMPLE   N = 658*
(Business and Government)
(This describes me)

	Very well	Somewhat	A little	Not at all	Total
Expert	82%	16%	1%	0%	100%
Helper	65	29	6	0	100
Defender	26	34	25	15	100
Institutional helper	46	38	12	4	100
Innovator	25	40	21	14	100
Self-developer	57	31	9	3	100

*N is the sample size, the number of people who answered the questionnaire.

APPROACHES TO WORK*
Significant Intercorrelation at 1% level of significance
Telecommunications sample: N = 295

	Expert	Helper	Institutional helper	Defender	Innovator	Self-developer
Expert	—	×	×	.16	.18	.24
Helper	×	—	.34	.28	×	.15
Institutional helper	×	.34	-	.34	.29	×
Defender	.16	.28	.34	—	.37	.17

	Expert	Helper	Institutional helper	Defender	Innovator	Self-developer
Innovator	.18	×	.29	.37	–	.24
Self-developer	.24	.15	×	.17	.24	–

*This table reports product moment correlations based on a scale of identification with each type ranging from very well (4) to not at all (1). I report those correlations which are significant at the one percent level (meaning that there is less than one chance in a hundred that they are caused by chance). The significant correlations indicate which combinations of types people tend to choose. They show that many people identify with more than one type. They also describe patterns of choice that are explained in this book. For example, innovators tend to identify with all types except helpers, but they do tend to identify with institutional helpers. Institutional helpers tend to identify with helpers on the one hand and with defenders and innovators (leaders) on the other. Self-developers identify most with innovators and experts, very little with helpers, and not at all with institutional helpers.

+N is the sample size, the number of people who answered the questionnaire.

THE AT&T MANAGERIAL INTERVIEW QUESTIONNAIRE

I. INTRODUCTION

Describe your current job.

II. MANAGERIAL APPROACH

1. What are the main goals of your organization? Do you think your subordinates see the goals as you do? How do you communicate them?

2. How do you give feedback and evaluation to your subordinates, and how do you get it from your own boss?

3. How do people in your organization give you feedback?

4. Describe your activities as a manager—what do you actually do?

5. How are decisions made in your organization? Do you have any process for involving others in the decisions you make? (Give examples.) What decisions have you delegated?

6. What are your views about sharing sensitive information with those who work for you?

7. To what extent are lower-level people involved in the work usually allotted to senior individuals?

8. What is it that is challenging in the work in your organization for employees? Is it different for different types or groups of people? What do you do about it?

9. How do you apportion new work that arises that doesn't fit the existing structure?

10. How do you conceive of your role regarding the morale of your organization?

11. How do you share credit? Give examples.

12. Do you have a managerial philosophy? What is it? How did you develop it? (Reading, etc.)

13. What is your definition of leadership? What words and/or behavior most inspires employees in AT&T?

14. Is it important, useful, or necessary in your leadership role to have symbols of authority, rank, and prestige?

15. What individuals have been the greatest influence on you and your managerial approach, either as role models or in what they have said to you or taught you?

16. What are the criteria you use to evaluate subordinate managers? Do you communicate these criteria? If so, how?

17. Do you talk about management with subordinates? (Give examples.)

18. What specifically are you doing to help the people who report to you to develop themselves?

19. What do you see as your role in regard to the development of those two levels down from you, and of others down to the lowest levels?

20. Assuming a responsibility on the part of supervisors, do you think that any other part(s) of the organization has a responsibility to help individuals develop their capabilities? What should be the nature of that help?

21. In your experience, are there some individuals whose management style makes them good leaders in one situation but poor leaders in a different situation? (Give examples.)

III. STRUCTURAL CONSTRAINTS

1. Are there things you believe you ought to be accomplishing in your position, things you feel you could do and that the organization needs to have done, that you are not doing? If so, what are these things, and why are you not doing them?

2. If you are accomplishing what you feel needs to be done, are you doing it with satisfaction, and as efficiently and effectively as you would like? Do you have a sense of accomplishment? If not, what are the reasons (institutional and personal)? What needs to be changed?

3. Do you have what you need in the way of authority to struc-

ture the work and organize people to accomplish the tasks at hand (e.g., determining the proper number of positions and the areas to which they are allocated)? If not, what would have to be changed for you to have what you need?

4. In general, when you think about the things you feel should be done, do you feel blocked by structural constraints? If so, what needs to be changed?

5. What are the strengths and values in AT&T that we need to protect, that should be preserved?

IV. BACKGROUND AND CAREER DEVELOPMENT
1. Describe your family background and work history.
2. What experiences or training would you like to have had to prepare you for what you are doing now? Is it possible for you to provide such experiences or training now for the people who work for you? (Give examples.)
3. What strategies have you employed in planning your own career?

V. What are your views of the goals of AT&T in the broadest sense? (Describe the company's strategy and your organization's role in achieving it.)

NOTES

PREFACE

1. Anders Edström, Michael Maccoby, Jan Erik Rendahl, and Lennart Strömberg, *Ledare for Sverige* (Lund: Liber, 1985). The CEOs included Pehr
   Gyllenhammer of Volvo, Jan Carlzon of SAS, Bjorn Svedberg of LM Erics-
   son, and Percy Barnevik of ASEA, among others. Political leaders included Ingvar Carlsson, currently Prime Minister.

2. Anders Edström, Lars Erik Norbäck, and Jan Erik Rendahl, "Leadership
   and Corporate Development: The Case of the Scandinavian Airline System (SAS) (Stockholm: The Swedish Council for Management and Worklife Issues, working paper, 1984).

INTRODUCTION

1. Edward A. Feigenbaum, and Pamela McCorduck, *The Fifth Generation*
   (Reading, Mass.: Addison-Wesley, 1983). Michael Maccoby, "A New Way
   of Managing," *IEEE Spectrum*, June 1984, pp. 60–72. See also other arti-
   cles in this issue on expert systems and new modes of work.

2. *USA Today*, January 31, 1985, p. 3D.

3. William F. Whyte, et al., *Worker Participation and Ownership* (Ithaca,
   N.Y.: ILR Press, 1983).

NOTES

4. Abraham Maslow, *Motivation and Personality* (New York: Harper & Row, 1954).

5. T. J. Peters and R. H. Waterman Jr., *In Search of Excellence* (New York: Harper & Row, 1982).

6. Ken Follet, *On the Wings of Eagles* (New York: William Morrow, 1983).

7. Daniel Yankelovich, *New Rules* (New York: Random House, 1981). Yankelovich has been a pioneer in identifying the new value orientation. See also D. Quinn Mills, *The New Competitors* (New York: Wiley, 1983), for a discussion of the new generation as managers.

8. Quoted by Garry Wills in *Nixon Agonistes* (New York: New American Library, 1979), p. 330.

CHAPTER 1

1. David Ingvar, "Memory of the Future: An Essay on the Temporal Organization of Conscious Awareness," *Human Neurobiology* (1985) 4.

2. *American Heritage College Dictionary*, 1976.

3. Rene A. Spitz, *The First Year of Life* (New York: International Universities Press, 1965). Margaret S. Mahler, Fred Pine, and Anni Bergman, *The Psychological Birth of the Human Infant* (New York: Basic Books, 1974). John Bowlby, *Separation: Anxiety and Anger*, vol. 2 (New York: Basic Books, 1973). Mary D. Ainsworth, "Attachment: Retrospect and Prospect," in *The Place of Attachment in Human Behavior*, eds. C. M. Parkes and J. Stevenson-Hinde (New York: Basic Books, 1982).

4. William James, *Principles of Psychology* (Cambridge, Mass.: Harvard University Press, 1983).

5. Michael Maccoby and George M. Foster, "Methods of Studying Mexican Peasant Personality," *Anthropological Quarterly*, vol. 43, October 1979, pp. 225–242.

6. Study reported in *The Wall Street Journal*, March 30, 1987, p. 21.

7. David G. McClelland, *The Achieving Society* (Glencoe, Ill.: The Free Press, 1967).

8. Jean Piaget, *Play, Dreams and Imitation in Childhood* (London: Heinemann, 1951).

9. Michael Maccoby, "The Game Attitude" (unpublished doctoral dissertation, Harvard University, 1960).

10. Heinz Kohut, *The Restoration of the Self* (New York: International Universities Press, 1977).

11. Plato, *Laws*, II, 671, trans. B. Jowett (Princeton, N.J.: Bollingen Foundation; Princeton University Press, 1973). Aristotle, *Nicomachean Ethics*, IV, 9, (Indianapolis: Bobbs-Merrill, 1962).

12. Erik H. Erikson, *Gandhi's Truth* (New York: W. W. Norton, 1969), pp. 184, 197, 207ff.

13. Emile Durkheim, *Suicide: A Study in Sociology*, trans. J. Spaulding and G. Simpson (Glencoe, Ill.: The Free Press, 1951).

14. Harry Stack Sullivan, *The Interpersonal Theory of Psychiatry* (New York: W. W. Norton, 1953). See pp. 28ff for a discussion of syntaxic (culturally given), prototaxic (universal), and parataxic (private) meanings.

15. Jean Piaget, *The Child's Conception of Physical Causality*, trans. Marjorie Gabain (Paterson, N.J.: Littlefield, Adams, 1960).

CHAPTER 2

1. Erich Fromm, *To Have Or to Be* (New York: Harper & Row, 1976).

2. Stephen Potter, *The Theory and Practice of Gamesmanship: The Art of Winning Without Actually Cheating* (New York: Holt, 1948).

3. Johann Huizinga, *Homo Ludens* (Boston: The Beacon Press, 1955).

4. Jean Piaget, *The Moral Judgment of the Child* (Glencoe, Ill.: The Free Press, 1955).

5. Michael Maccoby, "The Game Attitude."

6. Sigmund Freud, *Beyond the Pleasure Principle* (1920) (London: The Hogarth Press, 1950).

7. Michael Maccoby, Nancy Modiano, and Patricia Lander, "Games and Social Character in a Mexican Village," *Psychiatry*, 26:150–62, 1964.

8. Interviewed in *INC*, August 1985, p. 27.

CHAPTER 3

1. Kenneth Blanchard and Spencer Johnson, *The One-Minute Manager* (New York: Berkley Books, 1984).

2. "Lessons from Major Accidents: A Comparison of the Three Mile Island Nuclear Core Overheat and the North Sea Platform Bravo Blowout," Executive Report 6, based on the work done by David W. Fischer of the International Institute of Applied Systems Analysis (IIASA), A-2361, Laxenburg, Austria, 1981. National Transportation Safety Board, "Marine Ac-

cident Report: Capsizing and Sinking of the U.S. Mobile Offshore Drilling Unit OCEAN RANGER," Washington, D.C., 1983, pp. 47–50, 69–72.

3. Glenn C. Kinney et al., *The Human Element in Air Traffic Control* (McLean, Va.: MITRE Corporation, April 1983), pp. 4–21.

4. Donald A. Schön, *The Reflective Practitioner: How Professionals Think in Action* (New York: Basic Books, 1983), pp. 300–302.

CHAPTER 4

1. Carol Gilligan, *In a Different Voice: Psychological Theories and Women's Development* (Cambridge, Mass.: Harvard University Press, 1982).

CHAPTER 5

1. Doris Kearns, *Lyndon Johnson and the American Dream* (New York: Harper & Row, 1976). Garry Wills, *Nixon Agonistes*. Laurence Leamer, *Make-Believe: The Story of Nancy and Ronald Reagan* (New York: Dell, 1983).

2. John A. Justice, "The Right Tough," *The Ambassador* (TWA flight magazine), January 1985, p. 54.

CHAPTER 7

1. Rene A. Spitz, *The First Year of Life*, pp. 277–281.

2. For example, see Harry Gunrip, *Schizoid Phenomena: Object Relations and the Self* (New York: International Universities Press, 1969); W. R. D. Fairburn, *An Object Relations Theory of the Personality* (New York: Basic Books, 1952).

3. Erich Fromm, *Escape from Freedom* (New York: Rinehart, 1941).

4. See also Michael Maccoby, *The Leader*, Chapter 8; Douglas LaBier, *Modern Madness: The Emotional Fallout of Success* (Reading, Mass.: Addison-Wesley, 1986).

CHAPTER 8

1. Robert H. Hayes, "Strategic Planning: Forward in Reverse?" *Harvard Business Review*, November–December 1985, pp. 111–119. For a good text on business strategy, see Michael E. Porter, *Competitive Advantage* (New York: The Free Press, 1985).

2. Robert J. Smith, *Japanese Society: Tradition, Self and the Social Order* (Cambridge, England: Cambridge University Press, 1983).

3. Jan Borgbrant and Michael Maccoby, "Beyond Negotiation: Leadership for Change" (unpublished paper, 1987).

INDEX

accountants, 118, 123, 130
achievement, 52, 55, 56, 57, 84, 203
  as mastery, 66, 67
  self-developers and, 188, 189–90
ACTION Agency, 145, 149, 185–87
activity pleasure, 64
Acton, Lord, 67
addictive needs, 56, 57, 58, 64, 66, 67
administrative leadership, 13,
  215–16, 232, 235–37
age distribution, 45–46
Ainsworth, Mary, 61
air traffic controllers, 128–29, 193
Alcoa, 228
American Revolution, 151
American Transtech, 14, 25, 85,
  87–95, 166, 220–21
  organizational levels of, 93–95
anthropology, 14
appetite, 64
Aristotle, 70
Arvonen, Jouko, 53n
assembly-line workers, 62, 67
AT&T, 13–14, 15, 72, 76, 228,
  231–32
  before Bell System breakup,
    88n–89n
  customization at, 220, 221
  helpers at, 142
  management style of, 215–16
  production at, 25–26
  Stock and Bond, 88–93
AT&T managerial interview
  questionnaire, 13, 251–53
auditing, 106–11, 139, 154, 155, 159
Australia, 112
authority, 68, 80, 85, 90
  criticism of, 47, 63
  experts' ambivalence toward, 120,
    130
  self-developers and, 167, 177, 178,
    198
auto industry, strategic thinking in,
  222

automation, 22–27, 219–222
autonomy, see independence

Bahr, Morton, 63
Baily, Martin Neil, 25n
balance:
  of self-developers, 175–76
  strategic self-development and,
    201, 206–11
banks, 25, 221
Barnes, Harry G., Jr., 12
Barometer Questionnaire, 91–95
Bearse, Peter J., 27n
Bell Laboratories, 118
Bell System, 15, 75–76, 82, 88, 118
  see also AT&T
Berkeley, University of California at,
  47
Bernstein, Michael, 47
Blue Knight, The (Wambaugh), 153
Boston Consulting Group, 216
Bowlby, John, 61
brain:
  hope and, 52
  information and, 65
Bravo blowout, 128
Bricklayers and Allied Craftsmen
  (BAC), 228n–29n
bureaucracy, 19–20, 21, 88–90
  political critiques of, 47
  see also industrial bureaucracy
Bureau of Labor Statistics, U.S., 24
Burr, Donald, 114
Burt, Dan, 159

care, 201–3, 208
Carlzon, Jan, 96–101, 111, 115, 116,
  195
  background of, 96, 113
  as entrepreneurial leader, 216–17,
    218, 224, 228, 229
  power as viewed by, 100–101
  timing of, 99–100
  two-phase approach of, 98–99

261

Carter, Jimmy, 214
Castle, The (Kafka), 121
Challenger space shuttle, 128
challenges, experts and, 121–22
Chaplin, Charlie, 72
character formation:
   of defenders, 156–59
   of experts, 119–21
   of helpers, 137–38
   of innovators, 111–14
   of self-developers, 176–78
character types, see social character
   theory
chief executives (CEOs), 34, 45, 63,
   83, 85, 225, 230–31
   at American Transtech, 94–95
   as economic men, 29
   as innovators, 88–105
children:
   dignity of, 203, 205, 206
   discipline and, 205–6
   freedom of, 203–4
   play of, 68, 112–13
   value drives and, 61, 66, 68–71
   see also infants
Churchill, Winston, 158
civil rights, 47
Civil Service, U.S., Merit Protection
   Board of, 11
clerks, 25, 39
clients, see customers and clients
College Interns sample, 43, 44, 46,
   248
Commerce Department, U.S., 154,
   159, 164
commitment, 51, 81, 114
   self-developers and, 168, 188, 189,
   191, 193, 195
   strategic self-development and,
   201, 207–11
Communication Workers of America
   (CWA), 15, 63, 171
company men, 37, 38, 40
competence, 12, 19, 66, 67, 169
   discipline and, 205–6
   responsibility and, 79, 80
competition, 9, 23, 221
   dignity and, 72–73
   global, 21, 25–26, 96, 97, 215
computer-aided design (CAD)

systems, 102, 220
computer networks, 21, 22, 24, 27
computer technicians, 121, 122, 130
   self-developer, 176, 178, 179
conflict:
   helpers and, 148–49
   self-developers' views on, 183
   strategic dialogue and, 227
conformity, 61–62, 112–13
Constitution, U.S., 229
consultants, 13–15, 89–90, 170, 172
   types of, 14
control:
   experts and, 118–19, 126, 127,
   129–30
   responsibility and, 79
cooperation, 20, 22, 27, 35, 82, 112
   defenders and, 161
   in Japan, 130–31
   self-developers and, 182
   see also teamwork
craftsmen, 37, 39, 40
creativity, 52, 56, 57, 64
   play and, 67, 68
   of self-developers, 173–74, 190
Crozier, Michael, 31n
culture:
   corporate, entrepreneurial
   leadership and, 217, 229–31
   value drives and, 53–54, 61–62,
   65, 70, 71–72, 75
Curie, Marie, 178
customers and clients, 9, 20, 74
   industrial-bureaucratic, 22
   satisfaction of, 9, 21, 28, 97, 98
   technoservice and, 21, 23, 25, 27
customization, technoservice and,
   22–23, 25, 27, 219–22

Death of the Bell System, The (film),
   89
defenders, 39–40, 41, 44, 151–66
   character formation of, 156–59
   entrepreneurial, 87, 232, 233, 235–
   237
   innovators as viewed by, 115
   jungle fighters vs., 39, 164
   management and, 160–63
   power and, 67, 159–60, 165–66
   rewards of, 81, 159–60

self-developers vs., 168
service approach of, 151, 153–55
in technoservice, 152, 164, 165–66
value drives of, 65–66, 67, 74, 159–60
weaknesses of, 163–65
democracy, 99, 112, 168, 223, 229
development, human, 9, 32, 33
see also self-developers; strategic self-development
developmental needs, 56, 57–58
dialogue, strategic, 226–28
dignity, 55, 57, 59, 69–74, 79, 84, 85, 90, 160
rewards and, 80, 81
discipline , 201, 205–6, 209
divorce, 189–90, 193
doctors, 27, 28, 39, 86
helper, 136, 141
self-developer, 182–83
dreams, 118, 165
drives, see value drives
Durkheim, Emile, 75

economic man, theory of, 28, 29–30, 32, 34
education, 26, 80, 168, 170
effectiveness at work, 9, 30, 154, 198
egocentrism, 75, 112, 113
Einstein, Albert, 178, 179
Eisenhower, Dwight D., 214
Ekvall, Goran, 53n
Emerson, Ralph Waldo, 168
Employee Involvement (EI), 69, 228
entrepreneurial leadership, 13, 63
administrative leadership vs., 215–16, 232, 235–37
functions of, 216–31
implementation and, 217–18
meaning of, 216
motivating corporate culture and, 217, 229–31
strategic thinking and, 217–23
styles of, 231–37
teamwork and, 217, 223–28
entrepreneurs, 87, 171, 210
gamesmen as viewed by, 111
equality, dignity and, 73–74
Erikson, Erik, 55, 201n
expert-entrepreneurs, 87, 232–37

experts, 39–41, 45, 117–32
character formation for, 119–21
communication problems of, 126–27, 129
defined, 119
dreams of, 118
gamesmen as viewed by, 111
helpers vs., 136
helping as viewed by, 118
ideal boss of, 122–24
innovators as viewed by, 99, 115, 117
reasons and, 84
rewards of, 80–81, 83, 121–22
self-developers as viewed by, 48–49, 117, 184
self-developers vs., 170, 177, 193
self-development of, 168
service approach of, 117–19
in technoservice, 127–32
transferential attachments of, 85–86
value drives of, 58, 61, 63, 65, 67, 69, 117, 132, 206

facilitator-entrepreneurs, 233–37
facilitators, 94, 181, 183–84
Fairburn, W. R. D., 203–4
fairness, 83
family, 20, 47–48, 61, 70, 195
of experts, 119–20, 177
of helpers, 137
of innovators, 113
organization as, 63
of self-developers, 175–78, 189, 198
fantasy, 61, 67, 68, 70
father figures, 63, 86, 120, 177
Federalist Paper No. 10, 229
feedback, 66, 181–82
Ford, Gerald, 105
Ford Motor Co., 73, 228
Foreign Service, U.S., 144–45
Foster, George, 61–62
Founding Fathers, 168, 229
Francis, Saint, 193
Franklin, Benjamin, 168
freedom, 47, 55, 56, 68, 74
discipline for, 205
of employees, 25, 91

freedom (cont.)
  money and, 30
  play and, 68
  strategic self-development and,
      201, 203–5, 209
Freud, Anna, 201n
Freud, Sigmund, 61, 112, 242
Fromm, Erich, 35n, 55, 101
front-line workers, 94
frustration, 57, 61, 66, 70, 80
  neglect and, 202
  of self-developers, 173–74, 190

Gamesman, The (Maccoby), 35,
      37–40, 71, 111, 131n, 193
gamesmen, 37–40
  balance lacking in, 206–7
  innovators as, 111–16
  rewards and, 81, 83
  use of term, 111
  value drives of, 61, 69, 71
Gandhi, Mohandas K., 71, 138
Gaynor, Robert H., 13
General Mills, 62
General Motors (GM), 67, 73, 215, 228
Germany, Federal Republic of,
      rewards in, 81
Gilligan, Carol, 146
global market:
  competition in, 21, 25–26, 96, 197,
      215
  demands of, 19–20
"Goldwater Manifesto" (Bernstein),
      47
golf, 121
government:
  innovators in, 44, 105–11
  strategic thinking and, 222
  see also specific departments and
      agencies
Government Accounting Office, 124
Government sample, 43, 246–47
Guntrip, Harry, 203–4
Gyllenhammar, P. G., 111

Harlow, Harry, 83
Harris poll, 28
Hayden, Tom, 47
Hayes, Robert H., 223–24
helpers, 39–40, 41, 133–49

character formation of, 137–38
as entrepreneurs, 87, 232, 233,
      235–37
experts vs., 136
innovators as viewed by, 115
institutional, 41n
management and, 141–46, 148–49
reasons and, 84
relationships and, 138–40, 145
rewards of, 81, 140–42
self-developers as viewed by,
      48–49, 184
self-developers vs., 170, 177, 183,
      193
self-development of, 168–69
service approach of, 134–35
technoservice and, 149
value drives of, 58, 61, 63, 65, 74
weaknesses of, 147–49
helpfulness, 27, 28, 118
Herman Miller, 103
Hewlett-Packard, 37
hierarchy, 73
  industrial-bureaucratic, 20, 21,
      26–27, 30, 31
  of needs, 28, 31–34
  value drives and, 55
High-Tech sample, 43, 44, 88, 152,
      246
Hirschorn, Larry, 26n
Hitler, Adolf, 214
Homo Ludens (Huizinga), 112
hope, 52–53, 65, 68, 207
  rewards and, 80
Huizinga, Johann, 112
Humphrey, Hubert, 138

Iacocca, Lee, 41
implementation, 217–18
independence, 63, 117, 204–5
  of experts, 120–21
  of self-developers, 167, 168, 171
individuation, 61–62
indulgence, 205–6
industrial bureaucracy:
  dignity in, 73–74
  experts and, 119
  of government, 105–6
  hierarchy of, 20, 21, 26–27, 30, 31
  motivation in, 20, 28–35, 80

rewards in, 82
service and, 23–28
strategic thinking, 218–23
infants:
  care of, 201–2
  value drives and, 61, 64, 66
information, 21, 91
  self-developers and, 169, 170, 184, 191
  as value drive, 55, 59, 65–66, 79, 84
Ingvar, David, 52
innovation:
  play and, 67, 68, 69
  strategic dialogue and, 227
innovator-entrepreneurs, 234–37
innovators, 39–40, 41, 45, 87–116
  in business vs. government, 44
  case studies of, 88–105
  character formation of, 111–14
  experts' views on, 99, 115, 117
  as gamesmen, 111–16
  government, 44, 105–11
  motivation of, 90, 100, 115
  organizational form as viewed by, 95
  reasons and, 84
  relationships of, 85
  rewards of, 81
  self-developers vs., 115
  self-development of, 168–69
  use of term, 39
  value drives of, 66, 67, 74
  weaknesses of, 114–16
In Search of Excellence (Peters and Waterman), 34, 37
institutional helpers, 41n
interactive consultants, 14
Internal Revenue Service (IRS), 43, 44, 45, 88, 154, 170–71, 182
International Business Machines (IBM), 37, 80–81
International Institute of Applied Systems Analysis, 128
interviews, 10–13
  questionnaire for, 239–40

Jaikumar, Ramchandras, 26n
James, William, 61, 168, 242
Japan, 83, 238

dignity in, 71
management in, 126, 130–31
teamwork in, 225–26
Jobs, Steven, 41
Johnson, Clifford M., 29n
Johnson, Lyndon B., 156
Joyce, Jack, 228n–29n
Jung, Carl, 36
jungle fighters, 37–40
  defenders vs., 39, 164
  value drives of, 60
Justice Department, U.S., 154–55

Kafka, Franz, 121
Karasek, Robert A., 27n
Kellogg Foundation, 152
Kennedy, John F., 138, 156, 214
Kennedy, Joseph, 206
King, Martin Luther, Jr., 138, 158
Kissinger, Henry A., 162
Kohn, Melvin L., 31n
Kohut, Heinz, 70

Labor Market Board, Swedish, 106
labor unions, 15, 63, 103, 104, 114, 160, 171
  strategic dialogue and, 228n–29n
language, 65, 75
Larsson, Allan, 106n
Lasch, Christopher, 188n–89n
lawyers, 27–28, 39, 118, 171–72
  self-developer, 171–72, 189
Leader, The (Maccoby), 35, 39, 46, 62, 111, 146, 188
leadership, 15, 213–38
  administrative, 13, 215–16, 232, 235–37
  consultants' work with, 14
  entrepreneurial, see entrepreneurial leadership
  fear of, 213–14
  function of, 213
  hope and, 52–53
  institutional helpers and, 41n
  self-developers' views on, 185
  State Department study of, 12
  Swedish study of, 12–13
  value drives and, 60
Lemasters, Larry, 13–14, 88–95, 111, 115, 116, 195

Lemasters, Larry (*cont.*)
    backround of, 89, 113
    as entrepreneurial leader, 216–17, 218, 224, 228, 229
    motivation of, 90
Levitan, Sar A., 29n
Library of Congress, 182
Lincoln, Abraham, 138, 158
Linjeflyg, 96

McClelland, David, 67
Machiavelli, Niccolò, 30
machismo, 71
Madison, James, 229
Mahler, Margaret, 61
maintenance needs, 56–57
management, managers, 11
    of American Transtech, 90–95
    conservative, 32
    defenders and, 160–63
    dignity and, 72, 73
    etymology of term, 77
    experts as, 124–27
    experts' views on, 122–24
    helpers and, 141–46, 148–49
    industrial-bureaucratic, 22
    information and, 65
    laissez-faire, 180, 215–16
    liberal, 32
    mastery and, 67
    matrix, 124
    meaning and, 75–76
    middle, 34, 45
    motivation tools in, 77–86
    new work demands and, 19–20
    participative, 131–32
    of Scandinavian Airlines, 99, 100
    scientific, 30
    self-developers and, 179–88
    style of, 12–13, 215–16
    technoservice and, 21, 27
    third-level at American Transtech, 94
    top, *see* chief executives
    see also self-management
Management Style Matrix, 235–37
marriage, self-developer's view of, 193–94
Marx , Karl, 31
Marxism, 30–31

Maslow, Abraham, 31–34
mastery, 55, 59, 64, 66–67, 79, 90
    experts and, 58, 67, 117, 206
    play and, 68
meaning:
    of power, 67
    reasons and, 84, 85
    rewards and, 80, 83
    self-developers and, 169, 191, 192
    types of, 75
    as value drive, 55, 59, 74–76, 79, 80, 84, 85, 169
medical model, helper's critique of, 136
mentors, 63, 64
Merit Protection Board (U.S. Civil Service), 11
methodology, summary of, 9–15
Mexico, play in, 112–13
money, 20, 160
    as motivation, 28, 29–30, 32, 52, 80–81, 83, 171–72
    as reward, 80–81, 83, 171–72
Moore, Mary Tyler, 47
motivation, 15, 51–86
    entrepreneurial leadership and, 223–24, 229–31
    feeling of, 57–58
    importance of, 19
    in industrial bureaucracy, 20, 28–35, 80
    of innovators, 90, 100, 115
    management and, 65, 67, 72, 73, 75–86, 89–95
    outmoded theories of, 28–35
    reasons and, 78, 84–85
    relationships and, 78–79, 85–86
    responsibilities and, 78, 79–80
    rewards and, 78, 80–84
    of self-developers, 20, 34, 168
    for technoservice, 35–41, 77–86
    traditional, decline of, 20
    value drives and, 53–78

Nader, Ralph, 41, 156, 158–59
Nagel, Russell, 13, 101–5, 111, 116, 130, 195
background of, 103, 113
as entrepreneurial leader, 216–17, 218, 224, 228, 229

philosophy of, 102
narcissism, 70, 188, 202
NASA (National Aeronautics and
    Space Administration) sample,
    43, 44, 247
National Transportation Safety Board,
    128
needs:
    addictive, 56, 57, 58, 64, 66, 67
    hierarchy of, 28, 31–34
    types of, 56–58
neglect, 201–4
    care vs., 201–3
neurotics, 61
Newhart, Bob, 47
Nixon, Richard M., 156, 214
Novelle, Theirry J., 27n
Nuclear Regulatory Commission, 155
Nummi (New United Motor
    Manufacturing Inc.), 67
nurses, 41, 202–3
    as experts, 123–24

off-the-shelf consultants, 14
Ohio Bell, 89
One–Minute Manager, The
    (Blanchard and Johnson), 122
oppression, 203–4, 206
optimism, 52–53
ownership, worker, 30–31

Packard, David, 111
paranoics, 55, 164–65
partial man theories, 28–35
participant study, 10, 13–15
participation, 99, 104, 131–32, 185
participatative consultants, 14
peasants, 65
People Express, 28, 79, 114
Pericles, 151
Perot, Ross, 38
perversion:
    defined, 201
    power vs., 201–7
Peters, Tom, 34, 63
Piaget, Jean, 75, 112, 113, 201n
Plato, 70
play, 55, 58, 59, 67–69, 79
    of children, 68, 112–13
    self-developers and, 184

strategic self-development and,
    209–10
pleasure, 52, 55, 58–59, 64
    types of, 64
policemen, 121–22, 123, 126
    defender, 153, 164
    helper, 139–41
policy implementation, 217–18
political man, theory of, 28, 30–31
Position Emission Tomography (PET
    Scan), 52
positive thinking, 52–53
Potter, Stephen, 111
power, 20, 28, 30–31, 32, 52, 57, 77
    defenders and, 67, 159–60, 165–66
    gamesmen and, 111
    innovators and, 88, 90, 100–101,
        160
    as mastery, 66, 67
    perversion vs., 200–207
    sadomasochism and, 204
    self-developers and, 185, 198
    strategic self-development and,
        199–207
powerlessness, 31, 67, 199
problem solving, 25, 35
    consultants and, 14
    hope and, 52
    rewards vs. punishments and, 83
    self-developers and, 20, 169–71,
        182
production:
    Marxist views of, 30–31
    service vs. technoservice and, 24–
        26
productivity, 19, 24, 28, 185
    in industrial bureaucracy, 27
    in technoservice, 27–28
    at Westinghouse Furniture Systems,
        102, 104
professionalism, 136
Project on Technology, Work, and
    Character, Seminar on Social
    Character of, 10, 11
Project 2000, 228n–29n
promotion, 20, 30, 80, 160
protector-entrepreneurs, 232, 233,
    235–37
protectors, see defenders
psychiatrists, as experts, 118–19

psychoanalysis, 14, 54–55
psychological man, theory of, 28, 31–34
psychostructures, 44
psychotics, 61
punishment, 82–84, 204
Puritan Ethic, 64

Quality of Worklife (QWL) programs, 69, 72, 102, 103, 142, 154, 228
questionnaires:
　AT&T, 13, 251–53
　Barometer, 91–95
　survey, see Values at Work Questionnnaire

rage, 70, 71
Ransom, John Crowe, 159
Reagan, Ronald, 52–53, 105, 156, 157
Realpolitik, 30
reasons, 78, 84–85
relatedness, 55, 58, 61–64
relationships, 78–79, 85–86
　of experts, 129–30
　of helpers, 138–40, 145
　of self-developers, 86, 169, 182–83
repression, 57, 58, 68
respect, 73, 74, 85, 183
responsibilities, 78, 79–80
　defenders and, 151–52
　experts' views on, 120
　helpers and, 147–48
　self-developers and, 167, 168, 178, 184
rewards, 52, 78, 80–84
　criteria for, 83–84
　of defenders, 81, 159–60
　of experts, 80–81, 83, 121–22
　of helpers, 81, 140–42
　of self-developers, 81, 171–73
Riesman, David, 55
risk-taking, 198
　of gamesmen, 111
　of innovators, 169
Rockefeller, John D., 206
role models, 198
　of self-developers, 178–79
Roosevelt, Eleanor, 137–38, 178–79
Roosevelt, Franklin D., 138, 156
Rorschach test, 14n

sadomasochism, 204
Scandinavian Airlines (SAS), 28, 87, 96–101, 220
　participation in, 99
　philosophy of, 98
schizoid character, 202
Schlumberger, 37
Schön, Donald A., 36n, 132
Schooler, Carmi, 31n
Schweitzer, Albert, 178
scientific management, 30
secretaries, 25, 141–42, 169, 180, 185
self-actualization, 32–33
self-developers, 20, 33, 39–40, 44, 45, 167–95
　age of, 45, 197
　at American Transtech, 93
　balanced life of, 175–76
　character formation of, 176–78
　as entrepreneurs, 87, 171
　experts' views on, 48–49, 117, 184
　family background of, 20, 48
　frustrations and, 173–74, 190
　gamesmen as viewed by, 111
　ideal boss of, 179–82
　innovators as viewed by, 115
　innovators compared with, 113–14
　as managers, 183–88
　motivation of, 20, 34, 168
　negative views of, 48–49
　reasons and, 84–85
　relationships of, 86, 169, 182–83
　rewards of, 81, 171–73
　role models of, 178–79
　service approach of, 41, 169–71
　value drives of, 61, 63–64, 66, 74, 76, 167–68, 169
　weaknesses of, 168, 188–95
　see also strategic self-development
self-esteem, 34, 57, 68, 167
　dignity and, 70, 72
　self-developers and, 189, 193, 194
self-expression, 52, 61–62, 68, 79
self-management, 19, 80, 88
self-worth, 51
Seminar on Social Character (Project on Technology, Work, and Character), 10, 11
service:
　defender approach to, 151, 153–55

defined, 23–24
expert approach to, 117–19
self-developer approach to, 41,
    169–71
technoservice vs., 23–28
Service Sector sample, 43, 44, 88,
    152, 248
shame, 69, 70
Simenon, Georges, 153
Sjöwall, Maj, 153
skills:
    competency and, 12
    of self-developers, 20
sociability at work, 62–63, 183
Social Character Seminar (Project on
    Technology, Work, and
    Character), 10, 11
social character theory, 35–41
    modern changes and, 46–48
    see also defenders; experts; helpers;
        innovators; self-developers
social/human criteria, work
    relationship improvements and,
    9–10
social problems, self-developer's
    views on, 194–95
social workers, 63, 139
    defender, 151, 153, 160–61
sociological man, theory of, 28, 30
Spitz, Rene, 61, 202
Stanback, Thomas M., Jr., 27n
State Department, U.S., 12, 81, 148
    Passport Office of, 106
status, 20, 28, 30, 32, 34, 80
    of helpers, 142
Steelcase, 103
stewards, union, 171
strategic dialogue, 226–28
strategic self-development, 197–211
    balance and, 201, 206–11
    care and, 201–3, 208
    commitment and, 201, 207–11
    discipline and, 201, 205–6, 209
    freedom and, 201, 203–5, 209
    need for, 197–99
    power vs. perversion in, 200–207
    technoservice and, 197–98, 211
    wholeness and power and,
    199–200
strategic thinking, 217–23

strategy, use of term, 218
stress, Japanese experts and, 131
Sullivan, Harry Stack, 75
surveys, 10–12
    reliability of, 11
    validity of, 11
    see also Values at Work
        Questionnaire
survival, 55, 58–61
    reasons and, 84
suspiciousness, 164
Sweden, 83, 86, 112
    dignity in, 71
    Labor Market Board in, 106n
    leadership study in, 12–13
Swedish Council on Management
    and Worklife Issues, 12–13
Switzerland, 113

Taylor, Frederick Winslow, 30
teachers, 27, 41, 44
teamwork:
    of defenders, 154
    entrepreneurial leadership and,
        217, 223–28
    equality and, 73
    Lemasters' use of, 89, 90
    relatedness and, 63
    rewards and, 82, 84
    of self-developers, 169, 170, 177,
        182–83, 184, 186, 192
    strategic dialogue and, 226–28
    technoservice and, 22–23, 27
    at Westinghouse Furniture Systems,
        103
technology, 31, 47
    experts' clashes with, 128
    organizational form as, 95
    of technoservice, 21–23
    traditional, 22
    at Westinghouse Furniture Systems,
        105
technoservice, 21–28, 67
    defenders in, 152, 164, 165–66
    defined, 21
    experts in, 127–32
    helpers in, 149
    Maslow's theory and, 32–34
    motivation for, 75–76

technoservice *(cont.)*
  self-developers in, 167, 182, 185–86
  service vs., 23–28
  strategic self-development and, 197–98, 211
  strategic thinking and, 218–23
Telecommunications sample, 43, 45, 152, 246
telematics, 21
tension reduction, 64
Texas Instruments, 37
thinking, strategic, 217–23
Thoreau, Henry David, 168
Three Mile Island, 128
Thucydides, 151
timing, of innovators, 99–100
Toffler, Alvin, 62
To Have Or to Be (Fromm), 101
Toyota, 67
transference, 63, 85–86
travel, 175–76
Trial, The (Kafka), 121
Truman, Harry S., 163
trust, 164, 167, 183, 186, 193–94, 197
  care and, 201–2
  dignity and, 73

unions, *see* labor unions
United Kingdom, 112
United Steelworkers, 103

value drives, 53–78
  dignity, *see* dignity
  information, 55, 59, 65–66, 79, 84
  mastery, *see* mastery
  meaning, 55, 59, 74–76, 79, 80, 84, 85, 169
  needs and, 56–57
  play, *see* play
  pleasure, 52, 55, 58–59, 64
  relatedness, 55, 58, 61–64
  survival, 55, 58–61, 84
  use of term, 53n, 241–43
values, 10, 11
  at American Transtech, 90–91
  defined, 53

employee, 14, 20, 34
  gaps in, 90–91
  leadership and, 12
  modern changes and, 46–48
  of self-developers, 20
  traditional vs. new, 48–49
Values at Work Questionnaire, 10–11, 41n, 42–46
  follow-up interview questionnaire on, 239–40
  sample of, 42–43
  statistical results from, 45, 245–49
Vermont Asbestos Company, 31
Vingressor/Club 33, 96
volunteer work, 138, 141–42, 145

Wahlöö, Per, 153
Walton, Richard, 26n
Wambaugh, Joseph, 153
Washington, George, 213–14
Waterman, R. H., 34, 63
Watson, Thomas, Jr., 111
Westinghouse Furniture Systems, 25, 87, 101–5, 130, 166, 220
Westmoreland, William, 159
whistle-blowers, 39, 41, 151, 155, 161
wholeness, 199–200
women, 39, 45, 47–48
  as experts, 120
  as helpers, 133, 136–38, 145–46
  as mothers, 120, 137, 168, 177
  as self-developers, 175
word processors, 185
work:
  meaning of, 15, 31, 34
  motivation for, *see* motivation
  new demands of, 19–23
  play vs., 68–69
  values and, *see* values
  volunteer, 138, 141–42, 145
  see also specific topics
workaholics, 57, 175

Yankelovich, Daniel, 46
Young Leaders sample, 43, 88, 152, 247
Yugoslavia, worker ownership in, 31